全球金融竞争力报告2021
Global Financial Competitiveness Report 2021

全球金融竞争力课题组
中国社会科学院世界经济与政治研究所　著
中国社会科学院国家全球战略智库

Global Financial Competitiveness Research Group

Institute of World Economics and Politics,
Chinese Academy of Social Sciences (CASS)

National Institute for Global Strategy,
Chinese Academy of Social Sciences (NIGS, CASS)

中国社会科学出版社

图书在版编目(CIP)数据

全球金融竞争力报告.2021 = Global Financial Competitiveness Report 2021：英文 / 全球金融竞争力课题组，中国社会科学院世界经济与政治研究所，中国社会科学院国家全球战略智库著．—北京：中国社会科学出版社，2021.12

(国家智库报告)

ISBN 978-7-5203-9426-0

Ⅰ.①全… Ⅱ.①全…②中…③中… Ⅲ.①金融—竞争力—研究报告—世界—2021—英文 Ⅳ.①F831

中国版本图书馆 CIP 数据核字(2021)第 265632 号

出 版 人	赵剑英
项目统筹	王 茵　喻 苗
责任编辑	张 潜
责任校对	季 静
责任印制	李寡寡

出　　版	中国社会科学出版社
社　　址	北京鼓楼西大街甲 158 号
邮　　编	100720
网　　址	http://www.csspw.cn
发 行 部	010-84083685
门 市 部	010-84029450
经　　销	新华书店及其他书店
印刷装订	北京君升印刷有限公司
版　　次	2021 年 12 月第 1 版
印　　次	2021 年 12 月第 1 次印刷
开　　本	787×1092　1/16
印　　张	15.5
插　　页	2
字　　数	201 千字
定　　价	89.00 元

凡购买中国社会科学出版社图书，如有质量问题请与本社营销中心联系调换
电话：010-84083683
版权所有　侵权必究

项目组成员名单

项目负责人　刘东民

项目组成员　（按照拼音顺序）

　　　　　　　高海红　陆　婷　倪淑慧　宋　爽
　　　　　　　夏广涛　杨盼盼　杨子荣　张梓润

目 录

一 引言 …………………………………………………………（1）

二 金融竞争力的评价方法综述 ………………………………（2）

三 全球金融竞争力评价指标体系 ……………………………（4）
 （一）指标选取 …………………………………………………（4）
  1. 金融业竞争力 ……………………………………………（4）
  2. 货币竞争力 ………………………………………………（4）
  3. 金融基础设施竞争力 ……………………………………（5）
  4. 金融科技竞争力 …………………………………………（6）
  5. 国际金融治理竞争力 ……………………………………（7）
 （二）评级样本 …………………………………………………（8）

四 全球金融竞争力指数构建 …………………………………（9）
 （一）金融业竞争力的指数构建 ………………………………（9）
  1. 指标选择 …………………………………………………（9）
  2. 数据处理 …………………………………………………（14）
 （二）货币竞争力的指数构建 …………………………………（19）
  1. 指标选择 …………………………………………………（19）
  2. 数据处理 …………………………………………………（22）
 （三）金融基础设施竞争力的指数构建 ………………………（26）
  1. 指标选择 …………………………………………………（26）

2. 数据处理 ……………………………………………… (27)
　(四)金融科技竞争力的指数构建 ……………………………… (28)
　　1. 指标选择 ……………………………………………… (28)
　　2. 数据处理 ……………………………………………… (30)
　(五)国际金融治理竞争力的指数构建 …………………………… (30)
　　1. 指标选择 ……………………………………………… (30)
　　2. 数据处理 ……………………………………………… (36)

五　全球金融竞争力评价 ………………………………………… (38)
　(一)总指数 ………………………………………………………… (38)
　(二)一级指标 ……………………………………………………… (40)
　　1. 金融业竞争力 ………………………………………… (40)
　　2. 货币竞争力 …………………………………………… (42)
　　3. 金融基础设施竞争力 ………………………………… (44)
　　4. 金融科技竞争力 ……………………………………… (45)
　　5. 国际金融治理竞争力 ………………………………… (48)

附　录 ………………………………………………………………… (50)
　(一)金融业竞争力分项结果 ……………………………………… (50)
　　指标1.1　金融体系规模 ………………………………… (50)
　　指标1.2　金融体系活力 ………………………………… (54)
　　指标1.3　金融体系效率 ………………………………… (57)
　　指标1.4　金融体系稳定性 ……………………………… (61)
　　指标1.5　金融服务可得性 ……………………………… (69)
　　指标1.6　国际金融中心地位 …………………………… (75)
　(二)货币竞争力分项结果 ………………………………………… (76)
　　指标2.1　价值储存 ……………………………………… (76)
　　指标2.2　交易媒介 ……………………………………… (79)
　　指标2.3　计价单位 ……………………………………… (82)

（三）金融基础设施竞争力分项结果 ……………………（86）
    指标3.1　金融基础设施硬件 …………………………（86）
    指标3.2　金融基础设施软件 …………………………（94）

（四）金融科技竞争力分项结果 ………………………………（98）
    指标4.1　算力 …………………………………………（98）
    指标4.2　用户接入度 …………………………………（102）
    指标4.3　产业发展潜力 ………………………………（103）

（五）国际金融治理竞争力分项结果 …………………………（107）
    指标5.1　全球金融组织竞争力 ………………………（107）
    指标5.2　非正式协调平台竞争力 ……………………（111）
    指标5.3　区域多边金融组织竞争力 …………………（115）

CONTENTS

I INTRODUCTION ··· (121)

II REVIEW ON THE EVALUATION METHODS OF
   FINANCIAL COMPETITIVENESS ···················· (122)

III EVALUATION INDICATOR SYSTEM OF THE GLOBAL
    FINANCIAL COMPETITIVENESS ···················· (124)
   i Selection of indicators ································ (124)
      1. The competitiveness of financial industry ············ (124)
      2. The competitiveness of currency ······················ (124)
      3. The competitiveness of financial infrastructure ······ (125)
      4. The competitiveness of financial technology ········· (126)
      5. The competitiveness in international financial governance ··· (127)
   ii Rating samples ······································· (128)

IV CONSTRUCTION OF INDICATORS FOR GLOBAL
   FINANCIAL COMPETITIVENESS ···················· (130)
   i Construction of the indicators for the competitiveness
      of financial industry ··································· (130)
      1. Selection of indicators ································ (130)
      2. Data processing ······································· (134)
   ii Construction of the currency competitiveness indicators ············ (140)
      1. Selection of indicators ································ (140)
      2. Data processing ······································· (143)
   iii Construction of indicators for the competitiveness of
      financial infrastructure ································ (146)
      1. Selection of indicators ································ (146)
      2. Date Processing ······································· (149)
   iv Construction of the indicators for the competitiveness of the
      financial technology ··································· (149)
      1. Selection of indicators ································ (149)
      2. Date processing ······································· (152)

  v Construction of the indicators for the competitiveness in
international financial governance ·················· (152)
    1. Selection of indicators ························· (152)
    2. Data processing ································ (158)

V EVALUATION OF THE GLOBAL FINANCIAL COMPETITIVENESS ································ (160)

  i General indicators ································ (160)
  ii Primary indicators ································ (162)
    1. The competitiveness of financial industry ················ (162)
    2. The competitiveness of currency ······················ (164)
    3. The competitiveness of financial infrastructure ··········· (166)
    4. The competitiveness of financial technology ·············· (167)
    5. The competitiveness in international financial governance ··· (170)

APPENDIX ································ (172)

  i Sub-indicators for the competitiveness of financial
industry ································ (172)
    Indicator 1.1: Scale of financial system ······················ (172)
    Indicator 1.2: Vitality of financial system ···················· (175)
    Indicator 1.3: Efficiency of financial system ·················· (179)
    Indicator 1.4: Stability of financial system ··················· (183)
    Indicator 1.5: Availability of financial services ··············· (190)
    Indicator 1.6: Status of the international financial center ········ (196)
  ii Sub-indicators for the competitiveness of currency ············ (197)
    Indicator 2.1: Store of value ································ (197)
    Indicator 2.2: Medium of exchange ·························· (199)
    Indicator 2.3: Unit of account ······························ (202)
  iii Sub-indicators for the competitiveness of financial
infrastructure ································ (206)
    Indicator 3.1: Hardware of the financial infrastructure ··········· (206)
    Indicator 3.2: Software of the financial infrastructure ············ (213)
  iv Sub-indicators for the competitiveness of financial
technology ································ (218)
    Indicator 4.1: Computing power ···························· (218)
    Indicator 4.2: User access ································· (222)
    Indicator 4.3: The potential of the industry ··················· (223)
  v Sub-indicators for the competitiveness in international
financial governance ································ (227)

Indicator 5.1: Competitiveness of global financial organizations ……………………………………… (227)

Indicator 5.2: Competitiveness over the informal coordination platforms …………………………………… (231)

Indicator 5.3: Competitiveness in regional multilateral financial organizations …………………………………… (235)

参考文献 ………………………………………………… (238)

一 引言

作为现代经济的核心,金融是推动经济发展、促进科技创新、提升国民福祉的重要力量,而金融竞争力则成为支撑国家竞争力的关键要素之一。

金融体系最基本也是最重要的功能是配置金融资源和管理风险。在全球化时代,一国金融体系必然要进入国际金融市场,融入全球化进程,才能更好地完成配置资源和管理风险的目标。因此,考察全球化时代的国家金融竞争力需要整合国内和国际市场,并引入全球金融治理的视角,才能得出较为可靠的结论。

本报告将"全球金融竞争力"界定为:一个经济体的金融体系相较于其他经济体而言,在全球范围内更有效地配置金融资源和管理风险并以此促进经济增长与社会发展的能力。通过考察金融业竞争力、货币竞争力、金融基础设施竞争力、金融科技竞争力和国际金融治理竞争力五个维度共57个指标,本报告试图较为全面地衡量32个国家或地区的全球金融竞争力。

目前,中国的金融体系在规模上已经处于世界领先水平,其全球竞争力持续增强。伴随新一轮的金融改革与开放,中国的金融业将会在国内与国际市场上与全球金融机构开展更加全面而深度的竞争与合作。全球金融竞争力评价指标体系的构建,有助于我们通过国际比较与量化分析来研判一国金融体系的竞争优势与不足,从而为政府推出新的金融改革与开放措施提供参考,为金融机构的创新发展提供借鉴。

二　金融竞争力的评价方法综述

一些国际机构已经建立了包含金融竞争力维度的国家竞争力评价体系，并具有较大国际影响力，如 IMD（瑞士洛桑国际管理学院）发布的《世界竞争力年度报告》(*World Competitiveness Yearbook*) 和 WEF（世界经济论坛）发布的《全球竞争力报告》(*The Global Competitiveness Report*)。

IMD 从经济表现、政府效率、业务效率、基础设施四个方面衡量一国的整体实力，其中金融部分主要考察银行和资本市场两个维度，通过银行部门、金融服务、股票市场、企业经营四个方面共 19 个指标来评价金融竞争力。WEF 主要关注国别层面的整体竞争力，从机构、基础设施、采用信息和通信技术、宏观经济稳定、健康、技能、产品市场、劳动力市场、金融体系、市场规模、商业活力、创新能力十二个部分讨论，而对于金融体系的分解主要从银行和资本市场的深度以及银行业稳定性两个角度出发。

可以看出，在 IMD 和 WEF 的报告中，金融竞争力都是作为国家竞争力的一部分，并且仅仅是关注银行和资本市场，没有考虑货币、金融基础设施、金融科技与国际金融治理等其他因素。

国内也逐步对金融竞争力开展评价体系的研究。詹继生等（2007）认为，金融竞争力是在竞争性和开放性市场中，一国金融产业成功地将金融资源用于转换过程，比他国金融产业更有效地向市场提供产品和服务,实现更多价值的动态系统能力。根据这一定义,詹继生等在接受 IMD 评价金融竞争力的四项指标的基础上,增加了金融资产竞争力、金融创新竞争力、金融人力资本竞争力三项指标。倪鹏飞等(2016)与 IMD 类似,在进行国家竞争力评价时,建立了国家金融竞争力的分指标,包含货币优势、国际关系、金融体系、国内服务和金融监管 5 个一级指标。

关于数据处理的方式,目前国际上已经存在系统地对跨国经济体进行综合评估的方法。对于数据的标准化,IMD 采用 Z-score 标准化法,即标准差法(Standard Deviation Method)对数据进行标准化,这种方法虽然简单可行,但是依赖于原始数据的均值和方差;WEF 采用 Min-Max 标准化法,但由于一些指标的最小值、最大值不确定,同时为避免极端值和新数据加入对最值的影响,报告使用分位数等方式人为对其设定可接受的最值。对于缺失值的处理,IMD 直接使用该指标的均值替换缺失值,这种方法虽然简单可行,但是将各国的发展状况视为平均水平,不能表明不同国家发展的特征;WEF 则是利用线性回归填补缺失,或者按发展水平的高低对国别进行分组,使用同组均值替代缺失。这种方式对于数据量的要求较高,不适合样本数较少的情况。

三　全球金融竞争力评价指标体系

本报告以国家（或地区）为考察的基本单位，以金融业竞争力、货币竞争力、金融基础设施竞争力、金融科技竞争力和国际金融治理竞争力五个维度作为一级指标，建立全球金融竞争力评价指标体系。

（一）指标选取

1. 金融业竞争力

金融业是一国经济发展的重要组成部分。通过构建多层次、全面综合发展的金融体系，提高本国金融业竞争力，从而促进本国的实体经济发展，这是各国政策制定者的共同目标。本报告从金融体系规模、金融体系活力、金融体系效率、金融业稳定性、金融服务的可得性以及该经济体拥有的国际金融中心的地位六大维度衡量金融业竞争力。

2. 货币竞争力

正如总报告对于全球金融竞争力的界定，本报告非常强调"全球"这一概念，我们的货币竞争力同样关注一种货币在全球范围内的竞争力。从这个视角出发，对于货币竞争力的概念有两个关键之处需要明确：第一，本报告货币竞争力所关注的核心是某一货币的国际竞争力，也即一国货币职能在全球范围内的广泛使用。从国际货币研究的文献出发，货币的竞争力可被视为一种货币的职能跨越货币所辖区域在公共和私人部门的使用；第二，本报告关注基于结果的竞争力。从测度货币国际化的文献出发，对于货币竞争力的衡量可被分为基于原因和基于结果的竞争力，基于原因的竞争力关注使得货币具有竞争力的各类因素，例如经济规模、金融市场深度、通货膨胀水平等；基于结果的竞争力关注货币竞争力的结果，即某种货币在全球发挥不同职能的实际情况，本书在构建实际指标时确保所有的指标均反映结果竞争力。

在概念明确的基础上，我们对货币竞争力指标的构建按照货币职能划分为3个二级指标，分别为：价值储存、交易媒介和计价单位，在二级指标下设不同的子指标，刻画这些货币职能在全球视野下的运用，以全面反映货币竞争力。

3. 金融基础设施竞争力

根据2012年国际清算银行支付结算体系委员会（CPSS，2014年9月更名为CPMI）和国际证监会组织（IOSCO）联合发布的《金融市场基础设施原则》，金融市场基础设施主要包括中央交易对手、支付系统、中央证券存管系统、证券结算系统和交易数据库。2020年3月，人民银行等六部门联合印发《统筹监管金融基础设施工作方案》，对中国金融基础设施范围进行了界定。中国金融基础设施主要包括金融资产登记托管系统、清算结算系统（包括开展集中清算业务的中央对手方）、交易设施、交易报告库、重要支付系统、基础征信系统六类设施及其运营机构。这种侧重于从硬件设施的角度来定义金融基础设施的方式通常被视作狭义概念上的金融基础设施。

广义金融基础设施则主要指为金融活动提供公共服务并保证金融市场稳健、持续、安全运行的硬件设施及制度安排。具体来看，其不仅包括支付、清算、结算、存管等金融市场基础设施，也应包括金融会计准则、信用环境、定价机制等内容。近年来，随着金融与科技的深度融合，学者们着重从硬件设施与软约束条件相结合的角度对金融基础设施予以界定（如焦瑾璞等，2019）。考虑到金融基础设施硬件和软件的质量均与金融运行和经济发展有着密切的联系，这里将从两方面度量和考察金融基础设施竞争力指标。

良好的金融基础设施伴随着更大的金融市场深度、更高的金融服务效率、更好的金融资源可及性和更高的经济增长。不仅如此，良好的金融基础设施还可以提高金融系统的抗冲击能力，防止金融危机的发生和传染。例如可靠的支付系统能够大大降低金融交易中的信用、流动性和操作风险，而健全的破产清算体系则有助于保护抵押品价值，防止危机通过资产负债表的途径传染。鉴于此，世界各国与相关国际组织都将金融基础设施建设作为经济发展政策的重要内容，也正因为如此，在衡量一国金融竞争力时，金融基础设施应被视作不可或缺的重要指标之一。

4. 金融科技竞争力

金融科技竞争力指数是按照底层技术（算力）、中间接入（用户接入度）、终端产业（产业发展潜力）三个层次构建的反映一国金融科技整体竞争力的指数。在选取计算指数所需的具体指标时遵循以下逻辑：从底层技术看，金融科技产业发展需以强大的计算能力作为技术基础，底层技术决定金融科技行业和市场的长远发展，大部分技术属于慢产量。从应用领域看，随着金融科技产业的发展，越来越多的用户接入该产业，用户接入度本质上说明用户是否具备消费最新金融科技的手段与渠道，是沟通技术与市场的关键纽带；"变现"潜在用户的程度决定了底层技术的应用宽度，某种程度上可以衡量各国金融科技产业当前的发展水平；稳定的计算能力与较高的用户接入度支撑金融科技产业中终端行业的发展，终端行业的发展情况展现金融科技行业的未来潜力，而市场潜力又会反过来影响技术迭代更新速度。基于此逻辑构建三级指标体系，各子指标在原数据标准化处理的基础上乘以其权重加总得到 32 个样本国家或地区的金融科技竞争力指数。

5. 国际金融治理竞争力

国际金融治理亦称为全球金融治理，一般被视为全球治理在国际金融领域的延展与应用。这个概念在 1997 年亚洲金融危机后逐渐受到关注，并在 2008 年金融危机后成为国际社会研究的焦点。在 2003 年，牛津大学便设立全球经济治理研究项目（Global Economic Governance Programme），其中的金融板块以建立全球金融监管与改革的新政策议程为己任，将如何能够更好地满足发展中国家人民需求作为目标。同年剑桥大学也出版了一本名为《压力下的国际金融治理：全球机构与国内需要》的论文集，试图分析之前几次金融危机的原因并为国际金融体系改革提供建议。2008 年，由美国次贷危机引发的国内金融危机迅速蔓延，演变成了一次真正意义上的全球金融危机。其所造成的全球经济衰退之严重后果，又一次体现了现行国际金融体系的不合理性，改革当前国际金融体系与国际金融监管体制已经到了刻不容缓的时候。在这一背景下，全球金融治理（Global Financial Governance）或类似提法日益频繁地出现在新闻报道和学术讨论的范围内。

对国际金融体系进行有效的治理，需要从为什么治理，治理什么，如何治理等几个方面入手。其中，关于为什么治理大家基本已经达成共识。治理什么则主要包括要治理的对象有哪些以及要实现哪些治理目标，即国际金融治理的客体有哪些。如何去治理主要包括由谁来治理和以什么方式治理两方面重要内容。治理方式是参与主体共同参与、合作协商的机制，包括一系列的规则秩序和协调方式等，另外一个核心问题就是，到底由谁来主导对全球金融体系的治理,也就是国际金融治理的主体有哪些。

在上述维度上,各国在参与国际金融治理的能力,则体现为各国在国际金融治理主体中的地位以及决定治理客体的能力,即各国参与国际金融体系相关事项规则制定和协调过程中的代表权和话语权。本报告将根据全球金融治理的主体和客体范围来确定二级指标,选择衡量代表权和话语权的数据指标来确定三级指标。

(二) 评级样本

本报告选取了32个经济体作为评级样本(见表3-1),范围涉及G20成员国、金砖国家、大部分欧元区成员国等国家或地区,包含了大部分发达国家和少数经济体量较大的发展中国家。这些经济体大多拥有金融中心,经济发展程度高,金融活动在全球影响力大,具有较高的代表性。

表3-1　　　　　　　　经济体列表

经济体	代码	经济体	代码	经济体	代码	经济体	代码
阿联酋	ARE	中国大陆[①]	CHN	印度尼西亚	IDN	荷兰	NLD
阿根廷	ARG	德国	DEU	印度	IND	葡萄牙	PRT
澳大利亚	AUS	西班牙	ESP	爱尔兰	IRL	俄罗斯	RUS
奥地利	AUT	芬兰	FIN	意大利	ITA	沙特阿拉伯	SAU
比利时	BEL	法国	FRA	日本	JPN	新加坡	SGP
巴西	BRA	英国	GBR	韩国	KOR	土耳其	TUR
加拿大	CAN	希腊	GRC	卢森堡	LUX	美国	USA
瑞士	CHE	中国香港	HKG	墨西哥	MEX	南非	ZAF

① 本报告中的"中国大陆",不包括中国台湾、中国香港和中国澳门,后同。

四 全球金融竞争力指数构建

本报告对5个一级指标,即金融业竞争力、货币竞争力、金融基础设施竞争力、金融科技竞争力和国际金融治理能力,分别采用35%、35%、10%、10%和10%的权重。下文详细论述五个指标的构建方式。

(一)金融业竞争力的指数构建

1. 指标选择

对于金融业竞争力,报告使用金融体系规模、金融体系活力、金融体系效率、金融稳定性、金融服务可得性以及该经济体拥有的国际金融中心的地位6个二级指标衡量。该体系除了借鉴 Beck et al. (1999) 等文献的做法,从金融体系的规模、活力和效率三个维度衡量金融体系外,还进一步将金融体系的稳定性、获得金融服务的难易程度以及国际金融中心地位纳入了指标体系范畴。(见表4-1)

指标1.1 金融体系规模

金融体系规模从规模层面衡量了一国金融体系的发展程度。金融体系的规模越大,其服务实体经济的容量也越大。Merton (1995) 从金融功能视角总结了金融体系的六项基本功能。不同的金融机构能够为实体经济提供不同的金融服务,比如商业银行作为金融中介的典型代表,能够融通资金,实现资源跨时间、地域和产业间的转移,且在筛选项目、监督企业和风险管理方面具有业务优势(Diamond,1984；Rajan and Zingales,1998)；而股票市场作为直接融资的代表,则能够筹集资金,在信息披露、企业并购、技术进步和分散风险方面具有优势(Allen and Gale,2000；Levine,2005)。

本模型除了分银行、股票、央行资产、共同基金、保险、养老金等金融部门来衡量金融体系的规模外,还补充了流动性负债这一整体性衡量指标。模型选择使用各部门规模占GDP的比重来衡量,代表一国或地区金融体系规模占整个经济规模的大小,相对指标可以避免使用绝对指标时各国经济体量差异过大可能造成不可比的问题。因此,采用存款银行资产同GDP比率、股票市值同GDP比率、其他部门资产同GDP比率(包含央行资产、共同基金资产、保险公司资产和养老金资产)这3个三级指标衡量金融体系规模。

这些指标的数值越大,表明这些部门的相对规模越大,即金融体系规模越大。这7个指标的数据均来自世界银行的全球金融发展数据库(The Global Financial Development Database,GFDD)。

指标1.2 *金融体系活力*

金融体系活力从活力层面衡量了金融体系服务实体经济的动能。金融体系的活力越强,其服务实体经济的动能也越足。投向私营部门信贷通常是衡量金融中介活力的最全面指标,且大量文献证实私营部门信贷对经济增长存在显著、积极和稳健的影响(Levine et al.,2000；Beck et al.,2000)。另有文献发现,股票市场交易值是衡量股票市场活力的合理指标,它表明了股票市场向实体经济提供的流动性程度,且股票市场交易值是长期经济增长的稳健指示器(Levine and Zervos,1998)。限于数据的可得性,本模型仅选择了银行和股市两个部门,并分别用私人部门信贷同GDP比率、银行贷款同银行存款比率来衡量银行部门的活跃程度,用股票交易值同 GDP 比率来衡量股票市场的活跃程度。

这些指标的数值越大,表明这些部门的活力越强,即金融体系活力越强。这 3 个指标的数据均来自世界银行的全球金融发展数据库。

指标 1.3　金融体系效率

金融体系效率从运行效率角度来衡量金融服务实体经济的成本。金融体系的效率越高,其服务实体经济的成本越低。金融市场效率高通常意味着拥有较好的流动性,能够高效地为实体经济筹集与转换资金。本报告选择了银行和股市两个部门,银行部门选取银行非利息收入同总收入比率、银行营业费用同总资产比率和银行业资产回报率衡量银行的运营成本和盈利能力,股票市场选取股市换手率来衡量股票流动性的强弱和股票市场的融资效率。

银行营业费用同总资产比率越大,表明银行的效率越低,即金融体系效率越低。其他指标的数值越大,表明银行和股市的效率越高,即金融体系效率越高。这 4 个指标的数据均来自世界银行的全球金融发展数据库。

指标 1.4　金融稳定性

金融体系稳定性从稳定性层面衡量金融服务实体经济的可持续性和波动性。Schinasi G. J.（2004）将金融稳定性定义为金融体系促进经济体的表现,并且消除由内生或重大不利和意外事件导致的金融失衡。ECB（2016）认为金融稳定可以定义为金融体系抵御冲击和消除金融失衡的条件,减轻了金融中介过程中断的可能性,减少对实体经济活动的不利影响。IMF（2006）在《金融稳健指标编制指南》提到,金融稳健指标可以评估和监督金融体系的实力和脆弱性,提高金融体系的稳定性,减少金融体系崩溃的可能性。吴念鲁和郓会梅（2005）认为金融稳定有利于创造良好的环境实现金融功能,提高金的效率，从而促进经济和社会的发展。金融体系的稳定性越强，其服务实体经济的可持续性越强。与股票市场波动造成的经济波动相比，银行业部门危机的传染性和破坏性通常更强，因此本模型选取了银行 Z-score、不良贷款率、银行资本同总资产比率、银行监管资本同风险加权资产比率、流动资产同存款和短期融资比率、银行不良贷款准备金率和银行稳健性等多指标全面衡量银行系统的稳定性，并选取股市波动性来衡量股市的稳定性。

银行不良贷款率、股市波动率越大，表明银行/股市的稳定性越脆弱，即金融稳定性越差。其他指标的数值越大，表明银行的稳定性越强，即金融稳定性越高。银行稳健性指标的数据为调查数据，来自世界经济论坛（WEF）每年发布的《全球竞争力报告》，其余 7 个指标的数据均来自世界银行的全球金融发展数据库。

指标 1.5　金融服务可得性

除了从金融体系自身的特征出发来衡量金融体系服务实体经济的潜在能力外，本模型还考虑了金融服务可得性这一维度。Beck et al.（2009）认为缺乏融资渠道是造成长期收入不平等以及经济增长放缓的关键，Mookerjee and Kalipioni（2010）使用每十万人中的银行机构数量衡量金融服务可得性，发现金融服务可得性的提高可以有力地减少各国收入之间的不平等。本模型选取每十万成年人拥有的商业银行分支机构数量来衡量银行业服务的可得性，选取前十大上市公司之外的股市交易额同总交易额比率、前十大上市公司之外的公司市值同总市值比率、每百万人拥有的上市公司数量来衡量企业在股票市场融资的难易程度，选取中小企业融资来衡量中小企业获取资金的难易程度，选取风险资本可得性来衡量初创企业融资的难易程度。

这 6 个指标数值越大，均表明该经济体更容易获得金融服务。其中4个三级指标——每十万成年人拥有的商业银行分支机构数量、前十大上市公司之外的股市交易额同总交易额比率、前十大上市公司之外的公司市值同总市值比率、每百万人拥有的上市公司数量的数据来自世界银行的全球金融发展数据库，其余两个指标——中小企业融资和风险资本可得性的数据来自世界经济论坛每年发布的《全球竞争力报告》。

指标1.6 国际金融中心地位

国际金融中心地位指标衡量了国际金融中心的综合竞争力，一个国家或地区国际金融中心的地位越高，说明该国家或地区金融发展程度越高，在全球范围内配置金融资源和管理风险的能力越强，进而能够更好地服务实体经济。倪鹏飞（2004）认为国际金融中心具有良好的金融和商务环境，可以有力吸引跨国银行、跨国公司，从而实现对全球经济的有力控制。刘轶（2010）认为国际金融中心是能够提供便捷的国际融资服务、有效的国际支付清算系统和活跃的国际金融交易场所的城市，在世界范围内具有影响力。Solovjova et al.（2018）认为国际金融中心的建立与金融自由化进程以及金融市场的全球化有关，为国家的整体经济发展和增长做出了贡献，其地位取决于银行体系的发展、证券市场的发展、安全的银行系统以及政府的支持和完善的国家政策等。本报告使用英国Z/Yen集团与中国（深圳）综合开发研究院联合发布的《全球金融中心指数》（The Global Financial Centres Index，GFCI），将排名位列前30%的金融中心的指数得分作为所属国家或地区的指标。由于国家大小不同，所入选的城市数量也有差异，对于同一国家或地区本报告只取得分最高的金融中心，用来代表该国家或地区金融发展的程度。

2. 数据处理

（1）权重赋值

表 4－1　　　　　　金融业竞争力指标构建及权重概览　　　　（单位：%）

一级指标	二级指标及权重		三级指标及权重	
1. 金融业竞争力	1.1 金融体系规模	16.66	1.1.1 存款银行资产同 GDP 比率	33.33
			1.1.2 股票市值同 GDP 比率	33.33
			1.1.3 其他部门资产同 GDP 比率	33.33
	1.2 金融体系活力	16.66	1.2.1 私人部门信贷同 GDP 比率	25.00
			1.2.2 银行贷款同银行存款比率	25.00
			1.2.3 股市交易值同 GDP 比率	50.00
	1.3 金融体系效率	16.67	1.3.1 银行非利息收入同总收入比率	16.67
			1.3.2 银行营业费用同总资产比率	16.67
			1.3.3 银行业资产回报率	16.67
			1.3.4 股市换手率	50.00
	1.4 金融稳定性	16.67	1.4.1 银行 Z-score	7.14
			1.4.2 银行不良贷款率	7.14
			1.4.3 银行资本同总资产比率	7.14
			1.4.4 银行监管资本同风险加权资产比率	7.14
			1.4.5 流动资产同存款和短期融资比率	7.14
			1.4.6 不良贷款准备金率	7.14
			1.4.7 银行稳健性	7.14
			1.4.8 股市波动率	50.00
	1.5 金融服务可得性	16.67	1.5.1 每十万成年人拥有的商业银行分支机构数量	25.00
			1.5.2 前十大上市公司之外的股市交易额同总交易额比率	8.33
			1.5.3 前十大上市公司之外的公司市值同总市值比率	8.33
			1.5.4 每百万人拥有的上市公司数量	8.33
			1.5.5 中小企业融资	25.00
			1.5.6 风险资本可得性	25.00
	1.6 国际金融中心地位	16.67	1.6.1 全球金融中心指数	100

金融业竞争力下设 6 个二级指标，分别给予同等权重，即 16.67%。对于二级指标下属的三级指标的权重，由于各部门的指标数量之间存在差异，本报告按照其所属的部门进行平均分配。例如，二级指标 1.2 金融体系活力下设 3 个三级指标——1.2.1 私人部门信贷同 GDP 比率、1.2.2 银行贷款同银行存款比率、1.2.3 股市交易值同 GDP 比率，其中指标 1.2.1 和 1.2.2 同属于银行业部门，权重分别为 25%，而指标 1.2.3 归属于股市部门，权重为 50%。（见表 4-1）

三级指标的数值与其权重分别相乘并加总得到对应的二级指标数值，再分别乘以二级指标权重，加总后即为金融业竞争力指数。例如，二级指标 1.2 金融体系活力的计算公式为：指标 1.2.1 的值 × 25% + 指标 1.2.2 的值 × 25% + 指标 1.2.3 的值 × 50%，金融业竞争力指数的计算公式为：指标 1.1 的值 × 16.67% + 指标 1.2 的值 × 16.67% + 指标 1.3 的值 × 16.67% + 指标 1.4 的值 × 16.67% + 指标 1.5 的值 × 16.67% + 指标 1.6 的值 × 16.67%。

（2）标准化方式

由于不同数据的量纲不同，需要先对数据进行标准化处理，使其转化为 [0, 1] 区间上的值。本报告借鉴 WEF 的做法，采用 Min-Max 标准化法对三级指标进行标准化。考虑到一些经济体的指标存在异常值，或者在经济学意义上某些指标应该有其合理值范畴，因此报告使用合理最值 X_{min}^*、X_{max}^* 替代数据原始最值 X_{min}、X_{max}。关于合理最值 X_{min}^*、X_{max}^* 的确定主要有以下两个原则：第一，从经济学意义上，界定该指标的合理取值范围；第二，从统计学意义上，在 10% 或 90% 分位对该指标进行缩尾处理，消除异常值。① 本报告根据各指标的属性，选择不同的原则确定合理最值的大小（见表4-2）。

表4-2 合理最值的选择

三级指标	可接受的最小值 X_{min}^*	可接受的最大值 X_{max}^*	说明
1.1.1 存款银行资产同GDP比率	0	150	最小值，90%分位数缩尾
1.1.2 股票市值同GDP比率	0	200	最小值，90%分位数缩尾
1.1.3 其他部门资产同GDP比率	0	400	最小值，90%分位数缩尾
1.2.1 私人部门信贷同GDP比率	0	160	最小值，90%分位数缩尾
1.2.2 银行贷款同银行存款比率	50	140	10%和90%分位数缩尾
1.2.3 股市交易值同GDP比率	0	130	最小值，90%分位数缩尾
1.3.1 银行非利息收入同总收入比率	0	50	最小值，90%分位数缩尾
1.3.2 银行营业费用同总资产比率	0	4	最小值，90%分位数缩尾
1.3.3 银行业资产回报率	0	2	最小值，90%分位数缩尾
1.3.4 股市换手率	0	130	最小值，90%分位数缩尾
1.4.1 银行Z-score	0	30	最小值，90%分位数缩尾
1.4.2 银行不良贷款率	0	15	最小值，90%分位数缩尾
1.4.3 银行资本同总资产比率	5	15	10%和90%分位数缩尾

① 部分发展中国家的指标明显偏离了合理值范畴。例如，中国大陆的股市市值占GDP比重仅为65.5%，远低于日本的113.1%，并低于多数发达国家；而中国大陆的股市交易值占GDP比重却高达144.7%，高于日本的112.3%，并高于多数发达国家。股市交易值占GDP比重越高，表明股票的交易越活跃和流动性越好，这对于一级市场的股票IPO存在正向激励作用。但是，中国大陆的股市交易值占GDP比重明显过高，超出了合理值范畴，不能正确地反映股市的真实功能。因此，本模型选择澳大利亚、加拿大、德国、瑞士、美国作为基准国，以这5国的"股市交易值/股市市值"的均值作为中国大陆和其他发展中国家的合理上限，修正发展中国家"股市交易值占GDP比重"的异常值；使用5个基准国家的"股市换手率"的均值修正发展中国家"股市换手率"的异常值。

续表

三级指标	可接受的最小值 X_{min}^*	可接受的最大值 X_{max}^*	说明
1.4.4 银行监管资本同风险加权资产比率	10	25	10%和90%分位数缩尾
1.4.5 流动资产同存款和短期融资比率	10	60	10%和90%分位数缩尾
1.4.6 不良贷款准备金率	30	150	10%和90%分位数缩尾
1.4.7 银行稳健性	1	7	最小值,最大值
1.4.8 股市波动率	10	25	10%和90%分位数缩尾
1.5.1 每十万成年人拥有的商业银行分支机构数量	0	50	最小值,90%分位数缩尾
1.5.2 前十大上市公司之外的股市交易额同总交易额比率	0	80	最小值,90%分位数缩尾
1.5.3 前十大上市公司之外的公司市值同总市值比率	0	80	最小值,90%分位数缩尾
1.5.4 每百万人拥有的上市公司数量	0	80	最小值,90%分位数缩尾
1.5.5 中小企业融资	1	7	最小值,最大值
1.5.6 风险资本可得性	1	7	最小值,最大值
1.6.1 全球金融中心指数	770	0	最小值,最大值

大部分指标与金融业竞争力正相关,对其标准化的计算公式如下,其中 X' 是缩尾后的数值:

$$Z = \frac{X' - X_{min}^*}{X_{max}^* - X_{min}^*}$$

另有3个三级指标与金融业竞争力负相关,即指标1.3.2银行营业费用占总资产比重、1.4.2银行不良贷款率和1.4.8股市波动率,对其标准化的公式为:

$$Z = 1 - \frac{X' - X_{min}^*}{X_{max}^* - X_{min}^*}$$

本报告其余四个一级指标的测算,均采用同样的数据标准化处理方法。

(3) 缺失值处理

表 4-3　　　　　　　　　　缺失指标的参考排序列表

缺失指标 A	参考排序指标 B
1.1.1 存款银行资产同 GDP 比率	流动性负债同 GDP 比率
1.1.2 股票市值同 GDP 比率	流动性负债同 GDP 比率
1.1.3 其他部门资产同 GDP 比率	流动性负债同 GDP 比率
1.2.1 私人部门信贷同 GDP 比率	流动性负债同 GDP 比率
1.2.2 银行贷款同银行存款比率	流动性负债同 GDP 比率
1.2.3 股市交易值同 GDP 比率	流动性负债同 GDP 比率
1.3.4 股市换手率	流动性负债同 GDP 比率
1.4.2 银行不良贷款率	1.4.1 银行 Z-score
1.4.3 银行资本同总资产比率	1.4.1 银行 Z-score
1.4.4 银行监管资本同风险加权资产比率	1.4.1 银行 Z-score
1.4.6 不良贷款准备金率	1.4.1 银行 Z-score
1.5.1 每十万成年人拥有的商业银行分支机构数量	1.2.2 银行贷款同银行存款比率
1.5.2 前十大上市公司之外的股市交易额同总交易额比率	1.1.2 股票市值同 GDP 比率
1.5.3 前十大上市公司之外的公司市值同总市值比率	1.1.2 股票市值同 GDP 比率
1.5.4 每百万人拥有的上市公司数量	1.1.2 股票市值同 GDP 比率

一些国家或地区的指标存在缺失值，对于这种情况，此处主要有两种处理方法：（1）替代法，若该国家或地区指标 A 上一年度的数据存在，则假设该年度和上一年度的状况相近，直接使用上一年度的数据进行替代；（2）排序法，若该国家或地区指标 A 上一年度的数据不存在，可能是因为这个指标在该国家或地区未纳入统计，则使用参考其他指标进行排序的方式。具体做法为：选取与缺失指标 A 含义相似的指标作为参考指标 B，对参考指标 B 排序，若排序后该国别的位次为 n，则选取位

次为 n-1 和 n+1 的两国对应的指标 A 的平均值作为缺失国指标 A 的数值。参考排序的列表见表 4-3。

本报告其余 4 个一级指标的测算，如无特殊说明，均采用同样的缺失值处理方法。

（二）货币竞争力的指数构建

1. 指标选择

在充分考虑数据可得性和相关文献研究的基础上，本报告为货币竞争力构建了 3 个二级指标，分别是"价值储存""交易媒介""计价单位"（见图 4-1），并平均赋权。3 个二级指标的设定，与文献中国际货币职能的划分保持一致，体现本报告货币竞争力指标创设的科学性。在二级指标下设的子指标选取方面，本报告重点参考了 IMF 每五年进行的特别提款权（SDR）

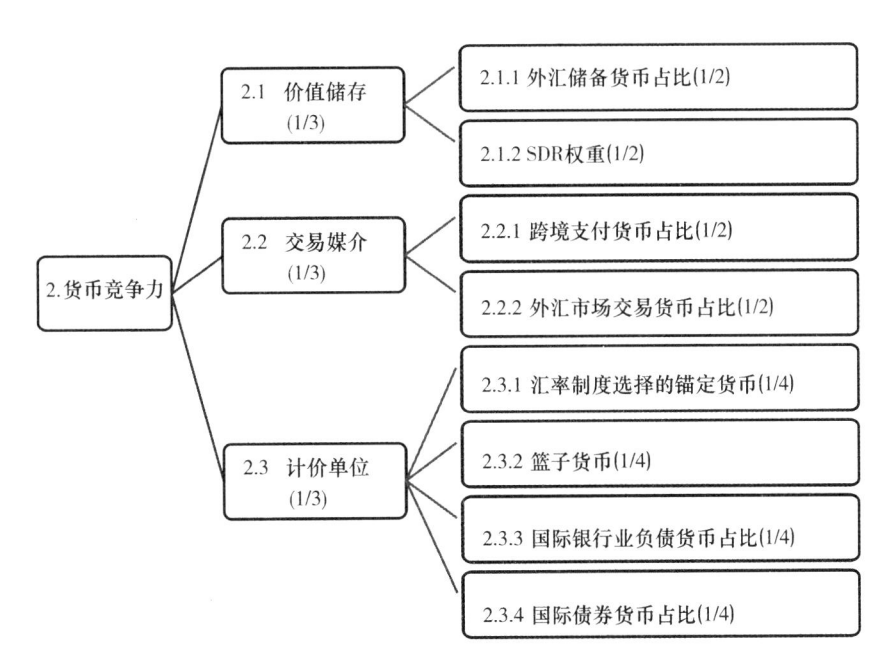

```
2. 货币竞争力
├── 2.1 价值储存 (1/3)
│   ├── 2.1.1 外汇储备货币占比 (1/2)
│   └── 2.1.2 SDR 权重 (1/2)
├── 2.2 交易媒介 (1/3)
│   ├── 2.2.1 跨境支付货币占比 (1/2)
│   └── 2.2.2 外汇市场交易货币占比 (1/2)
└── 2.3 计价单位 (1/3)
    ├── 2.3.1 汇率制度选择的锚定货币 (1/4)
    ├── 2.3.2 篮子货币 (1/4)
    ├── 2.3.3 国际银行业负债货币占比 (1/4)
    └── 2.3.4 国际债券货币占比 (1/4)
```

图 4-1 货币竞争力指标构建和权重概览

篮子份额审查（IMF，2015），并基于自身研究创设了货币锚指标，以便更全面地反映货币竞争力，也使得报告所形成的指数更具政策相关性。表4-4总结了各子指标衡量的不同货币职能在公共和私人部门的体现。

表4-4 货币竞争力各子指标与国际货币职能的对应关系

货币职能	政府	私人
价值储存	外汇储备	私人部门的货币替代行为
对应子指标	外汇储备货币占比、SDR权重	n. a.*
交易媒介	外汇市场干预的媒介货币	贸易和金融的交易货币
对应子指标	n. a.*	跨境支付货币占比、外汇市场交易货币占比
计价单位	一国汇率制度选择时的本币选择锚定的货币（Anchor Currency）	贸易和金融的计价货币
对应子指标	汇率制度选择的锚定货币、篮子货币	国际银行业负债货币占比、国际债券货币占比

说明：1. 国际货币职能的3×2矩阵图由 Kenen（1983）讨论美元国际货币地位时提出，本报告使用的版本源于 Chinn 和 Frankel（2007）。

2. 带*号的指标表示在该部门对应的货币职能难以找到国际可比的指标。

报告对于货币竞争力的测算基于货币而非基于主权国家，因此，人民币和港币将分别反映中国大陆和中国香港的货币竞争力。同时，在对欧元区的处理中，由于上述指标均难以设定欧元区国别层面的指标，因此货币竞争力中仅报告欧元区作为一个整体的指标，当加总至全球金融竞争力指标时，使用各成员国的出口占比分解欧元区的货币竞争力，进行打分。出口指标考虑货物贸易和服务贸易两个方面，采用最近5年的平均数，各赋权50%。具体的拆分方法是：以样本中欧元区国家在出口指标中的占比，对欧元区货币竞争力分值进行拆分得到最终欧元区各样本国家的分值。

"价值储存"包括了"外汇储备货币占比"和"SDR权重"两个三级指标,并进行平均赋权。理论上说,国际货币的价值储存功能在政府部门和私人部门均有所体现,但是从具体的指标来看,私人部门关注对于某一种国际货币对本币的货币替代,这一行为是相对灰色的,对于这一职能的刻画较难取得连续的量化数据。因此,在衡量价值储存的功能时,本报告侧重于对政府部门的刻画。外汇储备货币占比反映的是货币在国际层面的价值储存职能,是政府储备货币的币种选择。SDR是用于补充成员国官方储备的国际储备资产(IMF,2021),因此,处于SDR货币篮子中的五种货币可以发挥价值储存职能,且其规模取决于SDR货币篮子的权重。

"交易媒介"下设"跨境支付货币占比"和"外汇市场交易货币占比"两个三级指标,并进行平均赋权。两个三级指标均刻画的是私人部门的交易媒介角色,以更好地反映这一货币在国际金融市场和国际商务活动中作为交易货币的角色。政府部门的交易媒介职能关注外汇市场干预的媒介货币(Vehicle Currency),但是由于政府外汇市场干预的币种结构并不公开,因此这项职能较难采用指标进行刻画。

"计价单位"包含了"汇率制度选择的锚定货币""篮子货币""国际银行业负债货币占比""国际债券货币占比"四个三级指标,每个指标平均赋权。在这四个指标中,"汇率制度选择的锚定货币"和"篮子货币"反映一国汇率制度选择时的锚定货币,"汇率制度选择的锚定货币"(Exchange Rate Anchor)参考了IMF事实汇率分类的年度报告(IMF,2020),在这一体系中,对于非自由浮动制度的国家,汇率锚是其汇率政策制定和执行的重要组成;"篮子货币"指标由本报告作者测算,主要以Frankel和Wei(1994)为基准框架,基于徐奇渊和杨盼盼(2015)的研究拓展,测算一国货币驻锚篮子中每种货币的权重大小,并最终基于所有样本国的情况得出驻锚货币的权重,作为该项指标的打分。"国际银行业负债货币占比"和"国际债券货币占比"反映的是货币在私人部门履行的计价单位职能。

2. 数据处理

下面介绍各子指标的数据来源和处理方式。

指标2.1 价值储存

2.1.1 外汇储备货币占比

外汇储备货币占比的数据来源是IMF官方外汇储备货币构成调查(Currency Composition of Official Foreign Exchange Reserves survey,COFER)数据库。样本选取了报告编纂时可得的最新数值(2020年第四季度)。数据可得性方面,COFER数据库仅提供8种可确认币种的储备货币(Allocated Reserves)数据,分别为美元、欧元、日元、英镑、人民币、加拿大元、澳大利亚元、瑞士法郎。本报告将这8种货币的占比之和标准化为100%,然后再调整为百分制得分;对于没有数据的国家,该项指标打分为0。

2.1.2 SDR权重

SDR权重的数据来源是基金组织在2015年审查中确定的SDR权重(IMF SDR Weights determined in the 2015 Review),选取的时间是SDR最近一次调整生效时间,即2016年10月1日。由于SDR仅包含美元、欧元、人民币、日元和英镑五种货币,因此仅有这五种货币在这一指标下有得分,其得分以SDR权重为准,调整为百分制得分,其余货币没有得分。

指标2.2 交易媒介

2.2.1 跨境支付货币占比

跨境支付货币占比的数据来源为SWIFT(环球银行金融电信协会),指标衡量跨境支付的币种选择,选取时间为报告撰写时可获得的最新数据（2020年12月）。其中，印度、韩国、巴西、印度尼西亚、沙特阿拉伯、阿根廷、阿联酋没有数据，将这些货币的占比设为0，并将其他货币的占比标准化，然后调整为百分制得分。

2.2.2 外汇市场交易货币占比

外汇市场交易货币占比的数据来源为BIS的中央银行三年问卷（Triennial Central Bank Survey），这一问卷提供全球外汇市场交易数据，包含交易币种信息。选取的时间为2019年的最新可得数据。由于外汇交易数据同时包含了买卖双向信息，因此，理论上加总所有国家占比之后的值为200%，本报告在排序时将其标准化为加总之和为100%，之后再进行百分制调整。数据可得性方面，除阿根廷比索外，样本国家的货币均有数据。

指标2.3 锚定货币

2.3.1 汇率制度选择的锚定货币

汇率制度选择的锚定货币指标的数据来源是IMF汇率安排和汇率限制的年度报告（Annual Report on Exchange Arrangements and Exchange Restrictions 2019），报告中各国汇率制度选择是由基金组织工作人员识别的事实（de facto）汇率制度，而不是官方公布（de jure）的汇率制度。对于除了浮动和自由浮动汇率制度安排以外的国家，一些货币当局会采取买入或卖出外汇以使本币保持在预定水平或者一定区间的操作，对于这些国家而言，汇率就成为一个货币政策的名义锚或中间目标（IMF，2020）。IMF将汇率制度选择的锚定货币识别并进行统计，被锚定的货币主要是美元和欧元，也包括澳大利亚元、新加坡元、南非兰特、印度卢比等。数据截止时间为2019年4月30日。测算方法为先按锚定国家的数量对上述货币赋分，再调整为百分制得分。

2.3.2 篮子货币

篮子货币指标衡量的是某一种货币事实上锚定的货币篮子

成分。指标的测算以 Frankel 和 Wei（1994）为基准框架，基于徐奇渊和杨盼盼（2015）的研究拓展进行。其中货币篮子的货币与 SDR 保持一致，包括美元、欧元、日元、英镑和人民币，因此，篮子货币指标也只能反映这五种货币的排序，参考货币包括 26 种。① 具体的步骤如下：（1）将所有货币汇率日度数据标准化为对瑞士法郎的双边汇率；（2）由于美元仍然是人民币的重要参考货币，因此，首先使用其他主要参考货币（美元、欧元、日元和英镑）对人民币做回归，将人民币的非自主成分剔除，将回归的残差项作为人民币的自主波动成分，使用这一序列替代人民币汇率；（3）使用参考货币的汇率差分数据作为被解释变量，五个篮子货币汇率作为被解释变量，使用基于状态空间模型的时变参数估计，获得每一种货币随时间变动的货币篮子权重，将其标准化并取 2020 年平均值；（4）五种篮子货币对应每一种参考货币都有一个权重，将这些权重进行简单平均，就得到美元、欧元、日元、英镑和人民币的篮子货币排序。在得到了篮子货币权重后，对其进行百分制调整。

2.3.3 国际银行业负债货币占比

国际银行业负债货币占比的数据来源为国际清算银行（BIS）统计的反映跨境国际银行业务的本地银行业务统计（Locational Banking Statistics, LBS），该项统计关注以实际经营地（Residence）而非母公司所在国（Nationality）视角开展的国际银行业务。LBS 覆盖了约 95% 的跨境银行业务。本指标采用了其中对于国际银行业负债（International Banking Liabilities）中使用的不同类型计价货币规模的统计。选取时间为最新数据

---

① 参考货币包括：东亚地区：东盟 10 国、韩国、中国台湾、中国香港；其他 G10 经济体：澳大利亚、新西兰、加拿大、挪威、瑞典；其他 G20 发展中国家：阿根廷、巴西、印度、墨西哥、南非、俄罗斯、沙特阿拉伯、土耳其。

（2020年第四季度）。该数据库有5种货币的数据，分别为美国、欧元区、英国、日本和瑞士，对于其他国家的数据，采取如下处理方法：（1）对于人民币，基于IMF（2015年）的SDR份额评估报告，其公布了2015年第二季度除上述五种货币外人民币国际银行业负债的全球占比，为1.8%，假定这一占比与中国GDP在全球中的占比保持同比例的变化，那么2020年的占比为2.11%，本报告使用这一占比；（2）对于其他货币，按照2.2.1外汇市场成交量的对应规模进行分配，相应的指标介绍见下文；（3）假设所有样本货币份额之和为100%，除已知5种货币份额和人民币测算份额，其他货币占比为5.08%，按（2）中方法分配比例。最后，调整为百分制得分。

2.3.4 国际债券货币占比

国际债券货币占比的数据来源为BIS债券统计（Debt Securities Statistics）中的国际债券统计（International Debt Securities），BIS使用表4-5说明了国际债券（IDS）和国内债券（DDS）的区别，本指标使用了债券发行存量数据的币种信息，选取时间为指标编制时的最新数据（2020年第四季度）。在样本国中，除了南非兰特之外，其他币种均有数据，故将南非数据设为0，其余占比进行标准化后，调整为百分制得分。

表4-5　国际债券和国内债券的范畴

A国国民发行债券地点	A国国民的业务经营地	
	A国	B国
A国	国内债券	国际债券
B国	国际债券	国内债券
C国	国际债券	国际债券

（三）金融基础设施竞争力的指数构建

1. 指标选择

在金融基础设施硬件方面，我们的数据主要来源于国际清算银行（BIS）关于支付与金融市场基础设施的统计指标（即BIS红皮书统计指标）。具体使用指标包括：提供支付服务的机构数（每百万居民）、无现金支付金额占GDP比重、终端数（每个居民）、选定支付系统处理的支付交易额占GDP比重、国内使用SWIFT的机构数、选定中央对手方和清算所清算额占GDP比重、选定中央证券托管机构交付指令金额占GDP比重。选取这些指标主要依据是考虑到关于CPMI金融基础设施的定义中包括支付、清算、登记等各项设施。

衡量金融基础设施相关制度软件的指标主要来自于世界银行营商环境指数的分项指标。这些分项指标包括：（1）获得信贷指标，主要用来衡量一国征信系统的强弱和担保及破产法在促进借贷上的有效性；（2）投资者保护指标，主要用来衡量当董事滥用公司财务以获得私人利益时对于少数股东权利的保护力度，以及包括股权、治理保障和公司公开透明的要求在内的可降低股东利益受损风险的各项措施；（3）执行合同指标，用于衡量一家当地初级法院解决一起商业纠纷所花费的时间和费用，以及司法程序质量指标。其中司法程序质量指标衡量每个经济体是否采取了一系列的好的举措以提升法院系统的质量和效率。上述三项分项指标的打分方式完全依照世界银行营商环境指数方法论中所陈述的方法进行处理。

此外，本报告还加入国际财务报告准则（IFRS）应用范围指标作为会计准则质量的度量。根据IFRS使用标准，各国家及辖区所实施的会计准则可划分为：未采用IFRS标准（0分）、国内公众公司必须采用IFRS标准（2分）、国内公众公司可以采用 IFRS 标准但非强制要求（1 分）、外国公司在本国上市必须或允许采用 IFRS 标准（2 分）、小微企业必须或允许采用 IFRS 标准（2 分）、辖区正在考虑应用小微企业 IFRS 标准（1 分）。然后我们通过对一国 IFRS 标准应用程度打分并进行排名作为会计准则基础设施的比较与衡量。具体指标构建和权重分配见图 4–2。

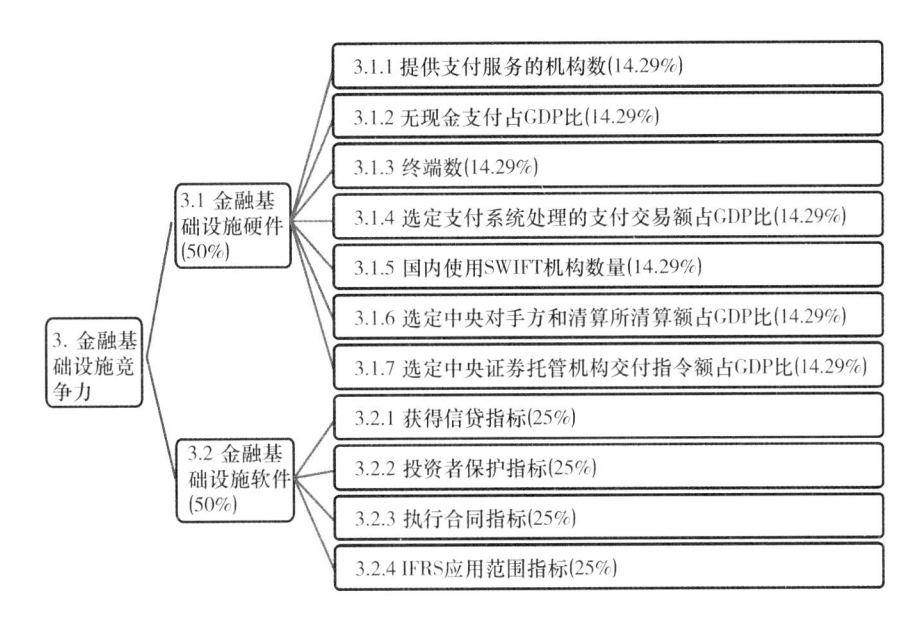

```
                              ┌─ 3.1.1 提供支付服务的机构数(14.29%)
                              ├─ 3.1.2 无现金支付占GDP比(14.29%)
                              ├─ 3.1.3 终端数(14.29%)
              3.1 金融基础设施硬件 ─┼─ 3.1.4 选定支付系统处理的支付交易额占GDP比(14.29%)
                  (50%)         ├─ 3.1.5 国内使用SWIFT机构数量(14.29%)
                              ├─ 3.1.6 选定中央对手方和清算所清算额占GDP比(14.29%)
3. 金融基础设施竞争力            └─ 3.1.7 选定中央证券托管机构交付指令额占GDP比(14.29%)
                              ┌─ 3.2.1 获得信贷指标(25%)
              3.2 金融基础设施软件 ─┼─ 3.2.2 投资者保护指标(25%)
                  (50%)         ├─ 3.2.3 执行合同指标(25%)
                              └─ 3.2.4 IFRS应用范围指标(25%)
```

图 4–2　金融基础设施竞争力指标构建和权重概览

2. 数据处理

金融基础设施硬件方面缺失值较多，针对这一问题，我们采取的解决方法为，倘若一个国家或地区某一单项指标缺失，则以余下指标值取等权重平均后参与排序；若该国家或地区所有指标均缺失，则我们依照各项指标的平均值予以补充，然后再取等权重平均进行排序。使用这一方式而非类似金融业竞争力相关指标的缺失值处理方式，主要由于各项指标国别差异性较大，若依照某一指标排序（如金融基础设施软件）后取前后排名平均值，则有可能显著高估/低估待填补指标的值，相

28　国家智库报告

比之下，取整体平均值则更为平滑。

随后我们对金融基础设施软件和硬件标准化后的分值等权重平均。

（四）金融科技竞争力的指数构建

1. 指标选择

金融科技领域的底层技术决定了该领域的发展潜能，市场发育程度反映了金融科技的应用前景。在底层技术之外，金融科技的应用领域进一步分为消费端和产业端，分别通过用户接入度和产业发展潜力来衡量。最终3个二级指标的权重为50∶25∶25（见图4-3）。

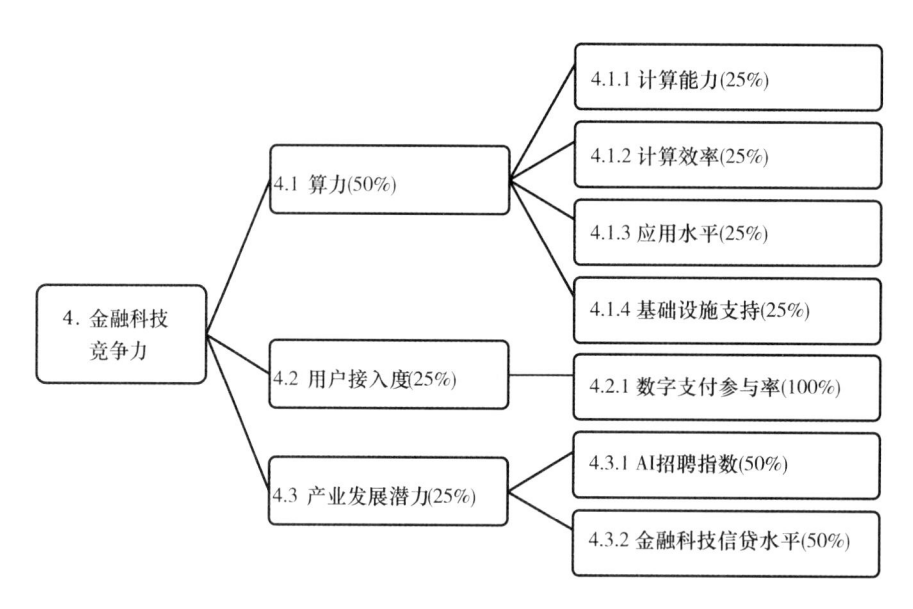

```
4. 金融科技竞争力
├── 4.1 算力(50%)
│   ├── 4.1.1 计算能力(25%)
│   ├── 4.1.2 计算效率(25%)
│   ├── 4.1.3 应用水平(25%)
│   └── 4.1.4 基础设施支持(25%)
├── 4.2 用户接入度(25%)
│   └── 4.2.1 数字支付参与率(100%)
└── 4.3 产业发展潜力(25%)
    ├── 4.3.1 AI招聘指数(50%)
    └── 4.3.2 金融科技信贷水平(50%)
```

图4-3　金融科技竞争力指标构建和权重概览

"算力指数"衡量各国金融科技产业的计算力，表现其技术基础的厚度。本报告引用IDC发布的《2020年全球计算力评估报告》中的算力指标作为计算"算力指数"的原始数据，该算力指标涵盖计算能力、计算效率、应用水平、基础设施支持四个维度，对2020年全球重点国家的算力发展水平和未来发展潜力进行评估。但原报告中只有美国、中国大陆、日本、德国、英国、法国、澳大利亚、巴西、南非、俄罗斯10个国家的数据，本报告尝试使用替代法与缺失法补齐全球另外24个主要国家或地区的指数。在补足"计算能力"数据时参考全球Top500超级计算机各国所占数量与排名以及各国智能手机普及率排名，补足"计算效率"等后三个指标时则借用"计算能力"指标排名，本报告采用标准化方法处理原始数据，各数据加权加总得出各国算力指数，故算力指数介于0—1之间，综合排名最前国家指数为1，最后的国家指数为0。一国算力指数数值越高，代表该国计算力越强大，在国际上计算力方面优势越大。

"用户接入度指数"衡量各国金融科技产业的普及程度以及用户基础，利用各国已接入金融科技产业的人数与金融科技产业所有潜在用户的比率来表现各国金融科技产业目前的用户接入度。本报告引用世界银行Findex数据库公布的2017年（最新数据）各国"过去一年中15岁及以上人口中使用或接受数字支付的比率"数据，原数据包含本报告所需32个国家，故只对原数据进行标准化处理即可得到用户接入度指数，用户接入度指数介于0—1之间，综合排名最前国家指数为1，最后的国家指数为0。一国用户接入度指数越高，代表其金融科技产业普及程度越高，"变现"潜在用户能力越强，用户群体数量相对其人口越庞大。

"产业发展潜力指数"利用金融科技产业中终端行业的发展状况衡量各国金融科技产业未来的发展空间，而决定一个产业发展潜力的两个关键因素是劳动力和资本的投入水平。基于此，本报告选取各国AI人才的招聘和储备水平来反映金融科技产业中的劳动力投入水平，选取各国金融科技信贷水平来反映金融科技产业中的资本投入水平。针对AI人才，本报告中综合斯坦福大学发布的2020

年各国 AI 招聘指数与牛津视野与国际研究中心发布的 2019 年各国 AI 准备指数，得出 32 个国家得分与排名；针对金融科技信贷水平，本报告选用 G. Cornelli 等发布的 Fintech Credit Data 中的 2018 年（最新数据）各国金融科技信贷人均规模为原数据。本报告通过对两个三级指标得分进行标准化处理再加权加总得出各国产业发展潜力指数。产业发展潜力指数介于 0—1 之间，一国产业发展潜力指数越高，说明该国金融科技终端行业发展状况越好，未来市场空间越大，有更高的获利可能性。

2. 数据处理

本节数据处理方式同金融业竞争力部分。

（五）国际金融治理竞争力的指数构建

1. 指标选择

（1）二级指标

根据联合国全球治理委员会的定义，治理是个人以及各种公共的或私人的机构管理共同事务的诸多方式的总和。全球治理理论的主要创始人之一詹姆斯·罗西瑙（James N. Rosenau）认为治理与政府统治相比，治理既包括政府机制，也包括非正式的、非政府的机制。全球治理包括在诸如超越国家的和国际其他层次上规则的建立和执行，同时也承认国家在国际系统中的作用。[1] 由此可见，尽管主权国家在过去、现在、将来都是国际治理的主角，但是其在国际治理体系框架中的作用和效果日益衰减，而各国际组织则突破初创时期的地域、领域的限制，在当今国际政治、经济、金融乃至社会各个领域发挥更大的作用。

---

[1] James N. Rosenau, *Governance in the Twenty First Century*, Global Governance Vol. 1, pp. 13–43.

由此可知，参与国际金融治理的主体至少包括以下几个部分：（1）各国政府以及相关政府部门，尤以各国财政部、中央银行部门、金融监管部门参与最为广泛；（2）正式的国际组织，尤以国际货币基金组织和国际清算银行等参与最为广泛和重要；（3）非正式组织和社会团体，比如 G20 和全球金融稳定委员会最为广泛，还有跨国公司、跨国运动以及众多非政府组织也会对国际金融治理施加影响。

鉴于国际正式或非正式组织满足了金融全球化的需求，其作为全球治理和金融治理主体的重要性日益增加，且各国政府以及相关政府部门亦是通过在国际正式或非正式组织中协商解决国际问题，因此本报告选择国际组织作为国际金融治理的主体。

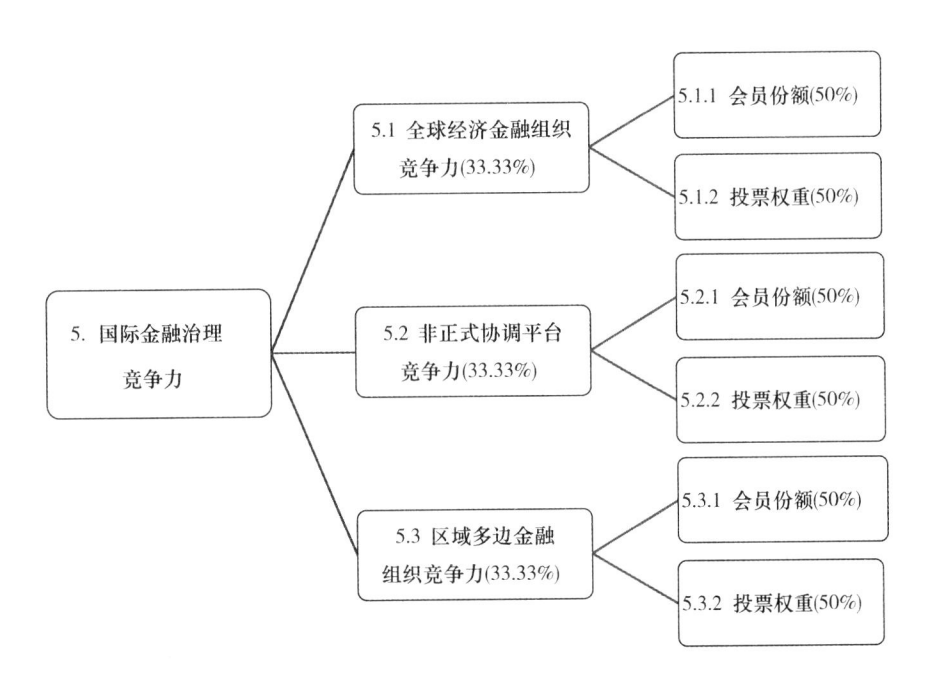

图 4-4　国际金融治理竞争力指标构建和权重概览

接下来，我们根据国际金融治理的客体来筛选哪些正式或非正式组织应纳入分析框架。根据联合国训练与研究所的课程对国际金融治理的理解，国际金融治理是为了维持一个可预测、稳定并有利于国际经济交易支付的国际货币体系；同时，国际金融治理旨在监督国际金融体系，保护世界各地储户与投资者的利益，并在所有潜在的借款人之间有效、公平地分配信贷。[①]有学者认为，国际金融治理至少除了包括国际货币体系和国际金融监管体系，还应包括国际金融治理机制的改革，包括国际货币金融机构的改革，也包括国际金融治理与改革的决策主体的改革，比如如何更好地发挥G20的作用。还有学者指出，除了国际货币体系改革、全球金融业监管和国际金融治理机构改革，国际金融治理应包括以下问题：国际宏观经济政策协调、区域金融合作、全球金融安全网建设和国际资本流动。[②]

据此，有学者指出第二次世界大战后布雷顿森林体系所建立的国际货币基金组织（International Monetary Fund，IMF）和世界银行集团（The World Bank，WB）、第一次世界大战之后建立的国际清算银行（Bank for International Settlements，BIS）、"七国集团"（G7）所建立的金融稳定论坛（Financial Stability Forum，FSF）以及在各地区建立的区域性开发银行，如欧洲复兴开发银行（European Bank for Reconstruction and Development，EBRD）、亚洲开发银行（Asian Development Bank，ADB）、非洲开发银行（African Development Bank，AfDB）、泛美开发银行（Inter-American Development Bank，IDB）等共同构成了当代全球金融组织体系，并将上述国际金融组织体系分为宏观稳定类、

[①] Daniel Bradlow, *Materials for A 4-Part On-Line Course on Global Financial Governance*, Offered by United Nations Institute on Training and Research (UNITAR), On-Line Training Courses in Public Finance and Trade, 2009.

[②] 张礼卿：《全球金融治理面临的八个问题》，《中国外汇》2021年第4期。

多边开发类、金融监管与标准制定类三个类别。① 熊北辰（2021）则认为参与国际金融治理的国际组织应该包括：国际货币基金组织、欧洲金融稳定基金、阿拉伯货币基金组织、东亚及太平洋中央银行行长会议组织、东加勒比中央银行、国际清算银行、金融稳定理事会、国际保险监督官协会、国际证监会组织、国际会计准则理事会、非洲开发银行、美洲开发银行和亚洲基础设施投资银行。除此之外，经济合作与发展组织（Organization for Economic Co-operation and Development，OECD）②、巴黎俱乐部（Paris FC）③、"清迈协议"（Chiang Mai Initiative，CMI）④、金砖国家新开发银行（New Development Bank，NDB）⑤、亚洲基础设施投资银行（Asian Infrastructure Investment Bank，AIIB）⑥ 等国际组织也常常被纳入分析框架。

综上，本报告选择以下国际正式或非正式机构作为国际金融治理的主体，包括国际货币基金组织（IMF）、世界银行（WB）、国际清算银行（BIS）、经济合作与发展组织（OECD）、二十国集团（G20）、金融稳定委员会（FSB）、巴黎俱乐部、泛

---

① 上海发展研究基金会全球金融治理课题组：《全球金融治理：挑战、目标和改革——关于2016年G20峰会议题的研究报告》，《国际经济评论》2016年第3期。

② 张庆麟、刘天姿：《全球金融治理若干凸显问题综述》，《金融法学家》（第四辑），2012年。

③ Tsingou Eleni, "The Club Rules in Global Financial Governance", *The Political Quarterly*, Vol. 85, No. 4, 2014.

④ 洪小芝：《全球金融治理改革的文献综述》，《西南金融》2012年第3期。

⑤ 潘庆中、李稻葵、冯明：《"新开发银行"新在何处——金砖国家开发银行成立的背景、意义与挑战》，《国际经济评论》2015年第2期。

⑥ 张茉楠：《AIIB影响全球金融治理格局的三个维度》，《金融博览》2016年第2期。

美开发银行（IDB）、非洲开发银行（AfDB）、欧洲复兴开发银行（EBRD）、欧洲投资银行（EIB）、亚洲开发银行（ADB）、亚洲基础设施投资银行（AIIB）和金砖国家新开发银行（NDB）。

区别于以往研究根据国际金融治理客体（即治理什么"问题"）对国际金融组织进行分类，本报告根据国际金融治理的层次进行分类：首先将国际金融治理分为全球层次和区域层次；其次根据国际组织机制，即是否有正式的协商机制，将全球层次分为全球金融组织和非正式协调平台；最后将国际金融治理竞争力分为全球经济金融组织竞争力、非正式协调平台竞争力和区域多边金融组织竞争力3个二级指标（见表4-6）。

表4-6　　　　　　　　国际金融治理竞争力二级指标

二级指标	覆盖机构	数量
全球经济金融组织竞争力	国际货币基金组织（IMF）、世界银行（WB）、国际清算银行（BIS）、经济合作与发展组织（OECD）	4
非正式协调平台竞争力	二十国集团（G20）、金融稳定委员会（FSB）、巴黎俱乐部	3
区域多边金融组织竞争力	美洲开发银行（IDB）、非洲开发银行（AfDB）、欧洲复兴开发银行（EBRD）、欧洲投资银行（EIB）、亚洲开发银行（ADB）、亚洲基础设施投资银行（AIIB）、金砖银行（NDB）	7

在全球化的时代，没有哪个国家或机构拥有充足的资源和知识可以独自解决所有的问题。全球的治理需要各种行为主体之间进行沟通和协商，共享各种资源和信息，采取协调一致的行动。如果一个机构会员覆盖全球主要国家，那么在这个机构相关机制下形成的决策、意见、方针等文件，将有可能在全球范围内实施和推广；而区域性金融机构则大概率只能在区域范围内实施；这是本报告采取层次对国际金融治理进行分类的原因。

进一步，国际机制分为正式和非正式两种类型：正式国际机制是指由国际组织通过法律制定的方式来建立，通过理事会、大会及其他实体方式来维持并由国际官僚机构来保障协议实施的国际机制，如国际货币基金组织、世界银行等；而非正式国际机制是指成员国依据彼此所追求目标之间能够达成的共识来建立，并根据彼此共同利益或"君子协定"以及相互之间的监督来保障协议实施的国际机制，如欧安会、八国集团等。在两种机制下，各成员国达成一致意见的方式和保障一致意见实施的途径存在较大差异，因此，本报告将全球性机构分为正式的全球金融组织和非正式的协调平台。

（2）三级指标

在选定国际金融治理主体（国际组织）和客体（议事范围）后，接下来我们将选择衡量各国在国际金融治理主体和客体中代表权和话语权的指标。

国际金融的"现实"在很大程度上是被"建构"的，谁具有国际金融"现实"建构权，谁就是话语实施者（或传播者）。在这个意义上，国际金融治理话语权的主要内容反映一个主权国家所关注的与自身金融利益相关的，或与之承担的国际责任、义务相关的观点和立场。因此，国际金融话语权体现为话语实施者凭借何种载体、渠道或方式表达并影响话语对象，其中，国际议程设置或被视为国际金融话语权的部分定义要素或被视为其获取手段。在现存的国际金融制度下，一国可以借助多层次的话语平台来凸显其国际金融话语权。双边话语平台主要包括两国间的直接接触，如经贸往来、监管合作、金融论坛、战略对话、资本交易、援助交流等途径。多边话语平台主要是透过正式的国际金融机构或者一定的国际金融机制进行。

根据前文对国际金融治理主体和客体的界定，本报告通过一国在国际组织中是否参与决策以及在多大程度上可以影响意见成为决策来衡量该国在国际组织中的代表权和话语权，即该国的国际金融治理竞争力。

以国际货币基金组织（IMF）为例，分析一国的代表权和话语权的表现方式。一国想获得IMF的会员（代表）资格，需要递交申请，基金的董事局审议通过后，再向管治委员会提交"会员资格决议"的报告，报告中会建议该申请国可以在基金中分到多少配额，管治委员会接纳申请后，申请国签署入会文件成为正式成员国。成员国的"配额"决定了一国的应付会费、投票力量、接受资金援助的份额以及特别提款权SDR的数量。这表明会员份额是成员国向IMF认缴的一定数额的资金，相当于成员国在IMF中所拥有的股份，是衡量各成员国在IMF相对地位的最重要的指标。由此可以看出，会员份额可以作为衡量一国在国际货币基金组织中代表权的指标。

在决策机制上，协商一致和投票表决是IMF的两种议事规则。虽然协商一致是IMF执行董事会广泛使用的原则，但它并非是一致同意的表现。它通常在非正式会议上进行，且被发达国家所主导。在进行重大事项决议时，IMF通常使用投票表决，并以多数票原则为基础。每个成员国的投票权由基本投票权和基于份额的投票权构成。加权投票制度和多数表决制度都有助于一项决策的尽快产生。由此可以看出，投票权重可以作为衡量一国在国际货币基金组织话语权的指标。

因此，本报告选择会员份额和投票权重作为国际金融治理竞争力的三级指标。

2. 数据处理

数据标准化方式同金融业竞争力部分。本节存在一些特殊的数据处理，方式如下。

首先，部分正式和非正式国际组织没有会员份额比重或投票权比重数据，按照是否为会员平均权利；比如非洲开发银行只有投票权比重，没有会员认缴份额比重，那么假定认缴会员份额在会员间平均分配，会员国家取值100，非会员国家取值0。

其次，对于二级指标中的会员份额比重指数和投票权比重指数各自赋权50%，得到单个机构或平台中样本国家的国际金融治理竞争力。然后，对每类机构中的单个机构或平台平均赋权，得到分类的竞争力指数。比如对国际货币基金组织（IMF）、世界银行（WB）、国际清算银行（BIS）和经济合作与发展组织（OECD）平均赋权，得到全球金融组织竞争力；对二十国集团（G20）、金融稳定委员会（FSB）和巴黎俱乐部平均赋权，得到非正式协调平台竞争力；对泛美开发银行（IDB）、非洲开发银行（AfDB）、欧洲复兴开发银行（EBRD）、欧洲投资银行（EIB）、亚洲开发银行（ADB）、亚洲基础设施投资银行（AIIB）和金砖国家新开发银行（NDB）平均赋权得到区域多边金融竞争力。

最后，对三个二级指标平均赋权，得到国际金融治理竞争力指数（IFGC）。

五 全球金融竞争力评价

(一) 总指数

表5-1展示了全球32个经济体的全球金融竞争力排名情况，欧美国家占据了前10名中的7位，其中美、英两国分列全球前2位；亚洲经济体当中有3个进入全球前10，日本排名第3，中国大陆排名第8，韩国排名第9。

表5-1 全球金融竞争力总指数

排名	经济体	全球金融竞争力分值	排名	经济体	全球金融竞争力分值
1	美国	85.1	17	卢森堡	28.9
2	英国	51.3	18	意大利	28.9
3	日本	44.8	19	阿联酋	28.5
4	德国	43.9	20	南非	27.2
5	加拿大	42.2	21	巴西	25.4
6	澳大利亚	41.3	22	沙特阿拉伯	25.3
7	法国	41.3	23	爱尔兰	25.2
8	中国大陆	41.2	24	奥地利	24.6
9	韩国	40.7	25	俄罗斯	22.9
10	瑞士	40.6	26	印度	22.4
11	荷兰	39.8	27	葡萄牙	22.2
12	新加坡	38.7	28	土耳其	21.5

续表

排名	经济体	全球金融竞争力分值	排名	经济体	全球金融竞争力分值
13	中国香港	38.4	29	墨西哥	19.1
14	西班牙	34.9	30	印度尼西亚	17.6
15	比利时	32.3	31	希腊	15.8
16	芬兰	31.6	32	阿根廷	15.0

注：表中分值经过"四舍五入"而得到，故存在分值相同而排名不同的情况，下同。

美国的全球金融竞争力排名世界第1，其分值比位居第2名的英国高出33.8分，这是相邻两个经济体分值差距最大的一组，显示出美国在全球金融领域拥有显著的竞争优势。从5个一级指标来看，美国在金融业竞争力、货币竞争力、金融科技竞争力和国际金融治理能力4个指标上均排名全球第1，只有金融基础设施一项排名第5。可以看出，支撑美国金融竞争力的基础是较为稳固的。此外，在美国领先的4个一级指标中，货币竞争力的优势最为突出，高出第2名欧元整体38.8分，这清楚地显示出，美元国际地位是美国维护其全球金融竞争力的最强大力量。

英国的全球金融竞争力排名世界第2，其竞争优势主要来自于金融基础设施和金融业竞争力两个一级指标。英国的金融基础设施竞争力排名全球第1，超出第2名的新加坡13.7分，这也是金融基础设施竞争力排名中相邻两个经济体分值差距最大的一组，充分显示出英国作为老牌资本主义国家在这一领域积累下来的优势。此外，英国的金融业竞争力排名世界第2，仅次于美国，这也是支撑英国成为世界金融强国的关键因素。

中国大陆的全球金融竞争力排名世界第8，以0.1分之差位于法国之后，以0.5分的优势高于韩国。在5个一级指标中，金融业竞争力是中国大陆与世界领先水平差距最小的，比排名第1的美国低16.2分。在近20年的时间里，中国的金融业实现了持续高速增长，培育出了全球规模最大、盈利能力最强的银行体系，建成了全球规模第二的股票市场与债券市场。除去规模外，中国金融体系的效率、活力与国际金融中心影响力均获得显著提升，三项分指标均进入世界前10位。我国的货币竞争力则是五项一级指标中与世界领先水平差距最大的，与美国相差90.2分。从2009年开始，我国逐步推进人民币国际化，2016年人民币纳入SDR货币篮子。可以说，人民币国际化在过去10年中也取得了重大进展，但是人民币的国际地位与中国的经济体量仍然不相匹配，与美元和欧元相比，人民币的国际化还有很大提升空间。

（二）一级指标

1. 金融业竞争力

表5-2展示了金融业竞争力得分及其排名情况。在所选择的32个经济体中，美国、英国和中国香港分别位居前三，新加坡和日本分别位居第5和第9，中国大陆、法国、德国分别位居第11、第12和第15。

表5-2　　　　　　　　金融业竞争力结果展示

排名	经济体	金融业竞争力分值	排名	经济体	金融业竞争力分值
1	美国	78.0	17	芬兰	53.4
2	英国	75.4	18	阿联酋	51.3
3	中国香港	75.4	19	南非	46.6
4	瑞士	75.1	20	沙特阿拉伯	38.6
5	新加坡	71.4	21	葡萄牙	36.7
6	韩国	69.4	22	印度	35.2
7	加拿大	68.8	23	巴西	33.9

续表

排名	经济体	金融业竞争力分值	排名	经济体	金融业竞争力分值
8	澳大利亚	68.5	24	土耳其	33.3
9	日本	67.9	25	奥地利	32.1
10	荷兰	63.5	26	印度尼西亚	31.7
11	中国大陆	61.8	27	墨西哥	30.3
12	法国	59.6	28	爱尔兰	29.3
13	卢森堡	57.3	29	意大利	28.3
14	西班牙	57.3	30	俄罗斯	27.2
15	德国	56.1	31	希腊	24.2
16	比利时	55.1	32	阿根廷	18.8

美国的金融业竞争指数排名世界第1，这与美国拥有全球最发达金融体系的地位相符，而且美国注重金融体系的全面与纵深发展，美国金融业的各项指标排名都相对靠前。基于细分指标来看，美国金融体系相对规模排名第10，金融体系活力排名第6，金融体系效率排名第2，金融稳定性排名第2，金融服务可得性排名第2，国际金融中心地位排名第1。

英国的金融业竞争指数排名第2。作为老牌资本主义国家，英镑仍是重要的国际货币，英国的金融体系在全球占有重要地位。基于细分指标，英国金融体系相对规模排名第4，金融体系活力第4，金融体系效率第5，金融稳定性第6，金融服务可得性第8，国际金融中心地位仅次于美国，排名第2。

中国大陆的金融业竞争指数排名世界第11。细分指标显示，中国大陆的金融体系相对规模排名第16，金融体系活力排名第10，金融体系效率排名第6，金融稳定性排名第22，金融服务可得性排名第17，国际金融中心地位排名第3。中国大陆的金融体系相对规模排名偏后，一方面是因为中国大陆的经济体量较大，另一方面，虽然中国大陆的银行业和股票市场发展较好，但共同基金、保险公司以及养老金等金融部门发展相对滞后。中国大陆的金融体系活力排名中等，反映了中国商业银行信贷活动和股票市场交易行为活跃，金融体系具有较高的活力。中国大陆的金融体系效率排名比较靠前，主要反映了银行业资产回报率和股市换手率较高，金融体系相对高效运转。中国大陆的金融稳定性排名比较靠后，一是因为股市的波动率过高，资本市场稳定性较差；二是间接融资比重很高，银行风险管控压力较大。中国大陆的金融服务可得性排名适中，反映了中国金融体系在为实体经济提供融资方面取得了明显的进步。中国大陆的国际金融中心地位排名比较靠前，主要是因为上海、北京和深圳等城市在全球重要的国际金融中心城市中已经具备较高的综合竞争力。

2. 货币竞争力

表5-3反映了各个国家/地区货币竞争力的综合排名情况。基于对价值储存、交易媒介和计价单位3个二级指标进行百分制标准化打分，最终得到美国的货币竞争力得分为100，排名第1；欧元区的货币竞争力得分为61.2，排名第2。英国、日本和中国大陆的货币竞争力得分较为接近，分列第3名至第5名，反映人民币的货币竞争力正在接近日元和英镑的水平。澳大利亚、加拿大和瑞士的货币竞争力排在第6名至第8名，且与前五大货币存在较大分数差距。中国香港排在第9，得分为1.5。

表5-3　　　　　　　　货币竞争力结果展示

排名	经济体	货币竞争力分值	排名	经济体	货币竞争力分值
1	美国	100	12	印度	0.8
2	欧元区	61.2	13	墨西哥	0.5
3	英国	13.6	14	韩国	0.4

续表

排名	经济体	货币竞争力分值	排名	经济体	货币竞争力分值
4	日本	10.6	15	土耳其	0.4
5	中国大陆	9.8	16	俄罗斯	0.4
6	澳大利亚	3.5	17	巴西	0.3
7	加拿大	2.6	18	印度尼西亚	0.1
8	瑞士	1.7	19	阿联酋	0
9	中国香港	1.5	20	沙特阿拉伯	0
10	新加坡	1.1	21	阿根廷	0
11	南非	1.0			

美国在货币竞争力排名中居于首位，且具有绝对优势。由于我们的货币竞争力打分是参照各指标的最高值进行百分制处理，因此，美元的货币竞争力在价值储存、交易媒介和计价单位领域均处于全球第一位置。随着布雷顿森林体系的建立，美元确立了在国际货币体系的核心地位。即使之后布雷顿森林体系解体，美元在最近半个世纪以来仍然发挥着主要国际货币的职能，被广泛应用于国际储备和交易结算。全球已经建立起一套完整的美元体系，这使美元能够在国际上充分发挥货币的三个基本职能。

排在美国之后的是欧元区。由于货币竞争力的测算是基于货币而非基于主权国家，因此本部分不对欧元区做进一步拆分。自欧盟国家于1999年开始实行单一货币欧元和在实行欧元的国家实施统一货币政策，欧元区至今已有19个成员国。单一货币不仅有利于欧元区国家间的国际贸易，作为世界第三大经济体的欧元区也与区外国家保持着广泛的贸易联系。欧元自启用以来，国际地位不断提升，在各项二级指标中仅次于美元，均排在第2。

英镑、日元和人民币的货币竞争力排在第3—5位，成为国际货币的第二梯队。英国曾在19世纪成为国际货币体系的中心国家,因此英镑至今仍在一定程度上发挥着国际货币的职能,在"交易媒介"和"计价单位"两个二级指标下均排在第3,在"价值储存"项下排名第5。日本在20世纪60—80年代的赶超,则助力日元获得今日的国际地位,在"价值储存""交易媒介"和"计价单位"三项二级指标下分别排在第3、第4和第6。相比之下,中国大陆属于后起之秀,随着人民币国际化自2009年以来不断推进,与英国和日本的货币竞争力差距逐渐缩小。从二级指标来看,人民币在"价值储存"和"计价单位"两项下均排在第4,在"交易媒介"项下则排在第7。

3. 金融基础设施竞争力

表5-4反映了金融基础设施竞争力的排名状况,英国位居全球第1,美国排名第5,中国大陆排名第10。

排名居于首位的英国,其标准化后的得分远超位居第2的新加坡,显示作为老牌金融帝国,英国在金融基础设施方面仍占据较大的优势,无论是软件还是硬件排名都位居前列(详见附录分项指标排名)。

由于近几年营商环境波动较大,美国金融基础设施软件评分排名较为靠后,拖累了美国金融基础设施的总体表现,导致美国排名第5。

中国香港和中国大陆排名则分别位居第3和第10,其中,中国香港金融基础设施软件排名第2,仅次于新加坡,金融基础设施硬件排名第3,显示香港无论是在金融制度环境还是在金融基础设施硬件方面都具有较强国际竞争力。中国大陆则在金融基础设施硬件方面占优,排名第2,仅次于英国,彰显了近些年中国大陆在金融基础设施建设方面所取得的成就。但金融基础设施软件方面,中国大陆排名较为靠后,位居第23,表明中国未来在金融基础设施软件建设仍有较大上升空间。

表 5-4　　　　　　　　金融基础设施竞争力结果展示

排名	经济体	金融基础设施竞争力分值	排名	经济体	金融基础设施竞争力分值
1	英国	72.6	17	沙特阿拉伯	40.1
2	新加坡	58.9	18	西班牙	39.5
3	中国香港	58.4	19	瑞士	39.2
4	韩国	50.2	20	巴西	38.9
5	美国	49.7	21	南非	37.8
6	澳大利亚	47.7	22	芬兰	36.8
7	爱尔兰	46.3	23	墨西哥	35.3
8	比利时	44.8	24	葡萄牙	34.9
9	加拿大	44.5	25	日本	34.0
10	中国大陆	43.4	26	荷兰	33.2
11	德国	43.0	27	意大利	32.7
12	阿联酋	41.5	28	希腊	32.0
13	奥地利	41.4	29	阿根廷	29.5
14	法国	41.1	30	卢森堡	29.0
15	土耳其	40.9	31	印度	21.6
16	俄罗斯	40.7	32	印度尼西亚	18.3

4. 金融科技竞争力

表 5-5 反映了全球金融科技竞争力的排名情况，美国排名全球第 1，德国位居第 2，中国大陆的排名是全球第 10。

直观来看，32 个样本中，美国以显著优势领先于其他国家，而其他国家整体竞争力指数较为平均地分布在 0—70 之间。美国作为世界唯一超级大国，其金融产业和高科技产业都十分发达。其丰富的金融科技人才资源，结构完善而具有活力的金融科技发展机制以及庞大的资金基础成为其强大金融科技竞争力的来源。

表 5-5　　　　　　　　　金融科技竞争力结果展示

排名	经济体	金融科技竞争力分值	排名	经济体	金融科技竞争力分值
1	美国	93.1	17	奥地利	45.3
2	德国	69.2	18	中国香港	45.3
3	意大利	68.7	19	沙特阿拉伯	41.6
4	日本	67.4	20	卢森堡	40.0
5	加拿大	65.7	21	巴西	40.0
6	荷兰	64.8	22	西班牙	38.9
7	英国	64.6	23	俄罗斯	38.1
8	法国	62.5	24	南非	35.9
9	澳大利亚	61.0	25	比利时	30.7
10	中国大陆	60.3	26	印度	30.4
11	爱尔兰	57.6	27	葡萄牙	29.4
12	新加坡	54.2	28	希腊	22.2
13	阿联酋	53.2	29	土耳其	17.3
14	芬兰	51.9	30	阿根廷	15.6
15	韩国	51.6	31	印度尼西亚	12.4
16	瑞士	50.6	32	墨西哥	3.8

从离散程度来看，32个样本方差为377.41，方差数值大，代表各国金融科技整体竞争力差距很大，离散程度较高。32个样本国家涵盖地域辽阔，发达国家与发展中国家并存，经济实力千差万别，所依靠的支柱性产业也各不相同，具体而言，各国对于金融科技产业的重视程度以及发展能力差别巨大，造就了金融科技竞争力指数的明显差异。

从集中趋势来看，32个样本中位数为45.3，而平均数为45.6。由样本中位数和平均数可看出，金融科技属于新兴的金融服务模式，金融科技产业对于大部分国家而言仍属于新兴产业，产业体制的建设及产业规模仍处在初级阶段。金融科技产业发展需以强大的计算能力作为技术基础,然而大部分技术属于慢参量,获利周期较长,前期需要大量的人才与资金投入。目前全球金融业与高科技产业的集聚效应突出,具备足够条件投入金融科技产业的企业集中于少数几个国家。

随着金融科技产业的发展,越来越多的用户接入该产业,"变现"潜在用户的程度决定了底层技术的应用宽度,某种程度上可以衡量各国金融科技产业当前发展水平。稳定的计算能力与较高的用户接入度支撑金融科技产业的发展,产业的发展情况展现金融科技行业的未来潜力。对于大部分国家而言,传统金融机构缺乏足够先进的技术手段,对于大数据、人工智能等技术的应用广度仍有待提升,而科技创新企业则缺乏研发金融科技产品所需的雄厚资金,用户亦对其产品获利水平与可靠性缺乏信心。总体而言,用户对于金融科技产品的接触面较窄,对于金融科技产品的认可度仍有待提高。如何实现金融业与高科技产业的有效互通,提升高科技在金融行业中的应用效率仍为未解之谜。

在32个样本国家或地区中,整体竞争力指数排名前十的国家或地区分别为美国(93.1)、德国(69.2)、意大利(68.7)、日本(67.4)、加拿大(65.7)、荷兰(64.8)、英国(64.6)、法国(62.5)、澳大利亚(61.0)、中国大陆(60.3)。其中,除中国之外,第一梯队全部为发达国家,并且以欧洲国家居多;第二梯队也以发达国家和地区为主。由此可见,发达国家在金融科技上具有明显优势。值得注意的是,意大利排名第三,高于英国和法国。这是因为意大利的产业发展潜力较强,其金融科技信贷水平仅次于美国。

与欧美前列国家相比,中国在计算力方面具有优势,计算能力和计算效率均在世界前列。这有利于金融行业进行技术创新,在金融产品、服务模式、业务流程、组织形态方面实现敏捷式改变,提升金融业整体效率与盈利水平。中国与欧美先进国家差距主要存在于用户接入度与产业发展潜力上,原因有两点:一是中国金融科技仍处于发展阶段,其普惠程度与监管灵活度较低,阻碍了金融科技产业市场的拓展空间;二是中国存在金融科技消费端数据缺失的问题。因此,对该领域中国金融科技的发展水平很可能存在显著的低估。

5. 国际金融治理竞争力

表 5-6 反映了国际金融治理竞争力的排名情况,美国排名全球第 1,日本位居第 3,中国大陆的排名是全球第 9。

表 5-6　　　　　　国际金融治理竞争力结果展示

排名	经济体	国际金融治理竞争力分值	排名	经济体	国际金融治理竞争力分值
1	美国	85.1	17	墨西哥	44.2
2	德国	73.0	18	土耳其	39.5
3	日本	72.5	19	比利时	38.9
4	法国	69.5	20	阿根廷	38.8
5	意大利	67.5	21	奥地利	37.8
6	英国	64.1	22	芬兰	37.1
7	加拿大	62.2	23	沙特阿拉伯	35.8
8	韩国	60.3	24	印度尼西亚	33.8
9	中国大陆	57.7	25	南非	31.4
10	巴西	55.9	26	爱尔兰	29.6
11	俄罗斯	53.5	27	葡萄牙	25.5
12	澳大利亚	52.9	28	新加坡	20.2
13	西班牙	52.2	29	希腊	15.6
14	荷兰	50.8	30	卢森堡	12.0
15	瑞士	47.3	31	中国香港	11.5
16	印度	46.4	32	阿联酋	0.6

从排名情况可以看出，以美国为代表的发达国家，仍在国际金融治理竞争力中占据绝对优势，其中最具国际金融治理竞争力的美国，指数得分高达85.1，在排名前10的国家中，发达国家获得8个席位，其中G7国家正好占据了全球前7名。

相比之下，发展中国家未获得与其相符的国际金融治理竞争力；在排名前10的国家中只有中国大陆和巴西两个发展中国家，且排名仅为第9和第10。

该排名较好地印证了美国在国际金融治理中仍具有主导性的话语权，以美国为首的西方发达国家整体上占据强势地位，而包括广大新兴市场国家、经济转型国家和发展中国家在内的非西方世界则处于弱势地位。

附　　录

（一）金融业竞争力分项结果

指标1.1　金融体系规模

表6-1展示了各经济体金融体系规模的具体分值，这里的规模是指"相对规模"。该指标越高，表征金融体系能够配置的金融资源越多，为一国国民提供金融服务的能力越强。从结果中可以发现，排名靠前的基本为发达经济体，其中中国香港和新加坡排名并列第1，比排名第3的瑞士高出8.2分；中国大陆的金融体系规模排名第16，就分项而言，中国大陆存款银行资产同GDP比率排名并列第1，股票市值同GDP比率排名第18，其他部门资产同GDP比率排名第27。可以看出，中国大陆的银行业资产同GDP比率超过了英美等发达国家，而共同基金、养老金和保险公司等的发展规模相对滞后。

表6-1　　金融业竞争力二级指标排名：金融体系规模

排名	经济体	金融体系规模分值	排名	经济体	金融体系规模分值
1	中国香港	100.0	17	西班牙	45.7
2	新加坡	100.0	18	比利时	42.6
3	瑞士	91.8	19	巴西	40.0
4	英国	81.5	20	德国	39.7

续表

排名	经济体	金融体系规模分值	排名	经济体	金融体系规模分值
5	荷兰	79.4	21	阿联酋	38.9
6	卢森堡	75.1	22	意大利	38.7
7	澳大利亚	74.6	23	葡萄牙	37.8
8	加拿大	74.1	24	奥地利	35.0
9	日本	70.0	25	印度	30.4
10	美国	65.7	26	希腊	30.3
11	南非	60.8	27	沙特阿拉伯	26.4
12	法国	59.4	28	俄罗斯	20.8
13	韩国	58.6	29	土耳其	20.6
14	爱尔兰	51.4	30	印度尼西亚	19.5
15	芬兰	50.9	31	墨西哥	18.0
16	中国大陆	47.4	32	阿根廷	10.0

1.1.1 存款银行资产同 GDP 比率

表 6-2 金融业竞争力三级指标排名：存款银行资产同 GDP 比率

排名	经济体	存款银行资产同 GDP 比率分值	排名	经济体	存款银行资产同 GDP 比率分值
1	中国香港	100.0	17	卢森堡	72.7
2	日本	100.0	18	巴西	70.2
3	中国大陆	100.0	19	芬兰	66.9
4	瑞士	100.0	20	奥地利	64.8
5	新加坡	100.0	21	德国	60.7
6	韩国	94.3	22	比利时	53.9
7	澳大利亚	93.6	23	南非	52.0
8	英国	87.8	24	土耳其	48.6

续表

排名	经济体	存款银行资产同GDP比率分值	排名	经济体	存款银行资产同GDP比率分值
9	西班牙	86.6	25	印度	45.6
10	加拿大	85.2	26	沙特阿拉伯	43.6
11	葡萄牙	83.9	27	美国	41.6
12	荷兰	82.2	28	俄罗斯	38.7
13	意大利	78.7	29	爱尔兰	33.9
14	法国	75.3	30	墨西哥	27.5
15	希腊	74.8	31	印度尼西亚	25.4
16	阿联酋	73.1	32	阿根廷	13.9

1.1.2 股票市值同 GDP 比率

表6-3　金融业竞争力三级指标排名：股票市值同 GDP 比率

排名	经济体	股票市值同GDP比率分值	排名	经济体	股票市值同GDP比率分值
1	中国香港	100.0	17	沙特阿拉伯	32.8
2	瑞士	100.0	18	中国大陆	32.7
3	新加坡	100.0	19	西班牙	30.3
4	南非	100.0	20	阿联酋	30.1
5	英国	82.2	21	德国	27.1
6	美国	76.6	22	印度尼西亚	23.3
7	加拿大	67.2	23	巴西	21.7
8	荷兰	58.0	24	俄罗斯	21.3
9	日本	56.5	25	爱尔兰	20.4
10	澳大利亚	53.1	26	墨西哥	16.5
11	卢森堡	52.6	27	奥地利	16.4
12	韩国	50.2	28	葡萄牙	15.3
13	芬兰	49.2	29	意大利	13.6

续表

排名	经济体	股票市值同GDP比率分值	排名	经济体	股票市值同GDP比率分值
14	法国	47.8	30	希腊	10.9
15	比利时	41.7	31	土耳其	10.8
16	印度	37.3	32	阿根廷	6.4

1.1.3 其他部门资产同GDP比率

表6-4 金融业竞争力三级指标排名：其他部门资产同GDP比率

排名	经济体	其他部门资产同GDP比率分值	排名	经济体	其他部门资产同GDP比率分值
1	中国香港	100.0	17	南非	30.3
2	爱尔兰	100.0	18	巴西	28.0
3	卢森堡	100.0	19	意大利	23.8
4	新加坡	100.0	20	奥地利	23.7
5	荷兰	98.1	21	西班牙	20.2
6	美国	79.0	22	葡萄牙	14.2
7	澳大利亚	77.1	23	阿联酋	13.6
8	瑞士	75.5	24	印度尼西亚	10.0
9	英国	74.4	25	墨西哥	10.0
10	加拿大	69.9	26	阿根廷	9.8
11	法国	55.1	27	中国大陆	9.4
12	日本	53.5	28	印度	8.2
13	芬兰	36.7	29	希腊	5.2
14	比利时	32.1	30	沙特阿拉伯	2.9
15	德国	31.2	31	俄罗斯	2.4
16	韩国	31.2	32	土耳其	2.3

指标1.2 金融体系活力

表6-5展示了各经济体金融体系活力的具体分值,该指标越大,表征金融体系聚集金融资源的动能越足。此项指标中,瑞士排名第1,英国第4,美国第6,中国大陆第10。就分项指标而言,中国大陆金融中介的深化程度较高,存款银行和其他金融机构发放的私人部门信贷同GDP比率排名第5,银行贷款同银行存款比率并列第1,股市交易值同GDP比率排名第15。

表6-5 金融业竞争力二级指标排名:金融体系活力

排名	经济体	金融体系活力分值	排名	经济体	金融体系活力分值
1	瑞士	89.0	17	希腊	43.5
2	南非	86.6	18	法国	42.8
3	芬兰	85.4	19	土耳其	38.8
4	英国	84.0	20	德国	37.5
5	韩国	82.9	21	比利时	35.4
6	美国	78.9	22	巴西	33.7
7	中国香港	77.9	23	奥地利	29.8
8	澳大利亚	70.4	24	意大利	29.8
9	日本	67.8	25	阿联酋	29.4
10	中国大陆	65.2	26	俄罗斯	29.2
11	加拿大	63.7	27	印度	28.5
12	荷兰	58.6	28	印度尼西亚	20.9
13	新加坡	58.5	29	墨西哥	18.3
14	葡萄牙	52.9	30	卢森堡	16.1
15	西班牙	52.1	31	爱尔兰	13.6
16	沙特阿拉伯	49.7	32	阿根廷	6.9

1.2.1 存款银行和其他金融机构发放的私人部门信贷同GDP比率

表6-6 金融业竞争力三级指标排名：存款银行和其他金融机构发放的私人部门信贷同GDP比率

排名	经济体	存款银行和其他金融机构发放的私人部门信贷同GDP比率分值	排名	经济体	存款银行和其他金融机构发放的私人部门信贷同GDP比率分值
1	瑞士	100.0	17	法国	60.5
2	美国	100.0	18	芬兰	57.8
3	中国香港	100.0	19	阿联酋	51.3
4	日本	100.0	20	意大利	51.2
5	中国大陆	94.1	21	奥地利	51.1
6	南非	88.7	22	德国	47.2
7	澳大利亚	87.8	23	土耳其	40.7
8	韩国	83.1	24	沙特阿拉伯	40.3
9	英国	82.3	25	俄罗斯	40.0
10	新加坡	79.9	26	巴西	39.9
11	荷兰	69.3	27	比利时	39.6
12	葡萄牙	65.7	28	印度	29.7
13	加拿大	65.7	29	爱尔兰	28.0
14	西班牙	65.6	30	印度尼西亚	23.4
15	卢森堡	64.0	31	墨西哥	21.0
16	希腊	63.6	32	阿根廷	8.4

1.2.2 银行贷款同银行存款比率

表6-7 金融业竞争力三级指标排名：银行贷款同银行存款比率

排名	经济体	银行贷款同银行存款比率分值	排名	经济体	银行贷款同银行存款比率分值
1	中国大陆	100.0	17	意大利	56.5
2	希腊	100.0	18	瑞士	56.1
3	沙特阿拉伯	100.0	19	奥地利	56.0
4	澳大利亚	99.2	20	巴西	50.7
5	芬兰	98.0	21	阿联酋	47.9
6	土耳其	92.3	22	德国	46.5
7	葡萄牙	82.2	23	印度尼西亚	46.2
8	法国	76.5	24	墨西哥	37.4
9	加拿大	73.5	25	印度	25.7
10	荷兰	71.5	26	阿根廷	17.8
11	南非	67.9	27	美国	15.4
12	西班牙	64.9	28	爱尔兰	14.5
13	韩国	63.8	29	中国香港	11.8
14	俄罗斯	61.8	30	比利时	8.6
15	新加坡	61.6	31	日本	0
16	英国	59.9	32	卢森堡	0

1.2.3 股市交易值同GDP比率

表6-8 金融业竞争力三级指标排名：股市交易值同GDP比率

排名	经济体	股市交易值同GDP比率分值	排名	经济体	股市交易值同GDP比率分值
1	瑞士	100.0	17	沙特阿拉伯	29.3
2	美国	100.0	18	印度	29.3
3	中国香港	100.0	19	德国	28.2

续表

排名	经济体	股市交易值同GDP比率分值	排名	经济体	股市交易值同GDP比率分值
4	英国	96.9	20	巴西	22.1
5	南非	94.8	21	法国	17.1
6	芬兰	93.0	22	土耳其	11.0
7	韩国	92.4	23	阿联酋	9.2
8	日本	85.6	24	俄罗斯	7.5
9	加拿大	57.7	25	墨西哥	7.3
10	澳大利亚	47.3	26	印度尼西亚	6.9
11	荷兰	46.8	27	奥地利	6.2
12	比利时	46.8	28	爱尔兰	6.0
13	新加坡	46.3	29	意大利	5.7
14	西班牙	38.9	30	希腊	5.2
15	中国大陆	33.4	31	阿根廷	0.6
16	葡萄牙	31.9	32	卢森堡	0.1

指标1.3 金融体系效率

表6-9展示了各经济体金融体系效率的具体分值，该指标越大，表征金融体系能够以较低的成本高效运转和聚集金融资源。此项指标中，韩国排名第1，美国第2，英国第5，中国大陆第6。就分项指标而言，中国大陆银行非利息收入同总收入比率排名第29（见表6-10），银行营业费用同总资产比率排名第2（见表6-11），银行业资产回报率排名第12（见表6-12），股市换手率与土耳其并列排名第8（见表6-13）。

表6-9 金融业竞争力二级指标排名：金融体系效率

排名	经济体	金融体系效率分值	排名	经济体	金融体系效率分值
1	韩国	75.7	17	比利时	46.7
2	美国	75.2	18	新加坡	45.9

续表

排名	经济体	金融体系效率分值	排名	经济体	金融体系效率分值
3	芬兰	74.0	19	荷兰	45.6
4	日本	70.4	20	意大利	43.7
5	英国	60.1	21	阿联酋	43.7
6	中国大陆	60.0	22	印度	43.0
7	土耳其	58.8	23	南非	40.8
8	德国	56.2	24	奥地利	40.0
9	中国香港	56.2	25	葡萄牙	36.7
10	西班牙	55.3	26	阿根廷	36.4
11	沙特阿拉伯	55.3	27	印度尼西亚	35.3
12	巴西	54.9	28	墨西哥	35.1
13	加拿大	54.4	29	爱尔兰	32.8
14	澳大利亚	50.1	30	卢森堡	32.6
15	法国	49.3	31	希腊	29.0
16	瑞士	46.8	32	俄罗斯	23.4

1.3.1 银行非利息收入同总收入比率

表6-10 金融业竞争力三级指标排名：银行非利息收入同总收入比率

排名	经济体	银行非利息收入同总收入比率分值	排名	经济体	银行非利息收入同总收入比率分值
1	瑞士	100.0	17	荷兰	79.2
2	芬兰	100.0	18	英国	77.3
3	比利时	100.0	19	阿联酋	75.9
4	葡萄牙	100.0	20	印度	73.9
5	法国	100.0	21	西班牙	72.2
6	阿根廷	100.0	22	俄罗斯	71.8
7	卢森堡	100.0	23	韩国	68.5

续表

排名	经济体	银行非利息收入同总收入比率分值	排名	经济体	银行非利息收入同总收入比率分值
8	意大利	98.9	24	爱尔兰	67.7
9	德国	96.3	25	美国	66.5
10	加拿大	93.7	26	土耳其	60.4
11	奥地利	90.3	27	墨西哥	55.8
12	巴西	88.4	28	沙特阿拉伯	54.5
13	日本	86.2	29	中国大陆	53.2
14	南非	84.9	30	澳大利亚	53.0
15	中国香港	82.9	31	印度尼西亚	52.4
16	新加坡	81.6	32	希腊	39.4

1.3.2 银行营业费用同总资产比率

表6-11 金融业竞争力三级指标排名：银行营业费用同总资产比率

排名	经济体	银行营业费用同总资产比率分值	排名	经济体	银行营业费用同总资产比率分值
1	日本	79.2	17	印度	45.8
2	中国大陆	78.4	18	英国	40.8
3	中国香港	76.2	19	奥地利	39.3
4	澳大利亚	73.2	20	比利时	37.6
5	阿联酋	70.9	21	美国	36.8
6	新加坡	68.4	22	西班牙	36.4
7	卢森堡	67.6	23	土耳其	31.6
8	沙特阿拉伯	66.3	24	瑞士	30.8
9	法国	61.0	25	葡萄牙	28.8
10	芬兰	59.8	26	爱尔兰	21.3
11	荷兰	55.8	27	印度尼西亚	18.6

续表

排名	经济体	银行营业费用同总资产比率分值	排名	经济体	银行营业费用同总资产比率分值
12	加拿大	55.1	28	南非	10.5
13	意大利	55.0	29	阿根廷	0
14	希腊	54.9	30	巴西	0
15	韩国	54.8	31	俄罗斯	0
16	德国	54.1	32	墨西哥	0

1.3.3 银行业资产回报率

表6-12 金融业竞争力三级指标排名：银行业资产回报率

排名	经济体	银行业资产回报率分值	排名	经济体	银行业资产回报率分值
1	阿根廷	100.0	17	澳大利亚	42.0
2	沙特阿拉伯	99.1	18	比利时	41.1
3	印度尼西亚	95.5	19	荷兰	37.0
4	墨西哥	88.9	20	意大利	34.7
5	土耳其	81.8	21	韩国	31.1
6	巴西	74.4	22	卢森堡	27.8
7	阿联酋	72.1	23	法国	20.6
8	南非	66.9	24	英国	20.6
9	爱尔兰	58.5	25	俄罗斯	18.8
10	中国香港	57.9	26	日本	14.1
11	新加坡	54.4	27	瑞士	9.1
12	中国大陆	49.3	28	西班牙	8.7
13	美国	48.2	29	德国	7.7
14	芬兰	47.4	30	希腊	0
15	加拿大	44.3	31	印度	0
16	奥地利	43.0	32	葡萄牙	0

1.3.4 股市换手率

表6-13　　金融业竞争力三级指标排名：股市换手率

排名	经济体	股市换手率分值	排名	经济体	股市换手率分值
1	美国	100.0	17	沙特阿拉伯	37.2
2	韩国	100.0	18	比利时	33.9
3	日本	80.9	19	荷兰	33.9
4	芬兰	79.0	20	葡萄牙	30.5
5	英国	73.9	21	南非	27.5
6	西班牙	71.5	22	希腊	26.5
7	德国	59.8	23	意大利	24.5
8	土耳其	59.6	24	新加坡	23.7
9	中国大陆	59.6	25	奥地利	22.5
10	巴西	55.4	26	墨西哥	21.9
11	瑞士	47.1	27	俄罗斯	16.6
12	印度	46.1	28	爱尔兰	16.5
13	加拿大	44.5	29	印度尼西亚	15.0
14	澳大利亚	44.4	30	阿联酋	14.4
15	中国香港	40.0	31	阿根廷	6.1
16	法国	38.1	32	卢森堡	0.1

指标1.4　金融体系稳定性

表6-14展示了各经济体金融体系稳定性的具体分值，该指标越大，表征金融体系聚集金融资源的可持续性越强。此项指标中，美国排名第1，英国第6，中国香港第12，中国大陆第22。就分项指标而言，中国大陆银行Z-score排名第7（见表6-15），银行不良贷款率排名第12（见表6-16），银行资本同总资产比率排名第17（见表6-17），银行监管资本同风险加权资产比率第29（见表6-18），流动资产同存款和短期融资比率第30（见表6-19），不良贷款准备金率并列第1（见表6-20），银行稳健

性第27（见表6-21），股市波动率第21（见表6-22）。尽管中国历史上并未发生过银行业危机，中国仍需要关注银行业体系的稳定性。

表6-14　金融业竞争力二级指标排名：金融体系稳定性

排名	经济体	金融体系稳定性分值	排名	经济体	金融体系稳定性分值
1	美国	75.8	17	印度	55.7
2	墨西哥	73.9	18	南非	55.6
3	新加坡	70.7	19	荷兰	55.0
4	加拿大	70.2	20	卢森堡	52.3
5	印度尼西亚	67.4	21	俄罗斯	51.3
6	英国	65.8	22	中国大陆	51.2
7	瑞士	64.8	23	奥地利	49.2
8	澳大利亚	63.3	24	葡萄牙	44.8
9	阿联酋	63.1	25	爱尔兰	44.1
10	沙特阿拉伯	60.5	26	土耳其	42.2
11	韩国	60.4	27	巴西	39.0
12	中国香港	58.3	28	日本	36.6
13	芬兰	56.7	29	西班牙	34.7
14	德国	56.5	30	阿根廷	32.1
15	比利时	56.3	31	希腊	13.3
16	法国	55.7	32	意大利	12.8

1.4.1　银行 Z-score

表6-15　金融业竞争力三级指标排名：银行 Z-score

排名	经济体	银行 Z-score 分值	排名	经济体	银行 Z-score 分值
1	卢森堡	100.0	17	澳大利亚	51.6
2	美国	99.3	18	巴西	50.8

续表

排名	经济体	银行 Z-score 分值	排名	经济体	银行 Z-score 分值
3	阿联酋	88.5	19	葡萄牙	47.2
4	德国	88.0	20	加拿大	47.1
5	奥地利	87.1	21	芬兰	46.3
6	法国	85.1	22	瑞士	42.0
7	中国大陆	76.4	23	意大利	40.2
8	新加坡	74.0	24	荷兰	36.2
9	沙特阿拉伯	68.8	25	韩国	35.1
10	墨西哥	67.3	26	英国	33.2
11	比利时	63.5	27	爱尔兰	32.2
12	西班牙	60.4	28	希腊	27.6
13	南非	55.6	29	土耳其	27.2
14	日本	54.3	30	俄罗斯	23.2
15	中国香港	53.3	31	阿根廷	21.7
16	印度	53.2	32	印度尼西亚	20.8

1.4.2 银行不良贷款率

表6-16　　金融业竞争力三级指标排名：银行不良贷款率

排名	经济体	银行不良贷款率分值	排名	经济体	银行不良贷款率分值
1	加拿大	97.0	17	印度尼西亚	83.0
2	芬兰	95.9	18	土耳其	81.0
3	中国香港	95.5	19	南非	80.9
4	瑞士	94.8	20	比利时	80.5
5	卢森堡	94.7	21	法国	79.5
6	澳大利亚	94.1	22	巴西	76.1
7	英国	93.7	23	德国	70.7
8	美国	92.5	24	西班牙	70.3
9	日本	92.1	25	阿联酋	57.1

续表

排名	经济体	银行不良贷款率分值	排名	经济体	银行不良贷款率分值
10	新加坡	90.7	26	印度	33.5
11	沙特阿拉伯	89.2	27	俄罗斯	33.3
12	中国大陆	88.4	28	爱尔兰	23.6
13	阿根廷	87.8	29	葡萄牙	21.1
14	墨西哥	86.1	30	意大利	0
15	荷兰	84.6	31	韩国	0
16	奥地利	84.2	32	希腊	0

1.4.3 银行资本同总资产比率

表6-17 金融业竞争力三级指标排名：银行资本同总资产比率

排名	经济体	银行资本同总资产比率分值	排名	经济体	银行资本同总资产比率分值
1	沙特阿拉伯	100.0	17	中国大陆	31.0
1	印度尼西亚	100.0	18	西班牙	26.2
3	爱尔兰	93.5	19	韩国	25.6
4	希腊	70.0	20	比利时	25.5
5	美国	66.5	21	奥地利	25.4
6	阿根廷	65.7	22	印度	23.9
7	土耳其	57.2	23	英国	20.3
8	俄罗斯	55.1	24	澳大利亚	18.8
9	墨西哥	54.0	25	瑞士	17.4
10	巴西	50.5	26	法国	15.9
11	中国香港	48.3	27	德国	13.3
12	新加坡	41.8	28	荷兰	10.8
13	阿联酋	39.9	29	芬兰	6.3
14	葡萄牙	34.2	30	意大利	4.9
15	卢森堡	33.5	31	日本	4.1
16	南非	32.0	32	加拿大	2.2

1.4.4 银行监管资本同风险加权资产比率

表 6-18 金融业竞争力三级指标排名：银行监管资本同风险加权资产比率

排名	经济体	银行监管资本同风险加权资产比率分值	排名	经济体	银行监管资本同风险加权资产比率分值
1	爱尔兰	100.0	17	希腊	46.8
1	卢森堡	100.0	18	土耳其	45.7
3	芬兰	87.2	19	瑞士	45.2
4	印度尼西亚	86.7	20	日本	44.4
5	荷兰	80.2	21	南非	39.5
6	英国	72.0	22	阿根廷	37.2
7	沙特阿拉伯	69.3	23	墨西哥	37.2
8	德国	62.5	24	西班牙	37.0
9	韩国	61.1	25	加拿大	32.1
10	中国香港	60.9	26	澳大利亚	30.3
11	比利时	59.8	27	美国	30.2
12	法国	59.4	28	意大利	25.0
13	奥地利	54.9	29	中国大陆	20.8
14	巴西	54.3	30	印度	18.8
15	阿联酋	54.0	31	葡萄牙	16.8
16	新加坡	47.2	32	俄罗斯	13.8

1.4.5 流动资产同存款和短期融资比率

表 6-19 金融业竞争力三级指标排名：流动资产同存款和短期融资比率

排名	经济体	流动资产同存款和短期融资比率分值	排名	经济体	流动资产同存款和短期融资比率分值
1	卢森堡	100.0	17	爱尔兰	33.5
2	瑞士	94.1	18	西班牙	28.4

续表

排名	经济体	流动资产同存款和短期融资比率分值	排名	经济体	流动资产同存款和短期融资比率分值
3	巴西	92.0	19	比利时	28.1
4	法国	90.0	20	荷兰	25.3
5	阿根廷	85.6	21	土耳其	23.8
6	德国	75.6	22	新加坡	20.1
7	英国	74.0	23	美国	18.3
8	墨西哥	51.2	24	南非	16.6
9	加拿大	49.9	25	澳大利亚	14.6
10	芬兰	49.3	26	葡萄牙	11.4
11	俄罗斯	43.5	27	印度尼西亚	11.4
12	意大利	42.9	28	沙特阿拉伯	10.5
13	日本	41.7	29	印度	6.2
14	奥地利	37.6	30	中国大陆	5.1
15	中国香港	36.3	31	韩国	0
16	阿联酋	35.4	31	希腊	0

1.4.6 不良贷款准备金率

表6-20　金融业竞争力三级指标排名：不良贷款准备金率

排名	经济体	不良贷款准备金率分值	排名	经济体	不良贷款准备金率分值
1	巴西	100.0	17	荷兰	15.6
1	墨西哥	100.0	18	韩国	15.6
1	沙特阿拉伯	100.0	19	希腊	15.5
1	中国大陆	100.0	20	印度	11.9
5	阿根廷	90.7	21	日本	11.7
6	土耳其	41.1	22	中国香港	11.7
7	阿联酋	37.6	23	南非	11.6

续表

排名	经济体	不良贷款准备金率分值	排名	经济体	不良贷款准备金率分值
8	俄罗斯	34.4	24	英国	11.4
9	葡萄牙	32.5	25	比利时	10.6
10	德国	29.3	26	新加坡	9.0
11	西班牙	23.4	27	卢森堡	5.8
12	美国	21.7	28	爱尔兰	4.0
13	奥地利	21.0	29	瑞士	3.9
14	印度尼西亚	21.0	30	加拿大	0
15	意大利	17.7	31	芬兰	0
16	法国	17.2	32	澳大利亚	0

1.4.7 银行稳健性

表6-21　　金融业竞争力三级指标排名：银行稳健性

排名	经济体	银行稳健性分值	排名	经济体	银行稳健性分值
1	芬兰	94.5	17	阿联酋	72.1
2	加拿大	92.0	18	比利时	71.3
3	新加坡	90.4	19	德国	70.3
4	澳大利亚	89.4	20	南非	69.3
5	中国香港	88.7	21	印度尼西亚	64.6
6	卢森堡	87.9	22	韩国	64.1
7	瑞士	86.0	23	西班牙	61.9
8	美国	79.9	24	阿根廷	61.0
9	日本	79.7	25	印度	60.5
10	巴西	78.8	26	土耳其	60.3
11	法国	77.8	27	中国大陆	58.1
12	沙特阿拉伯	77.7	28	爱尔兰	49.7
13	荷兰	76.5	29	俄罗斯	45.1

续表

排名	经济体	银行稳健性分值	排名	经济体	银行稳健性分值
14	奥地利	75.9	30	意大利	44.9
15	墨西哥	75.4	31	葡萄牙	38.7
16	英国	75.1	32	希腊	26.1

1.4.8 股市波动率

表6-22　　金融业竞争力三级指标排名：股市波动率

排名	经济体	股市波动率分值	排名	经济体	股市波动率分值
1	加拿大	94.7	17	中国香港	60.2
2	美国	93.2	18	芬兰	59.2
3	韩国	92.0	19	德国	54.5
4	新加坡	88.1	20	法国	50.6
5	澳大利亚	83.8	21	中国大陆	48.1
6	印度	81.6	22	沙特阿拉伯	47.3
7	墨西哥	80.4	23	奥地利	43.3
8	印度尼西亚	79.4	24	爱尔兰	40.2
9	英国	77.4	25	土耳其	36.3
10	瑞士	74.9	26	卢森堡	30.0
11	阿联酋	71.2	27	日本	26.3
12	南非	67.5	28	西班牙	25.5
13	俄罗斯	67.2	29	巴西	6.3
14	比利时	64.2	30	意大利	0.6
15	荷兰	63.0	31	阿根廷	0
16	葡萄牙	60.7	31	希腊	0

指标1.5 金融服务可得性

表6-23展示了各经济体金融服务可得性的具体分值,该指标越大,表征金融体系聚集金融资源和服务实体经济的能力越强,有研究发现金融服务可得性的提高可以有力地减少各国收入之间的不平等。此项指标中,卢森堡排名第1,美国第2,英国第8,中国大陆第17。就分项指标而言(见表6-24),中国大陆每十万成年人拥有的商业银行分支机构数量排名第29,前十大上市公司之外的股市交易额同总交易额比率排名并列第1(见表6-25),前十大上市公司之外的公司市值同总市值比率排名并列第1(见表6-26),每百万人拥有的上市公司数量排名第27(见表6-27),中小企业融资排名第18(见表6-28),风险资本可得性排名并列第5(见表6-29)。

表6-23　金融业竞争力二级指标排名：金融服务可得性

排名	经济体	金融服务可得性分值	排名	经济体	金融服务可得性分值
1	卢森堡	74.3	17	中国大陆	49.9
2	美国	72.4	18	韩国	48.8
3	西班牙	65.8	19	葡萄牙	48.0
4	日本	65.4	20	印度尼西亚	46.9
5	瑞士	63.8	21	意大利	44.9
6	中国香港	63.3	22	阿联酋	40.0
7	澳大利亚	62.5	23	沙特阿拉伯	39.6
8	英国	61.8	24	土耳其	39.4
9	比利时	60.5	25	奥地利	38.7
10	加拿大	59.8	26	俄罗斯	38.6
11	法国	58.0	27	墨西哥	36.7
12	新加坡	56.9	28	南非	35.8

续表

排名	经济体	金融服务可得性分值	排名	经济体	金融服务可得性分值
13	德国	53.8	29	巴西	35.7
14	印度	53.5	30	爱尔兰	33.6
15	芬兰	53.1	31	希腊	28.9
16	荷兰	51.2	32	阿根廷	27.3

1.5.1 每十万成年人拥有的商业银行分支机构数量

表6-24 金融业竞争力三级指标排名：每十万成年人拥有的商业银行分支机构数量

排名	经济体	每十万成年人拥有的商业银行分支机构数量分值	排名	经济体	每十万成年人拥有的商业银行分支机构数量分值
1	卢森堡	100.0	17	巴西	39.0
2	西班牙	100.0	18	土耳其	34.8
3	意大利	89.3	19	印度尼西亚	33.7
4	瑞士	81.5	20	韩国	30.9
5	葡萄牙	78.1	21	印度	29.4
6	法国	72.0	22	墨西哥	28.3
7	比利时	69.6	23	阿根廷	27.1
8	日本	68.1	24	德国	25.8
9	美国	62.4	25	奥地利	24.1
10	澳大利亚	59.2	26	荷兰	23.9
11	俄罗斯	58.4	27	阿联酋	22.6
12	英国	53.1	28	南非	20.9
13	希腊	45.7	29	中国大陆	17.6
14	中国香港	42.1	30	沙特阿拉伯	17.0
15	加拿大	41.6	31	新加坡	17.0
16	爱尔兰	41.5	32	芬兰	2.9

1.5.2 前十大上市公司之外的股市交易额总交易额比率

表6-25 金融业竞争力三级指标排名:前十大上市公司之外的股市交易额同总交易额比率

排名	经济体	前十大上市公司之外的股市交易额同总交易额比率分值	排名	经济体	前十大上市公司之外的股市交易额同总交易额比率分值
1	法国	100.0	17	德国	70.5
2	比利时	100.0	18	土耳其	68.0
3	日本	100.0	19	巴西	67.5
4	美国	100.0	20	瑞士	67.3
5	韩国	100.0	21	沙特阿拉伯	67.2
6	印度	100.0	22	南非	62.3
7	中国大陆	100.0	23	西班牙	61.3
8	芬兰	100.0	24	阿根廷	57.1
9	荷兰	99.7	25	墨西哥	52.5
10	加拿大	93.2	26	俄罗斯	39.1
11	卢森堡	91.9	27	意大利	36.9
12	英国	91.4	28	葡萄牙	36.9
13	中国香港	86.3	29	奥地利	36.9
14	澳大利亚	82.5	30	希腊	21.4
15	印度尼西亚	73.8	31	阿联酋	7.7
16	新加坡	72.3	32	爱尔兰	5.8

1.5.3 前十大上市公司之外的公司市值同总市值比率

表6-26 金融业竞争力三级指标排名：前十大上市公司之外的公司市值同总市值比率

排名	经济体	前十大上市公司之外的公司市值同总市值比率分值	排名	经济体	前十大上市公司之外的公司市值同总市值比率分值
1	日本	100.0	17	西班牙	72.7
2	中国大陆	100.0	18	印度尼西亚	65.0
3	荷兰	96.5	19	墨西哥	65.0
4	美国	95.8	20	新加坡	64.2
5	印度	95.0	21	瑞士	63.4
6	法国	89.4	22	南非	62.7
7	比利时	89.4	23	意大利	56.3
8	芬兰	89.4	24	葡萄牙	56.3
9	加拿大	85.6	25	奥地利	56.3
10	韩国	83.8	26	巴西	53.8
11	卢森堡	80.0	27	沙特阿拉伯	50.9
12	中国香港	80.0	28	希腊	47.5
13	英国	80.0	29	俄罗斯	46.3
14	澳大利亚	76.3	30	阿联酋	31.6
15	土耳其	74.8	31	阿根廷	24.4
16	德国	74.5	32	爱尔兰	11.3

1.5.4 每百万人拥有的上市公司数量

表6-27 金融业竞争力三级指标排名：每百万人拥有的上市公司数量

排名	经济体	每百万人拥有的上市公司数量分值	排名	经济体	每百万人拥有的上市公司数量分值
1	加拿大	100.0		爱尔兰	10.7
2	中国香港	100.0	18	奥地利	9.5
3	澳大利亚	100.0	19	法国	8.7
4	新加坡	100.0	20	荷兰	7.4
5	西班牙	83.4	21	沙特阿拉伯	7.1
6	英国	62.1	22	德国	6.8
7	卢森堡	58.7	23	南非	6.4
8	韩国	51.3	24	土耳其	5.8
9	日本	35.5	25	印度	5.2
10	瑞士	33.7	26	葡萄牙	5.2
11	芬兰	30.0	27	中国大陆	3.1
12	希腊	22.8	28	阿根廷	2.7
13	阿联酋	16.7	29	印度尼西亚	2.7
14	美国	16.7	30	巴西	2.0
15	意大利	14.0	31	俄罗斯	2.0
16	比利时	12.7	32	墨西哥	1.4

1.5.5 中小企业融资

表6-28　金融业竞争力三级指标排名：中小企业融资

排名	经济体	中小企业融资分值	排名	经济体	中小企业融资分值
1	美国	79.7	17	奥地利	57.9
2	德国	71.9	18	中国大陆	57.2
3	芬兰	71.7	19	沙特阿拉伯	53.3
4	新加坡	70.5	20	韩国	49.7
5	中国香港	66.8	21	西班牙	49.3
6	瑞士	66.3	22	法国	48.7
7	卢森堡	65.4	23	南非	45.6
8	日本	63.4	24	葡萄牙	45.5
9	印度	62.5	25	爱尔兰	44.8
10	澳大利亚	61.9	26	土耳其	44.5
11	阿联酋	61.7	27	墨西哥	43.2
12	荷兰	61.6	28	俄罗斯	39.0
13	加拿大	59.7	29	巴西	38.4
14	英国	59.5	30	意大利	33.6
15	印度尼西亚	59.5	31	阿根廷	30.1
16	比利时	58.4	32	希腊	22.7

1.5.6 风险资本可得性

表6-29　金融业竞争力三级指标排名：风险资本可得性

排名	经济体	风险资本可得性分值	排名	经济体	风险资本可得性分值
1	美国	76.7	17	法国	45.1
2	德国	66.8	18	加拿大	44.8

续表

排名	经济体	风险资本可得性分值	排名	经济体	风险资本可得性分值
3	芬兰	64.6	19	澳大利亚	42.5
4	新加坡	61.3	20	西班牙	41.6
5	阿联酋	57.0	21	奥地利	38.7
6	中国大陆	57.0	21	爱尔兰	38.7
7	英国	56.8	23	韩国	36.0
8	中国香港	55.7	24	墨西哥	35.9
9	印度	55.3	25	葡萄牙	35.5
10	卢森堡	54.9	26	南非	33.0
11	瑞士	52.4	27	土耳其	28.7
12	日本	51.5	28	俄罗斯	27.9
13	荷兰	51.4	29	巴西	24.3
14	印度尼西亚	47.0	30	阿根廷	24.1
15	比利时	46.8	31	意大利	21.0
16	沙特阿拉伯	46.3	32	希腊	16.8

指标1.6 国际金融中心地位

表6-30展示了各经济体国际金融中心地位的具体分值，该指标衡量了国际金融中心的综合竞争力，数值越大，表征金融体系聚集全球金融资源越丰富。此项指标中，美国以原始分值为770分的纽约为代表排名第1，英国以原始分值为766分的伦敦为代表排名第2，中国以原始分值为748分的上海为代表排名第3，日本东京为747分，仅有1分之差，排名第4。另外还有15个经济体的金融中心未进入榜单的前30%，因此得分为0。

表6-30　金融业竞争力二级指标排名：国际金融中心地位

排名	经济体	国际金融中心地位分值	排名	经济体	国际金融中心地位分值
1	美国	100.0	17	比利时	89.1
2	英国	99.5	18	阿根廷	0
3	中国大陆	97.1	19	奥地利	0
4	日本	97.0	20	巴西	0
5	中国香港	96.5	21	芬兰	0
6	新加坡	96.4	22	希腊	0
7	瑞士	94.0	23	印度尼西亚	0
8	卢森堡	93.4	24	印度	0
9	德国	92.9	25	爱尔兰	0
10	阿联酋	92.7	26	意大利	0
11	法国	92.6	27	墨西哥	0
12	荷兰	91.0	28	葡萄牙	0
13	加拿大	90.6	29	俄罗斯	0
14	韩国	90.3	30	沙特阿拉伯	0
15	澳大利亚	90.0	31	土耳其	0
16	西班牙	89.9	32	南非	0

（二）货币竞争力分项结果

指标2.1　价值储存

表6-31反映了各国货币在国际上发挥价值储存功能的情况。第一阵营由美国和欧元区构成，遥遥领先于其他国家。美元在外汇储备货币占比和SDR权重两个三级指标下均为第1（见表6-32和表6-33），故在"价值储存"二级指标下得分为100.0。欧元在两个三级指标下均排名第2，在"价值储存"项下也排名第2，得分为55.05。第二阵营由日本、中国大陆和英国构成。日本和中国大陆分列第3、第4位，得分不分伯仲；

英国略逊一筹，但与日本和中国大陆差距不大。第三阵营由加拿大、澳大利亚和瑞士构成，这三国的货币虽然也在一定程度上发挥着国际储备货币的职能，但是占比不高；而且未被纳入SDR篮子，因此总得分相对较低。其他国家的货币由于未在IMF官方外汇储备货币构成调查数据库中明确币种，且不属于SDR货币，因此在这一指标下的得分为零。

表6-31　　　　　货币竞争力二级指标排名：价值储存

排名	经济体	价值储存分值	排名	经济体	价值储存分值
1	美国	100.0	12	俄罗斯	0
2	欧元区	55.1	13	韩国	0
3	日本	15.1	14	墨西哥	0
4	中国大陆	15.0	15	南非	0
5	英国	13.7	16	沙特阿拉伯	0
6	加拿大	1.8	17	土耳其	0
7	澳大利亚	1.6	18	新加坡	0
8	瑞士	0.2	19	印度	0
9	阿根廷	0	20	印度尼西亚	0
10	阿联酋	0	21	中国香港	0
11	巴西	0			

2.1.1　外汇储备货币占比

从表6-32反映出，美元仍是国际储备中的主要货币。2020年第四季度，美元在外汇储备中占比59.02%，远超其他国家货币，因此得到满分。欧元在外汇储备中占比21.24%，得分为36.0，排名第2。日元和英镑也在外汇储备中占有一席之地，得分分别为10.2和8.0；人民币占比为2.25%，得分3.8，超过加拿大元和澳大利亚元，位居第5。

表6-32　货币竞争力三级指标排名：外汇储备货币占比（2020年Q4数据）

排名	经济体	外汇储备货币分值	排名	经济体	外汇储备货币分值
1	美国	100.0	12	俄罗斯	0
2	欧元区	36.0	13	韩国	0
3	日本	10.2	14	墨西哥	0
4	英国	8.0	15	南非	0
5	中国大陆	3.8	16	沙特阿拉伯	0
6	加拿大	3.5	17	土耳其	0
7	澳大利亚	3.1	18	新加坡	0
8	瑞士	0.3	19	印度	0
9	阿根廷	0	20	印度尼西亚	0
10	阿联酋	0	21	中国香港	0
11	巴西	0			

2.1.2　SDR权重

表6-33显示了IMF最近一次对SDR篮子货币权重的调整，五种篮子货币的排名分别为美元、欧元、人民币、日元和英镑。根据这五种货币在篮子中的权重，美元和欧元占据主要份额，占比分别超过40%和30%，得分为100.0和74.1；人民币首次入篮，占比10.92%，得分26.2，高于日元和英镑。

表6-33　货币竞争力三级指标排名：SDR权重（2016年10月数据）

排名	经济体	SDR权重分值	排名	经济体	SDR权重分值
1	美国	100.0	12	南非	0
2	欧元区	74.1	13	印度	0
3	中国大陆	26.2	14	墨西哥	0
4	日本	20.0	15	俄罗斯	0
5	英国	19.4	16	土耳其	0

续表

排名	经济体	SDR权重分值	排名	经济体	SDR权重分值
6	澳大利亚	0	17	巴西	0
7	加拿大	0	18	印度尼西亚	0
8	瑞士	0	19	沙特阿拉伯	0
9	中国香港	0	20	阿联酋	0
10	新加坡	0	21	阿根廷	0
11	韩国	0			

指标2.2 交易媒介

从表6-34可以看出各国货币在国际上作为交易媒介的情况。美国在跨境支付货币占比和外汇市场成交量占比两个三级指标下均位列第1，因此在交易媒介项下的总得分也为100.0。欧元区在两个三级指标下均排名第2（见表6-35和表6-36），于是在交易媒介项下得到65.7分。英国和日本分列第3、第4，落后欧元区各超过50分，但仍显著高于其他国家。中国大陆和中国香港排名第7、第8，落后于澳大利亚和加拿大，但是高于瑞士和新加坡，说明人民币和港币在交易媒介职能方面具有一定潜力。

表6-34　　　　　货币竞争力二级指标排名：交易媒介

排名	经济体	交易媒介分值	排名	经济体	交易媒介分值
1	美国	100.0	12	韩国	1.15
2	欧元区	65.7	13	南非	1.05
3	英国	15.65	14	俄罗斯	1
4	日本	14.15	15	土耳其	1
5	澳大利亚	5.7	16	印度	0.95
6	加拿大	5.15	17	巴西	0.65

续表

排名	经济体	交易媒介分值	排名	经济体	交易媒介分值
7	中国大陆	4.9	18	印度尼西亚	0.25
8	中国香港	3.85	19	阿联酋	0.1
9	瑞士	3.8	20	沙特阿拉伯	0.1
10	新加坡	2.25	21	阿根廷	0
11	墨西哥	1.3	—	—	—

2.2.1 跨境支付货币占比

表6-35显示了跨境支付活动中各国货币排名情况，美元和欧元仍然遥遥领先于其他国家货币。2020年12月，美元和欧元在跨境支付中的占比分别为40.83%和38.69%，得分分别为100和94.8，位居前两名；英镑和日元分列第3、第4，占比分别为6.85%和3.78%，得分16.8和9.3；中国大陆排名第5，人民币在跨境支付中的占比为1.98%，得分4.9，领先于加拿大元、澳大利亚元等。

表6-35 货币竞争力三级指标排名：跨境支付货币占比（2020年12月数据）

排名	经济体	跨境支付货币占比分值	排名	经济体	跨境支付货币占比分值
1	美国	100.0	12	土耳其	0.7
2	欧元区	94.8	13	墨西哥	0.7
3	英国	16.8	14	俄罗斯	0.7
4	日本	9.3	15	印度	0
5	中国大陆	4.9	15	韩国	0
6	加拿大	4.6	15	巴西	0
7	澳大利亚	3.7	15	印度尼西亚	0
8	中国香港	3.7	15	沙特阿拉伯	0
9	新加坡	2.5	15	阿根廷	0

续表

排名	经济体	跨境支付货币占比分值	排名	经济体	跨境支付货币占比分值
10	瑞士	1.9	15	阿联酋	0
11	南非	0.8			

2.2.2 外汇市场成交量

从表6-36来看，美元是外汇市场交易的主要货币，人民币与其他国家货币仍存在较大差距。在2019年的外汇市场交易中，美元交易在样本国家/地区货币总体交易中的占比为47.17%，稳居第1；欧元虽然排名第2，但是比美元低了30个百分点，得分仅为36.6；日元、英镑等国际货币也占有较高份额；中国大陆排名不及澳大利亚、加拿大和瑞士，仅排在第8。

表6-36 货币竞争力三级指标排名：外汇市场成交量占比（2019年数据）

排名	经济体	外汇市场成交量占比分值	排名	经济体	外汇市场成交量占比分值
1	美国	100.0	12	墨西哥	1.9
2	欧元区	36.6	13	印度	1.9
3	日本	19.0	14	俄罗斯	1.3
4	英国	14.5	15	南非	1.3
5	澳大利亚	7.7	16	土耳其	1.3
6	加拿大	5.7	17	巴西	1.3
7	瑞士	5.7	18	印度尼西亚	0.5
8	中国大陆	4.9	19	阿联酋	0.2
9	中国香港	4.0	20	沙特阿拉伯	0.2
10	韩国	2.3	21	阿根廷	0
11	新加坡	2.0			

指标 2.3 计价单位

从表 6-37 可以看出各国货币承担国际计价单位职能的情况。美国和欧元区依然稳居前两位,得分分别为 100.0 和 62.8。这是因为美国在汇率制度选择的货币锚、篮子货币、国际银行业负债货币占比和国际债券货币占比 4 个三级指标下均位列第 1;而欧元区除在篮子货币排名中位居第 3,在其他三级指标下均排在第 2。英国和中国大陆排在第 3、第 4 位,分数分别为 11.4 和 9.4,虽然与美国和欧元区相距甚远,但仍显著高于澳大利亚、日本等其他国家。

表 6-37　货币竞争力二级指标排名:计价单位

排名	经济体	计价单位分值	排名	经济体	计价单位分值
1	美国	100.0	12	中国香港	0.6
2	欧元区	62.8	13	墨西哥	0.2
3	英国	11.4	14	韩国	0.2
4	中国大陆	9.4	15	土耳其	0.2
5	澳大利亚	3.2	16	巴西	0.1
6	日本	2.5	17	俄罗斯	0.1
7	南非	2.1	18	印度尼西亚	0.1
8	印度	1.5	19	阿联酋	0
9	瑞士	1.2	20	沙特阿拉伯	0
10	新加坡	0.9	21	阿根廷	0
11	加拿大	0.8	—	—	—

2.3.1 汇率制度选择的货币锚

表 6-38 显示了根据 IMF 识别的事实汇率制度,各个国家

/地区的货币作为货币锚的排名情况,美元和欧元在国际上承担着主要的货币锚职能。在 IMF 调查的全部国家/地区中,有 38 个锚定美元,25 个锚定欧元,3 个锚定澳大利亚元,1 个锚定新加坡元,3 个锚定南非兰特,2 个锚定印度卢比,1 个跟踪欧元和美元篮子。按照各货币锚定国家的数量打分,美元得分为 100.0,欧元得分为 66.2,遥遥领先于其他国家/地区的货币。

表 6-38　货币竞争力三级指标排名：IMF 货币锚（2019 年数据）

排名	经济体	IMF 货币锚分值	排名	经济体	IMF 货币锚分值
1	美国	100.0	12	中国香港	0
2	欧元区	66.2	13	韩国	0
3	澳大利亚	7.8	14	墨西哥	0
4	南非	7.8	15	俄罗斯	0
5	印度	5.2	16	土耳其	0
6	新加坡	2.6	17	巴西	0
7	中国大陆	0	18	印度尼西亚	0
8	日本	0	19	沙特阿拉伯	0
9	英国	0	20	阿联酋	0
10	加拿大	0	21	阿根廷	0
11	瑞士	0			

2.3.2　篮子货币

表 6-39 显示了经测算作为篮子货币的各种货币得分情况。美元依然得到满分,为最重要的货币锚;人民币得到 32.4 分,超过欧元的 29.4 分,二者分列第 2、第 3;英镑得分 17.0,排

在第4。日元虽然包含在篮子货币中,但是其货币锚效应的总体打分为0。其他国家/地区货币不在测算中。

表6-39 货币竞争力三级指标排名:篮子货币(2016年10月数据)

排名	经济体	篮子货币分值	排名	经济体	篮子货币分值
1	美国	100.0	12	南非	0
2	中国大陆	32.4	13	印度	0
3	欧元区	29.4	14	墨西哥	0
4	英国	17.0	15	俄罗斯	0
5	日本	0	16	土耳其	0
6	澳大利亚	0	17	巴西	0
7	加拿大	0	18	印度尼西亚	0
8	瑞士	0	19	沙特阿拉伯	0
9	中国香港	0	20	阿联酋	0
10	新加坡	0	21	阿根廷	0
11	韩国	0			

2.3.3 国际银行业负债货币占比

表6-40显示了各国货币在国际银行业负债中的占比,美元和欧元遥遥领先于其他国家货币。截至2020年第四季度,国际银行业美元负债高达14.9万亿美元,占比49.65%,得分最高;国际银行业欧元负债为9.94万亿美元,占比33.12%,得分为66.7。经测算中国大陆的人民币在国际银行业负债中的份额约为2.11%,得分4.3,紧随英镑和日元之后,排名第5。

表 6-40   货币竞争力二级指标排名：国际银行业负债货币占比

(2020 年 Q4 数据)

排名	经济体	国际银行业负债货币占比分值	排名	经济体	国际银行业负债货币占比分值
1	美国	100.0	12	墨西哥	0.6
2	欧元区	66.7	13	印度	0.6
3	英国	10.9	14	俄罗斯	0.4
4	日本	6.3	15	南非	0.4
5	中国大陆	4.3	16	土耳其	0.4
6	瑞士	3.1	17	巴西	0.4
7	澳大利亚	2.5	18	印度尼西亚	0.2
8	加拿大	1.9	19	阿联酋	0.1
9	中国香港	1.3	20	沙特阿拉伯	0.1
10	韩国	0.7	21	阿根廷	0
11	新加坡	0.7	—	—	—

2.3.4 国际债券货币占比

从表 6-41 可以看出，美元和欧元也是国际债券融资的主要货币。截至 2020 年第四季度，国际债券融资中的美元债为 12.18 万亿美元，占比 45.8%，得到满分；欧元债为 10.82 万亿美元，占比 40.7%，得分 88.9；英镑也获得较高份额，约为 8.02%，得分 17.5。人民币在国际债券融资中占比仍然较低，仅为 0.42%，得分 0.9，排名第 9。

表 6-41　货币竞争力三级指标排名：国际债券货币占比

(2020 年 Q4 数据)

排名	经济体	国际债券货币占比分值	排名	经济体	国际债券货币占比分值
1	美国	100.0	12	土耳其	0.2
2	欧元区	88.9	13	俄罗斯	0.1
3	英国	17.5	14	印度	0.1
4	日本	3.7	15	巴西	0.1
5	澳大利亚	2.3	16	印度尼西亚	0.1
6	瑞士	1.7	17	沙特阿拉伯	0
7	加拿大	1.1	18	阿联酋	0
8	中国香港	1.0	19	韩国	0
9	中国大陆	0.9	20	阿根廷	0
10	新加坡	0.3	21	南非	0
11	墨西哥	0.3	—	—	—

（三）金融基础设施竞争力分项结果

指标 3.1　金融基础设施硬件

表 6-42 显示了各国金融基础设施硬件的排名情况。在金融基础设施硬件方面，英国排名位居首位，且其得分大幅领先于排名第 2 的中国大陆，表明英国作为全球老牌金融中心，其提供支付结算服务的系统和终端数量、使用 SWIFT 服务的金融机构数以及选定清算托管中心年内完成的业务规模都是首屈一指的。中国大陆依靠其体量优势，在支付结算领域的硬件设施发展迅猛，尤其是无现金支付相关的硬件基础设施，是唯一能与英国平分秋色的国家。2018 年，英国无现金支付规模是 GDP 的 42.8 倍，中国大陆无现金支付规模是 GDP 的 41.2 倍。相比之下，法国、德国、美国无现金支付规模分别是 GDP 规模的 11.5、16.6、4.7 倍。因此，就金融基础设施硬件数量和实现的

业务规模来看，中国大陆优势明显，丝毫不逊于除英国外的其他欧美等发达国家。

表6-42 金融基础设施竞争力二级指标排名：金融基础设施硬件

排名	经济体	金融基础设施硬件分值	排名	经济体	金融基础设施硬件分值
1	英国	62.0	17	葡萄牙	19.9
2	中国大陆	34.6	18	希腊	19.9
3	中国香港	33.3	19	卢森堡	19.9
4	美国	32.5	20	奥地利	19.9
5	比利时	31.4	21	日本	19.3
6	瑞士	28.7	22	加拿大	17.8
7	韩国	26.7	23	西班牙	15.9
8	德国	24.9	24	俄罗斯	15.4
9	新加坡	24.1	25	土耳其	10.8
10	荷兰	24.0	26	沙特阿拉伯	10.5
11	法国	23.5	27	墨西哥	7.2
12	澳大利亚	22.1	28	南非	6.6
13	意大利	21.3	29	阿根廷	5.3
14	巴西	20.2	30	印度	2.1
15	爱尔兰	19.9	31	印度尼西亚	1.0
16	芬兰	19.9	32	阿联酋	0.2

3.1.1 提供支付服务的机构数（每百万居民）

表6-43 金融基础设施硬件三级指标排名：提供支付服务的机构数

排名	经济体	提供支付服务机构数分值	排名	经济体	提供支付服务机构数分值
1	韩国	100.0	17	印度	1.1
2	瑞士	41.8	18	土耳其	1.0

续表

排名	经济体	提供支付服务机构数分值	排名	经济体	提供支付服务机构数分值
3	新加坡	39.4	19	沙特阿拉伯	0.4
4	中国香港	34.1	20	南非	0.1
5	俄罗斯	29.6	21	印度尼西亚	0
6	德国	27.2	N/A	英国	N/A
7	加拿大	23.4	N/A	阿联酋	N/A
8	比利时	12.5	N/A	美国	N/A
9	意大利	11.9	N/A	澳大利亚	N/A
10	法国	10.5	N/A	爱尔兰	N/A
11	西班牙	7.2	N/A	奥地利	N/A
12	荷兰	7.0	N/A	芬兰	N/A
13	巴西	6.9	N/A	葡萄牙	N/A
14	中国大陆	4.2	N/A	日本	N/A
15	墨西哥	2.5	N/A	希腊	N/A
16	阿根廷	2.0	N/A	卢森堡	N/A

注：提供支付服务的机构数为标准化后数值，原始数据来源于BIS。金融基础设施硬件方面缺失值较多，倘若一个国家或地区某一单项指标缺失，则以余下指标值取等权重平均后参与排序，若该国家或地区所有指标均缺失，则我们依照各项指标的平均值予以补充，然后再取等权重平均进行排序。使用这一方式而非类似金融业竞争力相关指标的缺失值处理方式，主要由于各项指标国别差异性较大，若依照某一指标排序（如金融基础设施软件）后取前后排名平均值，则有可能显著高估/低估待填补指标的值，相比之下，取整体平均值则更为平滑。下同。

3.1.2 无现金支付金额占 GDP 比重

表 6-44 金融基础设施硬件三级指标排名：无现金支付金额占 GDP 比重

排名	经济体	无现金支付金额占GDP比重分值	排名	经济体	无现金支付金额占GDP比重分值
1	英国	100.0	17	加拿大	3.7
2	中国大陆	96.1	18	新加坡	1.5
3	荷兰	56.9	19	阿根廷	0.6
4	沙特阿拉伯	37.3	20	印度尼西亚	0.2
5	德国	35.9	21	印度	0
6	比利时	34.1	N/A	中国香港	N/A
7	韩国	29.2	N/A	阿联酋	N/A
8	墨西哥	28.7	N/A	爱尔兰	N/A
9	法国	23.6	N/A	奥地利	N/A
10	西班牙	17.5	N/A	土耳其	N/A
11	巴西	14.7	N/A	瑞士	N/A
12	俄罗斯	14.1	N/A	芬兰	N/A
13	南非	11.1	N/A	葡萄牙	N/A
14	澳大利亚	11.1	N/A	日本	N/A
15	意大利	7.6	N/A	希腊	N/A
16	美国	6.7	N/A	卢森堡	N/A

3.1.3 终端数（每个居民）

表 6-45 金融基础设施硬件三级指标排名：终端数

排名	经济体	终端数分值	排名	经济体	终端数分值
1	意大利	100.0	17	沙特阿拉伯	18.0
2	新加坡	92.0	18	南非	10.0

续表

排名	经济体	终端数分值	排名	经济体	终端数分值
3	英国	78.0	19	墨西哥	10.0
4	巴西	78.0	20	印度尼西亚	2.0
5	瑞士	76.0	21	印度	0
6	澳大利亚	74.0	N/A	中国香港	N/A
7	加拿大	74.0	N/A	阿联酋	N/A
8	西班牙	66.0	N/A	韩国	N/A
9	土耳其	54.0	N/A	美国	N/A
10	荷兰	54.0	N/A	爱尔兰	N/A
11	法国	52.0	N/A	奥地利	N/A
12	中国大陆	44.0	N/A	芬兰	N/A
13	比利时	34.0	N/A	葡萄牙	N/A
14	俄罗斯	32.0	N/A	日本	N/A
15	阿根廷	30.0	N/A	希腊	N/A
16	德国	24.0	N/A	卢森堡	N/A

3.1.4 选定支付系统处理的支付交易额占GDP比重

表6-46 金融基础设施硬件三级指标排名：选定支付系统处理的支付交易额占GDP比重

排名	经济体	选定支付系统处理的支付交易额占GDP比重分值	排名	经济体	选定支付系统处理的支付交易额占GDP比重分值
1	中国香港	100.0	17	沙特阿拉伯	6.0
2	日本	36.6	18	俄罗斯	5.6
3	荷兰	34.2	19	西班牙	5.4
4	德国	26.1	20	墨西哥	3.7
5	韩国	25.3	21	阿根廷	3.5

续表

排名	经济体	选定支付系统处理的支付交易额占GDP比重分值	排名	经济体	选定支付系统处理的支付交易额占GDP比重分值
6	巴西	23.7	22	意大利	3.4
7	美国	23.4	23	印度	2.7
8	瑞士	23.0	24	印度尼西亚	2.5
9	中国大陆	22.7	25	比利时	0
10	新加坡	20.7	N/A	爱尔兰	N/A
11	英国	17.0	N/A	奥地利	N/A
12	法国	15.3	N/A	芬兰	N/A
13	南非	10.7	N/A	葡萄牙	N/A
14	澳大利亚	10.6	N/A	日本	N/A
15	加拿大	9.4	N/A	希腊	N/A
16	土耳其	8.5	N/A	卢森堡	N/A

3.1.5 国内使用SWIFT的机构数

表6-47 金融基础设施硬件三级指标排名：国内使用SWIFT的机构数

排名	经济体	国内使用SWIFT的机构数分值	排名	经济体	国内使用SWIFT的机构数分值
1	美国	100.0	17	印度	5.9
2	英国	65.2	18	加拿大	5.7
3	法国	45.7	19	韩国	5.1
4	德国	43.5	20	巴西	4.6
5	中国大陆	40.2	21	印度尼西亚	2.3
6	瑞士	27.0	22	沙特阿拉伯	1.2
7	俄罗斯	25.0	23	土耳其	0.8
8	日本	19.3	24	墨西哥	0.3
9	中国香港	18.7	25	阿根廷	0

续表

排名	经济体	国内使用SWIFT的机构数分值	排名	经济体	国内使用SWIFT的机构数分值
10	意大利	16.5	N/A	阿联酋	N/A
11	新加坡	14.6	N/A	爱尔兰	N/A
12	西班牙	12.7	N/A	奥地利	N/A
13	荷兰	10.9	N/A	芬兰	N/A
14	比利时	7.9	N/A	葡萄牙	N/A
15	澳大利亚	7.4	N/A	希腊	N/A
16	南非	6.6	N/A	卢森堡	N/A

3.1.6 选定中央对手方和清算所清算额占GDP比重

表6-48　金融基础设施硬件三级指标排名：选定中央对手方和清算所清算额占GDP比重

排名	经济体	选定中央对手方和清算所清算额占GDP比重分值	排名	经济体	选定中央对手方和清算所清算额占GDP比重分值
1	英国	100.0	17	西班牙	0.4
2	美国	30.4	18	新加坡	0.1
3	日本	17.4	19	韩国	0.1
4	德国	15.9	20	墨西哥	0
5	法国	13.5	21	印度尼西亚	0
6	中国香港	11.8	N/A	阿联酋	N/A
7	澳大利亚	7.6	N/A	爱尔兰	N/A
8	意大利	5.4	N/A	比利时	N/A
9	巴西	4.5	N/A	中国大陆	N/A
10	荷兰	4.3	N/A	奥地利	N/A
11	印度	4.0	N/A	沙特阿拉伯	N/A
12	瑞士	3.5	N/A	南非	N/A

续表

排名	经济体	选定中央对手方和清算所清算额占GDP比重分值	排名	经济体	选定中央对手方和清算所清算额占GDP比重分值
13	加拿大	1.8	N/A	芬兰	N/A
14	俄罗斯	1.2	N/A	葡萄牙	N/A
15	土耳其	0.5	N/A	希腊	N/A
16	阿根廷	0.4	N/A	卢森堡	N/A

3.1.7 选定中央证券托管机构交付指令金额占GDP比重

表6-49 金融基础设施硬件三级指标排名：选定中央证券托管机构交付指令金额占GDP比重

排名	经济体	选定中央证券托管机构交付指令金额占GDP比重分值	排名	经济体	选定中央证券托管机构交付指令金额占GDP比重分值
1	比利时	100.0	17	中国大陆	0.6
2	英国	12.0	18	荷兰	0.6
3	巴西	9.4	19	俄罗斯	0.4
4	加拿大	6.4	20	新加坡	0.4
5	墨西哥	5.3	21	韩国	0.3
6	意大利	4.6	22	土耳其	0.3
7	日本	4.0	23	印度尼西亚	0.1
8	法国	3.9	24	沙特阿拉伯	0.0
9	西班牙	2.2	N/A	阿联酋	N/A
10	中国香港	1.8	N/A	澳大利亚	N/A
11	美国	1.8	N/A	爱尔兰	N/A
12	德国	1.7	N/A	奥地利	N/A
13	印度	1.1	N/A	芬兰	N/A
14	瑞士	0.9	N/A	葡萄牙	N/A
15	南非	0.8	N/A	希腊	N/A
16	阿根廷	0.6	N/A	卢森堡	N/A

指标 3.2 金融基础设施软件

表 6-50 显示了各国金融基础设施软件的排名情况。在金融基础设施软件方面，排名第 1 的是新加坡。根据世界银行营商环境分项指标，新加坡的投资者保护和合同执行指标得分均为全球第 1，IFRS 应用范围指标亦获得了最高得分，表明新加坡健全的金融法律法规体系为其优越的金融基础设施软件奠定了基础。紧随新加坡之后的是中国香港和英国，二者均使用海洋法系。相比之下，中国大陆在金融基础设施软件指标中的排名较为靠后，指标得分为 52.3，列为第 23，较排名第 1 的新加坡低了 41.5 分，同时也低于大多数北美和西欧国家，表明在金融基础设施软件方面，中国大陆还有不少可进步的空间。美国由于近几年营商环境变数较多，在投资者保护指标上排名第 15，同时由于对国际会计准则 IFRS 应用程度较低，整体金融基础设施软件排名也跌出前 10，为第 12。但在信贷获取指标上，美国排名第 1，反映出美国整体企业融资环境较为宽松和优越（见表 6-51）。

表 6-50　金融基础设施竞争力二级指标排名：金融基础设施软件

排名	经济体	金融基础设施软件分值	排名	经济体	金融基础设施软件分值
1	新加坡	93.8	17	德国	61.2
2	中国香港	83.5	18	法国	58.8
3	英国	83.2	19	比利时	58.1
4	阿联酋	83.1	20	巴西	57.5
5	韩国	73.7	21	阿根廷	53.7
6	澳大利亚	73.2	22	芬兰	53.6
7	爱尔兰	72.7	23	中国大陆	52.3
8	加拿大	71.3	24	葡萄牙	49.8

续表

排名	经济体	金融基础设施软件分值	排名	经济体	金融基础设施软件分值
9	土耳其	70.9	25	瑞士	49.7
10	沙特阿拉伯	69.6	26	日本	48.6
11	南非	69.0	27	意大利	44.0
12	美国	66.9	28	希腊	43.9
13	俄罗斯	66.0	29	荷兰	42.4
14	墨西哥	63.3	30	印度	41.1
15	西班牙	63.2	31	卢森堡	38.0
16	奥地利	62.9	32	印度尼西亚	35.6

3.2.1 信贷获取

表6-51 金融基础设施软件竞争力三级指标排名：信贷获取

排名	经济体	信贷获取分值	排名	经济体	信贷获取分值
1	美国	100.0	17	瑞士	62.5
2	澳大利亚	100.0	18	中国大陆	56.3
3	墨西哥	93.8	19	芬兰	56.3
4	加拿大	87.5	20	沙特阿拉伯	56.3
5	印度	81.3	21	南非	56.3
6	俄罗斯	81.3	22	西班牙	56.3
7	中国香港	75.0	23	奥地利	50.0
8	新加坡	75.0	24	日本	50.0
9	土耳其	75.0	25	阿根廷	43.8
10	英国	75.0	26	巴西	43.8
11	德国	68.8	27	法国	43.8
12	印度尼西亚	68.8	28	希腊	37.5
13	爱尔兰	68.8	29	意大利	37.5
14	阿联酋	68.8	30	荷兰	37.5

续表

排名	经济体	信贷获取分值	排名	经济体	信贷获取分值
15	比利时	62.5	31	葡萄牙	37.5
16	韩国	62.5	32	卢森堡	0

注：数据经标准化，原始数据来源于世界银行营商环境指数分项指标。下同。

3.2.2 投资者保护

表6-52 金融基础设施软件竞争力三级指标排名：投资者保护

排名	经济体	投资者保护分值	排名	经济体	投资者保护分值
1	新加坡	100.0	17	印度尼西亚	55.6
2	沙特阿拉伯	100.0	18	比利时	50.0
3	加拿大	94.4	19	法国	50.0
4	中国香港	94.4	20	意大利	44.4
5	英国	94.4	21	澳大利亚	38.9
6	印度	83.3	22	日本	38.9
7	爱尔兰	83.3	23	阿根廷	33.3
8	南非	83.3	24	巴西	33.3
9	阿联酋	83.3	25	芬兰	33.3
10	土耳其	72.2	26	德国	33.3
11	韩国	66.7	27	墨西哥	33.3
12	中国大陆	61.1	28	葡萄牙	33.3
13	西班牙	61.1	29	俄罗斯	27.8
14	美国	60.0	30	荷兰	22.2
15	奥地利	55.6	31	卢森堡	11.1
16	希腊	55.6	32	瑞士	0

3.2.3 合同执行

表6-53　金融基础设施软件竞争力三级指标排名：合同执行

排名	经济体	合同执行分值	排名	经济体	合同执行分值
1	新加坡	100.0	17	墨西哥	59.6
2	韩国	99.1	18	芬兰	58.2
3	中国大陆	91.7	19	日本	55.7
4	澳大利亚	87.3	20	沙特阿拉伯	55.7
5	阿联酋	80.1	21	比利时	53.3
6	奥地利	79.2	22	巴西	52.9
7	德国	76.0	23	瑞士	52.9
8	法国	74.6	24	荷兰	43.2
9	美国	74.4	25	爱尔兰	38.6
10	卢森堡	74.1	26	阿根廷	37.6
11	俄罗斯	71.6	27	加拿大	36.7
12	土耳其	69.7	28	南非	36.3
13	西班牙	68.6	29	意大利	27.5
14	中国香港	64.4	30	印度尼西亚	18.2
15	英国	63.5	31	希腊	15.9
16	葡萄牙	61.7	32	印度	0

3.2.4 IFRS应用程度

表6-54　金融基础设施软件竞争力三级指标排名：IFRS应用程度

排名	经济体	IFRS应用程度分值	排名	经济体	IFRS应用程度分值
1	英国	100.0	17	德国	66.7
2	中国香港	100.0	18	希腊	66.7
3	新加坡	100.0	19	意大利	66.7
4	爱尔兰	100.0	20	韩国	66.7

续表

排名	经济体	IFRS应用程度分值	排名	经济体	IFRS应用程度分值
5	巴西	100.0	21	卢森堡	66.7
6	南非	100.0	22	墨西哥	66.7
7	阿联酋	100.0	23	荷兰	66.7
8	阿根廷	100.0	24	葡萄牙	66.7
9	俄罗斯	83.3	25	沙特阿拉伯	66.7
10	瑞士	83.3	26	西班牙	66.7
11	澳大利亚	66.7	27	土耳其	66.7
12	奥地利	66.7	28	日本	50.0
13	比利时	66.7	29	美国	33.3
14	加拿大	66.7	30	中国大陆	0
15	芬兰	66.7	31	印度	0
16	法国	66.7	32	印度尼西亚	0

（四）金融科技竞争力分项结果

指标4.1 算力

"算力指数"衡量各国金融科技产业的计算力，表现其技术基础的厚度。表6-55反映了32个国家在算力水平的排名情况，美国排名全球第1，中国大陆排名第2，日本排名第3，排名第4至第10的国家依次是：德国、英国、荷兰、法国、爱尔兰、加拿大和意大利。32个样本中，将排名第1的美国定基为100.0分，前10位的国家都在及格线60分以上，中国大陆（84.2分）的算力水平仅次于美国。美国的科技实力在全球长期保持领先地位，但是中国大陆作为发展中国家在基础科技方面的追赶速度相当可观。与美国相比，中国大陆在计算能力方面的差距较小（见表6-56），但在计算效率、应用水平和基础设施支持上还有一定差距（见表6-57、表6-58和表

6-59），需要进一步提高，尤其是应用水平和基础设施支持这两个方面。

表 6-55　　　　金融科技竞争力二级指标排名：算力

排名	经济体	算力分值	排名	经济体	算力分值
1	美国	100.0	17	阿联酋	42.2
2	中国大陆	84.2	18	南非	42.2
3	日本	73.1	19	芬兰	41.9
4	德国	70.4	20	巴西	41.4
5	英国	65.3	21	俄罗斯	39.1
6	荷兰	65.1	22	奥地利	34.2
7	法国	64.9	23	中国香港	31.2
8	爱尔兰	62.9	24	西班牙	29.2
9	加拿大	61.6	25	卢森堡	24.1
10	意大利	60.2	26	印度尼西亚	18.1
11	沙特阿拉伯	58.9	27	阿根廷	15.1
12	澳大利亚	57.5	28	葡萄牙	12.1
13	新加坡	43.6	29	希腊	9.1
14	瑞士	43.3	30	比利时	6.0
15	韩国	42.9	31	土耳其	3.0
16	印度	42.6	32	墨西哥	0

4.1.1　计算能力

表 6-56　　　　金融科技竞争力三级指标排名：计算能力

排名	经济体	计算能力分值	排名	经济体	计算能力分值
1	美国	100.0	17	印度	44.2
2	中国大陆	91.9	18	阿联酋	43.4
3	日本	63.5	19	芬兰	42.7

续表

排名	经济体	计算能力分值	排名	经济体	计算能力分值
4	德国	63.5	20	南非	41.9
5	英国	58.1	21	俄罗斯	40.5
6	荷兰	57.4	22	奥地利	37.2
7	法国	56.8	23	中国香港	33.8
8	爱尔兰	56.0	24	西班牙	32.1
9	加拿大	55.1	25	卢森堡	27.0
10	意大利	54.3	26	印度尼西亚	20.3
11	沙特阿拉伯	53.5	27	阿根廷	16.9
12	澳大利亚	52.7	28	葡萄牙	13.5
13	巴西	47.3	29	希腊	10.1
14	新加坡	46.5	30	比利时	6.8
15	瑞士	45.7	31	土耳其	3.4
16	韩国	45.0	32	墨西哥	0

4.1.2 计算效率

表6-57　　金融科技竞争力三级指标排名：计算效率

排名	经济体	计算效率分值	排名	经济体	计算效率分值
1	美国	100.0	17	韩国	61.0
2	日本	84.1	18	印度	60.8
3	德国	82.5	19	芬兰	60.5
4	中国大陆	81.0	20	阿联酋	60.3
5	英国	77.8	21	南非	55.6
6	荷兰	77.0	22	奥地利	51.1
7	法国	76.2	23	中国香港	46.4
8	爱尔兰	74.9	24	西班牙	44.1
9	加拿大	73.7	25	卢森堡	37.2
10	意大利	72.4	26	印度尼西亚	27.9

续表

排名	经济体	计算效率分值	排名	经济体	计算效率分值
11	沙特阿拉伯	71.1	27	阿根廷	23.2
12	澳大利亚	69.8	28	葡萄牙	18.6
13	俄罗斯	61.9	29	希腊	13.9
14	巴西	61.7	30	比利时	9.3
15	新加坡	61.4	31	土耳其	4.6
16	瑞士	61.2	32	墨西哥	0

4.1.3 应用水平

表6-58　金融科技竞争力三级指标排名：应用水平

排名	经济体	应用水平分值	排名	经济体	应用水平分值
1	美国	100.0	17	韩国	36.0
2	日本	83.5	18	印度	35.8
3	中国大陆	82.3	19	芬兰	35.6
4	德国	78.5	20	南非	35.4
5	法国	73.4	21	俄罗斯	25.3
6	荷兰	72.2	22	奥地利	23.4
7	英国	70.9	23	中国香港	21.4
8	爱尔兰	69.6	24	西班牙	19.5
9	加拿大	68.4	25	卢森堡	15.6
10	意大利	67.1	26	印度尼西亚	11.7
11	沙特阿拉伯	65.8	27	阿根廷	9.7
12	澳大利亚	64.6	28	葡萄牙	7.8
13	阿联酋	36.7	29	希腊	5.9
14	巴西	36.5	30	比利时	3.9
15	新加坡	36.3	31	土耳其	2.0
16	瑞士	36.2	32	墨西哥	0

4.1.4 基础设施支持

表6-59　金融科技竞争力三级指标排名：基础设施支持

排名	经济体	基础设施支持分值	排名	经济体	基础设施支持分值
1	美国	100.0	17	韩国	29.1
2	中国大陆	81.8	18	印度	29.0
3	日本	61.0	19	芬兰	28.8
4	德国	57.1	20	俄罗斯	28.6
5	英国	54.6	21	南非	27.3
6	荷兰	53.9	22	奥地利	25.2
7	法国	53.3	23	中国香港	23.1
8	爱尔兰	51.2	24	西班牙	21.0
9	加拿大	49.1	25	卢森堡	16.8
10	意大利	47.0	26	印度尼西亚	12.6
11	沙特阿拉伯	44.9	27	阿根廷	10.5
12	澳大利亚	42.9	28	葡萄牙	8.4
13	阿联酋	29.9	29	希腊	6.3
14	巴西	29.7	30	比利时	4.2
15	新加坡	29.5	31	土耳其	2.1
16	瑞士	29.3	32	墨西哥	0

指标4.2　用户接入度

"用户接入度指数"衡量各国金融科技产业的普及程度以及用户基础，利用各国已接入金融科技产业的人数与金融科技产业所有潜在用户的比率来表现各国金融科技产业目前的用户接入度。表6-60反映了32个国家在数字金融用户接入度（代指用户在金融科技领域的接入度）的排名情况，加拿大、荷兰、德国、卢森堡、芬兰靠前，接入度较高的国家包括：比利时、瑞士、澳大利亚、英国、奥地利、日本、爱尔兰、韩国、法国。

美国的接入度排名第15,中国大陆排名第24。美国的信用卡支付发展非常早、饱和度也很高,由于信用卡的支付使用习惯,美国的数字金融接入度偏低。中国作为刚刚完成脱贫攻坚任务的发展中国家和大型经济体,发展不平衡、不充分的问题依然存在,金融科技作为一个新兴业态和手段,其普及率有待提高,但潜在的用户规模却非常有竞争力。

表6-60　　金融科技竞争力二级指标排名:用户接入度

排名	经济体	用户接入度分值	排名	经济体	用户接入度分值
1	加拿大	100.0	17	西班牙	88.4
2	荷兰	100.0	18	意大利	88.4
3	德国	100.0	19	葡萄牙	82.6
4	卢森堡	100.0	20	中国香港	81.2
5	芬兰	100.0	21	阿联酋	79.7
6	比利时	98.6	22	希腊	65.2
7	瑞士	97.1	23	俄罗斯	60.9
8	澳大利亚	97.1	24	中国大陆	56.5
9	英国	97.1	25	土耳其	50.7
10	奥地利	97.1	26	沙特阿拉伯	46.4
11	日本	95.7	27	南非	44.9
12	爱尔兰	94.2	28	巴西	42.0
13	韩国	91.3	29	阿根廷	15.9
14	法国	91.3	30	印度尼西亚	8.7
15	美国	89.9	31	墨西哥	4.4
16	新加坡	88.4	32	印度	0

指标4.3　产业发展潜力

"产业发展潜力指数"利用金融科技产业中终端行业的发展状况衡量各国金融科技产业未来的发展空间,而决定一个产业发展潜力的两个关键因素是劳动力和资本的投入水平。基于此,本报告选取各国 AI 人才的招聘和储备水平（见表 6-62）来反映金融科技产业中的劳动力投入水平，选取各国金融科技信贷水平（见表 6-63）来反映金融科技产业中的资本投入水平。

表 6-61 反映了 32 个国家在金融科技产业发展潜力方面的排名情况，美国排名全球第 1，中国香港排名第 6，中国大陆排名第 19。美国在新兴产业投融资效率和高科技人才储备这两个方面的竞争力一直在全球保持领先地位，故而其金融科技产业的潜力巨大；但是中国在高科技人才尤其是高科技工程类人才的储备尚显不足，中国资本市场的产业投融资效率也是一个亟待提高的金融服务实体能力。

需要特别说明的是，意大利在金融科技领域的信贷水平非常高：作为传统的金融强国，意大利的佛罗伦萨是欧洲最早的金融中心之一，在历史上其贸易和金融领域长期居于领先地位，虽受欧债危机影响，意大利金融领域的传统优势和历史底蕴依然存在。面临金融科技这个新兴产业，意大利至少在信贷水平上尝试抓住这次新的产业发展机遇。此外，由于意大利在高端制造业方面储备大量人才，在统计口径的影响下，意大利 AI 招聘指数也相对较高（见表 6-62）。因此，虽然在数据可获得性和指标选取的限制下，意大利在金融科技产业上的发展潜力可能被高估了，但其在金融科技产业上的金融服务和人才服务能力依然不容小觑。

表 6-61　金融科技竞争力二级指标排名：**产业发展潜力**

排名	经济体	产业发展潜力分值	排名	经济体	产业发展潜力分值
1	美国	82.4	17	瑞士	18.7
2	意大利	65.8	18	阿根廷	16.1
3	阿联酋	48.5	19	中国大陆	16.1
4	新加坡	41.1	20	奥地利	15.6

续表

排名	经济体	产业发展潜力分值	排名	经济体	产业发展潜力分值
5	加拿大	39.7	21	南非	14.3
6	中国香港	37.5	22	俄罗斯	13.5
7	印度	36.6	23	比利时	12.3
8	德国	35.9	24	土耳其	12.3
9	巴西	35.2	25	卢森堡	11.8
10	澳大利亚	32.1	26	葡萄牙	10.9
11	英国	30.7	27	墨西哥	10.8
12	韩国	29.3	28	爱尔兰	10.5
13	荷兰	29.0	29	西班牙	9.0
14	法国	28.7	30	希腊	5.6
15	日本	27.8	31	印度尼西亚	4.9
16	芬兰	23.9	32	沙特阿拉伯	2.2

4.3.1 AI招聘指数

表6-62　金融科技竞争力三级指标排名：AI招聘指数

排名	经济体	AI招聘指数分值	排名	经济体	AI招聘指数分值
1	新加坡	78.6	17	阿联酋	30.3
2	加拿大	77.5	18	中国大陆	29.4
3	中国香港	75.0	19	南非	28.0
4	德国	67.2	20	阿根廷	26.9
5	印度	66.8	21	土耳其	24.4
6	巴西	65.6	22	比利时	23.6
7	美国	64.7	23	卢森堡	23.6
8	澳大利亚	62.2	24	韩国	23.4
9	英国	60.6	25	俄罗斯	22.3

续表

排名	经济体	AI招聘指数分值	排名	经济体	AI招聘指数分值
10	法国	50.6	26	葡萄牙	21.7
11	芬兰	45.3	27	墨西哥	21.4
12	日本	43.2	28	爱尔兰	20.0
13	意大利	40.8	29	西班牙	17.6
14	荷兰	32.7	30	希腊	11.1
15	奥地利	31.2	31	印度尼西亚	7.3
16	瑞士	30.4	32	沙特阿拉伯	0

4.3.2 金融科技信贷水平

表6-63 金融科技竞争力三级指标排名：金融科技信贷水平

排名	经济体	金融科技信贷水平分值	排名	经济体	金融科技信贷水平分值
1	美国	100.0	17	印度尼西亚	2.5
2	意大利	90.8	18	芬兰	2.5
3	阿联酋	66.7	19	澳大利亚	1.9
4	韩国	35.3	20	加拿大	1.8
5	荷兰	25.2	21	比利时	1.1
6	日本	12.4	22	爱尔兰	1.0
7	瑞士	6.9	23	英国	0.9
8	法国	6.9	24	南非	0.5
9	印度	6.5	25	西班牙	0.3
10	阿根廷	5.3	26	墨西哥	0.2
11	巴西	4.9	27	土耳其	0.2
12	俄罗斯	4.7	28	卢森堡	0
13	德国	4.5	29	葡萄牙	0
14	沙特阿拉伯	4.4	30	中国香港	0
15	新加坡	3.6	31	奥地利	0
16	中国大陆	2.7	32	希腊	0

(五) 国际金融治理竞争力分项结果

表 6-64、表 6-67 和表 6-70 给出了国际金融治理竞争力 3 个二级指标的排名情况。

指标 5.1 全球金融组织竞争力

表 6-64 国际金融治理竞争力二级指标排名：全球经济金融组织竞争力

排名	经济体	全球经济金融组织竞争力分值	排名	经济体	全球经济金融组织竞争力分值
1	美国	100.0	17	奥地利	40.8
2	日本	64.3	18	爱尔兰	39.9
3	德国	56.6	19	芬兰	39.8
4	英国	52.8	20	葡萄牙	39.4
5	法国	52.7	21	希腊	39.2
6	意大利	48.5	22	印度	33.6
7	加拿大	47.3	23	俄罗斯	33.0
8	西班牙	45.2	24	沙特阿拉伯	32.1
9	韩国	44.6	25	巴西	31.6
10	墨西哥	44.3	26	印度尼西亚	27.9
11	荷兰	43.9	27	阿根廷	27.6
12	澳大利亚	43.5	28	新加坡	26.6
13	比利时	42.9	29	卢森堡	13.6
14	瑞士	42.8	30	南非	2.1
15	中国大陆	42.2	31	阿联酋	1.1
16	土耳其	42.0	32	中国香港	0

表 6-64 可以看出，在全球经济金融组织竞争力这个二级指标中，发达国家的竞争力更为突出。其中美国排名第 1，且指

数得分为满分，可见美国在全球经济金融组织的强大话语权。以中国大陆和印度为代表的发展中国家，在这个维度仅排名为第15和第22。值得一提的是墨西哥，以44.3的分数位居第10，不仅高于中国大陆，还高于作为传统发达国家的澳大利亚。墨西哥高于中国大陆是因为，中国大陆在四大全球经济金融组织中，只位列三席。墨西哥高于澳大利亚是因为，尽管两国GDP规模相对持平，但是墨西哥对外贸易和国际储备均高于澳大利亚，而这三项是全球金融组织分配份额的主要依据。因此，墨西哥的排名略高于澳大利亚。

从全球经济金融组织竞争力这个维度上来看，国际金融治理并未从霸权模式走向真正的多边主义模式，表现为全球经济金融组织依然为发达国家所控制，新兴和发展中国家在国际金融事务中的发言权与其经济规模相比仍有较大差距。这表明，2008年金融危机后国际金融治理体系的一系列改革尚未取得显著进展，新兴和发展中国家在正式国际经济金融组织中话语权的提升是有限的。

5.1.1 全球经济金融组织会员份额

表6-65 国际金融治理竞争力三级指标排名：全球经济金融组织会员份额

排名	经济体	全球经济金融组织会员份额分值	排名	经济体	全球经济金融组织会员份额分值
1	美国	100.0	17	巴西	31.6
2	日本	57.5	18	瑞士	31.6
3	德国	48.5	19	比利时	31.3
4	英国	43.6	20	土耳其	30.8
5	法国	43.3	21	奥地利	29.1
6	中国大陆	42.1	22	爱尔兰	28.1
7	意大利	38.4	23	芬兰	28.0

续表

排名	经济体	全球经济金融组织会员份额分值	排名	经济体	全球经济金融组织会员份额分值
8	加拿大	36.9	24	印度尼西亚	27.9
9	西班牙	34.5	25	阿根廷	27.6
10	韩国	34.1	26	葡萄牙	27.5
11	印度	33.6	27	希腊	27.3
12	墨西哥	33.4	28	新加坡	26.6
13	俄罗斯	32.9	29	南非	2.0
14	澳大利亚	32.9	30	卢森堡	1.5
15	荷兰	32.1	31	阿联酋	1.1
16	沙特阿拉伯	32.0	32	中国香港	0

5.1.2 全球经济金融组织投票权重

表6-66 国际金融治理竞争力三级指标排名：全球经济金融组织投票权重

排名	经济体	全球经济金融组织投票权重分值	排名	经济体	全球经济金融组织投票权重分值
1	美国	100.0	17	爱尔兰	51.6
2	日本	71.1	18	芬兰	51.5
3	德国	64.8	19	葡萄牙	51.2
4	法国	62.1	20	希腊	51.1
5	英国	62.1	21	中国大陆	42.2
6	意大利	58.6	22	印度	33.6
7	加拿大	57.7	23	俄罗斯	33.0
8	西班牙	55.9	24	沙特阿拉伯	32.1
9	荷兰	55.8	25	巴西	31.7
10	墨西哥	55.2	26	印度尼西亚	27.9
11	韩国	55.1	27	阿根廷	27.7
12	比利时	54.4	28	新加坡	26.7

续表

排名	经济体	全球经济金融组织投票权重分值	排名	经济体	全球经济金融组织投票权重分值
13	澳大利亚	54.2	29	卢森堡	25.7
14	瑞士	53.9	30	南非	2.1
15	土耳其	53.2	31	阿联酋	1.2
16	奥地利	52.4	32	中国香港	0

以 IMF 为例分析正式国际组织改革举步维艰的原因。IMF 实施的是加权投票制度，即投票权由基本投票权和份额投票权组成。其中基本投票权考虑了国家主权平等原则并在成员国之间平均分配，但是随着 IMF 的多次增资和新成员的不断加入，基本投票权被逐步稀释，并让位于基于份额的投票权。而基金份额是根据一国的国民收入总值、经济开放度、经济波动性和国际储备等多种因素确定的，基本与一国经济实力挂钩。随着金融全球化的发展，发展中国家也不断壮大，产生新的大国。2008 年国际金融危机使得新兴市场和发展中国家的经济实力明显增强，正成为牵引世界经济复苏的火车头，然而它们在 IMF 的会员份额却被大大低估，代表性严重不足。2010 年 10 月，美国在国际货币基金组织的会员份额为 17.09%，投票权重 16.74%；日本会员份额为 6.12%，投票权重 6.01%，中国大陆的会员份额仅为 3.72%，投票权重为 3.65%。经过漫长的改革，截至 2020 年年底，尽管中国大陆的会员份额被提升至 6.41%，投票权重提升至 6.08%，但是日本的会员份额也略有提升至 6.48%，投票权重上升至 6.12%；美国的投票权重略有下降至 16.51%，会员份额反而上升至 17.51%。这使得在"一票否决权"（即超过 85% 投票权）制度下，美国仍具有绝对竞争力，日本等发达国家的竞争力也得到了维护。

指标5.2 非正式协调平台竞争力

从表6-67可以看出,在非正式协调平台竞争力这个二级指标中,各国竞争力排名相对平均,主要发达国家在第一档;新兴发展中国家出现分化,金砖国家的巴西和俄罗斯,率先在非正式协调平台中获得同发达国家持平的竞争力,而同为金砖国家的中国大陆和印度,则居于第二档。中国大陆和印度位居第二档主要是因为两国都不是巴黎俱乐部的永久会员,只是特别参与者。

表6-67　国际金融治理竞争力二级指标排名:非正式协调平台竞争力

排名	经济体	非正式协调平台竞争力分值	排名	经济体	非正式协调平台竞争力分值
1	澳大利亚	100.0	17	荷兰	66.7
2	巴西	100.0	18	沙特阿拉伯	66.7
3	加拿大	100.0	19	南非	66.7
4	法国	100.0	20	西班牙	66.7
5	德国	100.0	21	瑞士	66.7
6	意大利	100.0	22	土耳其	66.7
7	日本	100.0	23	奥地利	33.3
8	韩国	100.0	24	比利时	33.3
9	俄罗斯	100.0	25	芬兰	33.3
10	英国	100.0	26	中国香港	33.3
11	美国	100.0	27	爱尔兰	33.3
12	阿根廷	66.7	28	新加坡	33.3
13	中国大陆	66.7	29	希腊	0
14	印度	66.7	30	卢森堡	0
15	印度尼西亚	66.7	31	葡萄牙	0
16	墨西哥	66.7	32	阿联酋	0

5.2.1 非正式协调平台会员份额

表6-68　国际金融治理竞争力三级指标排名：非正式协调平台会员份额

排名	经济体	非正式协调平台会员份额分值	排名	经济体	非正式协调平台会员份额分值
1	澳大利亚	100.0	17	印度	66.7
2	巴西	100.0	18	墨西哥	66.7
3	加拿大	100.0	19	荷兰	66.7
4	德国	100.0	20	沙特阿拉伯	66.7
5	法国	100.0	21	土耳其	66.7
6	英国	100.0	22	南非	66.7
7	意大利	100.0	23	奥地利	33.3
8	日本	100.0	24	比利时	33.3
9	韩国	100.0	25	芬兰	33.3
10	俄罗斯	100.0	26	中国香港	33.3
11	美国	100.0	27	爱尔兰	33.3
12	阿根廷	66.7	28	新加坡	33.3
13	瑞士	66.7	29	阿联酋	0
14	中国大陆	66.7	30	希腊	0
15	西班牙	66.7	31	卢森堡	0
16	印度尼西亚	66.7	32	葡萄牙	0

5.2.2 非正式协调平台投票权重

表6-69　国际金融治理竞争力三级指标排名：非正式协调平台投票权重

排名	经济体	非正式协调平台投票权重分值	排名	经济体	非正式协调平台投票权重分值
1	澳大利亚	100	17	印度	66.7
2	巴西	100	18	墨西哥	66.7
3	加拿大	100	19	荷兰	66.7

续表

排名	经济体	非正式协调平台投票权重分值	排名	经济体	非正式协调平台投票权重分值
4	德国	100	20	沙特阿拉伯	66.7
5	法国	100	21	土耳其	66.7
6	英国	100	22	南非	66.7
7	意大利	100	23	奥地利	33.3
8	日本	100	24	比利时	33.3
9	韩国	100	25	芬兰	33.3
10	俄罗斯	100	26	中国香港	33.3
11	美国	100.0	27	爱尔兰	33.3
12	阿根廷	66.7	28	新加坡	33.3
13	瑞士	66.7	29	阿联酋	0
14	中国大陆	66.7	30	希腊	0
15	西班牙	66.7	31	卢森堡	0
16	印度尼西亚	66.7	32	葡萄牙	0

总体来说，相比全球金融组织竞争力，非正式协调平台竞争力受强国霸权影响较小，在一定程度上体现了多元治理和非正式机制的灵活性。以 G20 为例来说明，相比正式国际组织，非正式国际组织可以快速提升新兴发展中国家国际金融治理竞争力的原因。通常，在国际环境变化较快、不确定性程度较高时，国家经常会选择非正式机制，因为这样有利于国家修改甚至退出已达成的国际协议，保持机制的灵活性。[①] 在 2008 年金融危机后，G20 这种非正式性质的灵活性机制有助于在一定程度上提升新兴发展中国家的话语权，也为后续正式机制形成提供了时间窗口。可以说，G20 是金融危机后唯一能够兼顾议事效力和南北共同利益的

---

① Charles Lipson, "Why are Some International Agreements Informal?" *International Organization*, Vol. 45, No. 4, 1991, pp. 495–512.

全球性共治型经济治理平台,也是唯一的发达国家与发展中国家领导人平等对话的最高协调机制。体现了国际金融治理体系从霸权模式向多边模式的尝试,为新兴发展中国家参与国际金融治理和提升话语权,提供了平台和渠道。

2013年起,中国大陆在全球经济和国际金融治理中的话语权和影响力不断上升,更多包容性和可持续发展等问题逐步成为G20的合作议题和领域。G20虽扩大了新兴国家的参与权,但开展国际经济协调和决策的效率备受国际社会质疑。历届峰会除了不断重复危机期间各国达成的原则性共识、表明各成员国推动全球经济复苏的决心外,在行动上鲜有突破。这一方面是因为,G20是全球经济金融治理协商平台,但并非执行平台,它既没有常设秘书处,也没有执行或监管的治理实体;其在建立时没有以法律文件作为基础,其后所达成的国际协议也就没有法律约束力,所通过的各项公报、宣言和行动计划只发挥方向指引作用,不能对成员国构成国际法律义务。[①] 另一方面,G20仍在发达国家主导下运作,发展中国家依然处于次要地位,美欧国家试图保持甚至扩大自身在全球经济金融治理中的领导权,对G20转型态度转向消极,与新兴国家协调时的姿态渐趋强硬。再加上,新兴发展中国家缺乏凝聚力,未来想要切实提升在国际金融治理体系中的话语权仍面临较大障碍。

与此同时,作为一种非正式机制,要想保持领导人之间坦率、开放、有效的非正式交流,就必须限制参加会议的成员数量,即必须采取"选择性"的成员资格原则,保持成员构成的"小集团"特征。这种"选择性"成员资格原则也会给它带来严重的合法性缺陷,尤其是在选择成员的时候过于注重经济实力的标准,这会让广大发展中国家,尤其是非洲国家对该机制

---

① 刘宏松:《G20议题的扩展及其对机制有效性的影响》,《国际论坛》2015年第3期。

的合法性与代表性产生怀疑，客观上使得自身陷入"有效性"（要求减少成员）与"合法性"（要求增加成员）的两难困境。

指标5.3 区域多边金融组织竞争力

从表6-70可以看出，在区域多边金融组织竞争力这个二级指标中，发展中国家的排名显著提升。在区域多边金融组织竞争力中，中国大陆得分为64.2，位居第1，略高于排名第2的德国，在全球经济金融组织中拥有绝对话语权的美国，得分为55.3，仅位居第4。同样作为新兴发展中国家的印度和巴西的排名也从全球经济金融组织竞争力中的第22和第25跃升至第13和第17。

表6-70 国际金融治理竞争力二级指标排名：区域多边金融组织竞争力

排名	经济体	区域多边金融组织竞争力分值	排名	经济体	区域多边金融组织竞争力分值
1	中国大陆	64.2	17	巴西	36.0
2	德国	62.4	18	瑞士	32.5
3	法国	55.9	19	俄罗斯	27.5
4	美国	55.3	20	南非	25.4
5	意大利	54.0	21	卢森堡	22.3
6	日本	53.3	22	阿根廷	22.3
7	西班牙	44.6	23	墨西哥	21.5
8	荷兰	41.8	24	爱尔兰	15.7
9	比利时	40.5	25	澳大利亚	15.1
10	英国	39.6	26	土耳其	9.7
11	加拿大	39.5	27	沙特阿拉伯	8.6
12	奥地利	39.5	28	希腊	7.6
13	印度	38.8	29	印度尼西亚	6.8
14	芬兰	38.2	30	中国香港	1.1
15	葡萄牙	37.1	31	新加坡	0.6
16	韩国	36.2	32	阿联酋	0.6

5.3.1 区域多边金融会员份额

表6-71 国际金融治理竞争力三级指标排名：区域多边金融组织会员份额

排名	经济体	区域多边金融组织会员份额分值	排名	经济体	区域多边金融组织会员份额分值
1	中国大陆	63.2	17	芬兰	31.9
2	德国	61.1	18	葡萄牙	30.2
3	法国	58.8	19	阿根廷	28.6
4	意大利	57.9	20	南非	28.6
5	美国	57.1	21	俄罗斯	23.1
6	日本	55.0	22	沙特阿拉伯	15.5
7	英国	44.1	23	爱尔兰	15.1
8	西班牙	43.2	24	卢森堡	15.0
9	巴西	42.9	25	墨西哥	14.5
10	加拿大	38.7	26	澳大利亚	8.5
11	印度	38.4	27	印度尼西亚	6.6
12	荷兰	37.5	28	土耳其	3.2
13	韩国	36.4	29	希腊	0.9
14	比利时	36.2	30	中国香港	0.9
15	奥地利	34.3	31	阿联酋	0.6
16	瑞士	32.7	32	新加坡	0.4

5.3.2 区域多边金融组织投票权重

表6-72 国际金融治理竞争力三级指标排名：区域多边金融组织投票权重

排名	经济体	区域多边金融组织投票权重	排名	经济体	区域多边金融组织投票权重
1	中国大陆	65.2	17	瑞士	32.2
2	德国	63.6	18	俄罗斯	31.8
3	美国	53.4	19	卢森堡	29.7

续表

排名	经济体	区域多边金融组织投票权重	排名	经济体	区域多边金融组织投票权重
4	法国	53.0	20	巴西	29.2
5	日本	51.6	21	墨西哥	28.6
6	意大利	50.0	22	南非	22.3
7	西班牙	46.1	23	澳大利亚	21.7
8	荷兰	46.1	24	爱尔兰	16.3
9	比利时	44.7	25	土耳其	16.3
10	奥地利	44.6	26	阿根廷	15.9
11	芬兰	44.5	27	希腊	14.4
12	葡萄牙	44.0	28	印度尼西亚	6.9
13	加拿大	40.2	29	沙特阿拉伯	1.6
14	印度	39.1	30	中国香港	1.3
15	韩国	36.1	31	新加坡	0.9
16	英国	35.1	32	阿联酋	0.7

当全球层面的金融治理工作难以推动或者获得实质性进展时，区域金融治理便成为大家关注的对象，区域层面的金融治理的成功将在很大程度上推动全球层面金融治理的进行。可以说，区域金融合作也是国际金融治理改革的一个重要步骤或者是较为迂回的路径。从这个维度来看，中国大陆已经在区域多边治理中承担了与自身相匹配的责任，也在区域多边合作中取得了与主要发达国家持平的话语权，未来如何通过区域多边金融合作推动国际金融治理合作，是中国大陆参与国际金融治理、提升自身国际金融治理竞争力的关键。

Global Financial Competitiveness Report 2021

Global Financial Competitiveness Research Group
Institute of World Economics and Politics, Chinese Academy of Social Sciences(CASS)
National Institute for Global Strategy, Chinese Academy of Social Sciences (NIGS, CASS)

I Introduction

As the core of the modern economy, finance serves as an important engine promoting economic development and technological innovation and enhancing the well-being of people, and financial competitiveness has become one of the key elements to support national competitiveness.

The most fundamental and significant function of the financial system is to allocate financial resources and manage risks. In the era of globalization, a nation must involve its financial system in the international financial market and integrate into the process of globalization in order to better achieve the goal of resource allocation and risk management. Therefore, for a more reliable conclusion, we need to integrate domestic and international markets from the perspective of global financial governance in the investigation of national financial competitiveness in the era of globalization.

This report defines "global financial competitiveness" as the ability of an economy's financial system in allocating financial resources and managing risks more effectively worldwide than other economies, so as to promote economic growth and social development. This report attempts to comprehensively measure the global financial competitiveness of 32 countries or regions by examining 57 indicators in five dimensions: the competitiveness of financial industry, the competitiveness of currency, the competitiveness of financial infrastructure, the competitiveness of financial technology, and the competitiveness in international financial governance.

At present, with its global competitiveness ever increasing, China is leading the world concerning the size of its financial system. With the new round of financial reform and opening up, China's financial industry will carry out more comprehensive and in-depth competition and cooperation with global financial institutions in domestic and international markets. The construction of the indicator system for the evaluation of global financial competitiveness helps us to study and judge the competitive advantages and disadvantages of a country's financial system through international comparison and quantitative analysis, so as to provide a reference for the government in launching new financial reform and opening-up measures, as well as a reference for the innovative development of financial institutions.

II Review on the evaluation methods of financial competitiveness

Some international institutions have established evaluation systems with great international influence for national competitiveness including the dimension of financial competitiveness, such as the *World Competitiveness Yearbook* by International Institute for Management Development (IMD) and *The Global Competitiveness Report* by World Economic Forum (WEF).

IMD measures a country's overall strength in terms of economic performance, government efficiency, business efficiency and infrastructure, and for the financial part, IMD mainly examines the two dimensions of banking and capital market, and evaluates financial competitiveness through a total of 19 indicators in four aspects of the banking sector, financial services, stock market and enterprise operation. WEF, with its focuses mainly on the overall competitiveness at the national level, discusses the overall strength of a nation in 12 categories as institutions, infrastructure, adoption of information and communication technology, macroeconomic stability, health, skills, product market, labor market, financial system, market scale, business vitality and innovation ability, with the analysis of the financial system mainly starts from the depth of banks and capital markets and the stability of the banking industry.

It can be seen from the reports of IMD and WEF that they both take financial competitiveness as a part of national competitiveness with their attention merely focused on banks and capital markets, without considering other factors such as currency, financial infrastructure, financial technology and international financial governance.

Domestic research on the evaluation system of financial competitiveness is gaining momentum in recent years. Zhan Jisheng et al. (2007) believes that financial competitiveness represents a dynamic systematic ability with which a country's financial industry successfully provides products and services to the market more effectively than other countries' financial industries, and realizes more value in a competitive and open market through the conversion of financial resources. According to this definition, Zhan Jisheng et al. came up with three new indicators including financial asset competitiveness, financial innovation competitiveness and financial human capital competitiveness on the basis of the four accepted indicators of financial competitiveness by IMD, Switzerland. Similar to IMD, Ni Pengfei et al. (2016) established sub-indicators of national financial competitiveness in the evaluation of national competitiveness, including five primary indicators, namely, the strength of the currency, international relations, financial system, domestic services and financial supervision.

As for the way of data processing, there have already been systematic and comprehensive the evaluation methods of multinational economies in the world. For data standardization, Z-score, namely standard deviation method has been adopted by IMD to standardize the data, which is simple and feasible, but depends on the mean and variance of the original data. WEF takes the Min-max method, with minimum and maximum values in its reports artificially set acceptable by means liking using the quantile to avoid the effects on the min or max values from the uncertainty of them in some indicators or the addition of new data. For the missing values, IMD directly replaces the missing values with the mean value of the indicators, which can be simple and feasible but fails to indicate the characteristics of development in different countries when taking the average level as the development status of various countries. WEF uses linear regression to fill in the missing value, or groups countries according to the level of development, and replace the missing values with the mean value of the same group, which has high requirements on the amount of data and is not suitable for the situation with a small number of samples.

III Evaluation indicator system of the global financial competitiveness

This report takes the countries (or regions) as the basic units of investigation, and establishes evaluation indicator system of the global financial competitiveness within the competitiveness of financial industry, the competitiveness of currency, the competitiveness of financial infrastructure, the competitiveness of financial technology and the competitiveness in international financial governance as the primary indicators.

i Selection of indicators

1. The competitiveness of financial industry

The financial industry serves as a significant part of a country's economic development. It is the common goal of policymakers of all nations to promote the development of their real economy through enhancing the competitiveness of their financial industry upon the construction of a multi-level and comprehensive financial system. This report measures the competitiveness of the financial industry in six dimensions, namely, the size of the financial system, the activity of the financial system, the efficiency of the financial system, the stability of the financial industry, the availability of financial services and the status of the international financial center(s) of the economy.

2. The competitiveness of currency

Since the report measures financial competitiveness in a global context, the measurement of currency competitiveness also focuses on the competitiveness of a currency in the global context. From this perspective, two key points need to be made clear about the concept of competitiveness of the currency: firstly, the core of the competitiveness of the currency in this report is the international competitiveness of a currency, that is, the wide use of the currency of a certain country in the world. Based on the literature of international monetary research, the competitiveness of a currency can be regarded as the utilization of the function of a currency in the public and private sectors out of the jurisdiction of currency; secondly, this report focuses on result-based competitiveness. Starting from the literature on measuring currency internationalization, the measurement of currency competitiveness can be divided into factor-based and result-based competitiveness. Factor-based competitiveness focuses on various factors that make one currency competitive, such as economic scale, financial market depth, inflation level, etc., while result-based competitiveness concentrates on the results of the competitiveness of the currency, that is, the actual functions one currency plays in the world. When constructing the indicators, this report ensures that all indicators reflect the result-based competitiveness. Based on a clear concept, the construction of the indicators for the competitiveness of currency is divided into three secondary indicators according to the functions of the currency, namely, store of value, media of exchange and unit of account. Different sub-indicators are set under the secondary indicators to describe the international functions of one currency to fully reflect the competitiveness of the currency.

3. The competitiveness of financial infrastructure

According to the *Principles for Financial Market Infrastructures* jointly issued by Committee on Payment and Settlement Systems (CPSS, renamed as Committee on Payments and Market Infrastructures, CPMI, in September 2014) and International Organization of Securities Commissions (IOSCO), financial market infrastructures mainly include central counterparties, payment systems, central securities depository systems, securities settlement systems and trade repositories. In March 2020, the *Work Plan for Overall Supervision and Regulation of Financial Infrastructures* jointly issued by the People's Bank of China and other six departments classified the scope of China's financial infrastructures into six types of facilities and their operating institutions: financial asset registration and custody system, clearing and settlement system (including the central counterparties carrying out centralized clearing business), transaction facilities, trade repositories, important payment system and basic credit system. This way of defining financial infrastructures from the perspective of hardware facilities is usually regarded as financial infrastructures in a narrow sense.

Financial infrastructures, in the broad sense, mainly refer to the hardware facilities and institutional arrangements that provide public services for financial activities which ensure the stable, sustainable and safe operation of financial market. Specifically, they not only include financial market infrastructures such as payment, clearing, settlement and depository, but financial accounting standards, credit environment, pricing mechanism and so on. In recent years, with the deep integration of finance and technology, scholars have mainly defined financial infrastructure from the perspective of the combination of hardware facilities and soft constraints (such as Jiao Jinpu et al., 2019). Considering that the quality of the hardware and software for financial infrastructure is closely related to the financial operation and economic development, the competitiveness indicators of financial infrastructures will be measured and investigated from two aspects in this report.

Sound financial infrastructures will guarantee greater financial market depth, higher financial service efficiency, better access to financial resources and greater economic growth. Moreover, sound financial infrastructures can also improve the resistance of the financial system against shocks and prevent the occurrence and infection of a financial crisis. For example, a reliable payment system can greatly reduce the credit, liquidity and operational risks in financial transactions, while a sound bankruptcy liquidation system helps to protect the value of the collateral and prevent the crisis from being transmitted through the balance sheet. In view of this, countries and relevant international institutions all over the world regard the construction of financial infrastructures as an important part of economic development policies. Therefore, when measuring a country's financial competitiveness, financial infrastructure should be regarded as one of the indispensable and critical indicators.

4. The competitiveness of financial technology

The financial technology competitiveness indicator reflects the overall competitiveness of a country's financial technology based on the construction of three levels of bottom technologies (computing power/hush rate), intermediate access (user access) and terminal industry (industrial development potential). The following logic will be adhered to in selecting the specific indexes required for the calculation of the indicators. From the perspective of the underlying technology, the development of fintech industry needs strong computing power as its technical basis. Underlying technologies determine the long-term development of fintech industry and market, and most of such technologies fall into slow production. From the perspective of the application, with the development of the fintech industry, more users access the industry. User access essentially indicates whether users have the means and channels to consume the latest financial technology, which is an important key link between technology and the market. The degree of "realizing" potential users determines the application width of the underlying technology, which can measure the current development level of the fintech industry in various countries to some extent. Stable computing power and high user access support the development of the terminal industry in the fintech industry. The development of terminal industry shows the potentials of fintech industry, and the market potential will in turn affect the pace of technology iteration and update. Based on this logic, a system of tertiary indicators is constructed. The indicators of the competitiveness of financial technology of 32 sample countries or regions have been obtained through the multiplication of each sub-indicator by its weight on the basis of standardized processing of the original data.

5. The competitiveness in international financial governance

International financial governance, also known as global financial governance, is generally regarded as the extension and application of global governance in the field of international finance. This concept gradually attracted attention after the Asian financial crisis in 1997 and became the focus of international research after the financial crisis in 2008. In 2003, the Global Economic Governance Programme was established in Oxford University, of which the financial sector took it its responsibility to establish a new policy agenda for global financial regulation and reform, and to the way to better meet the needs of people in developing countries as its goal. In the same year, Cambridge University also published a collection of papers entitled *International Financial Governance under Stress: Global Structures versus National Imperatives*, with attempts to analyze the causes of previous financial crises and put forward suggestions for the reform of the international financial system. In 2008, the domestic financial crisis triggered by its subprime mortgage crisis in the US spread rapidly and evolved into a global financial crisis in its real sense. The serious consequences of the global economic recession once again reflect the irrationality of the current international financial system, which makes it urgent to reform the current international financial system and international financial supervision system. In this context, Global Financial Governance or similar notions are gaining frequent popularity in the scope of news reports and academic discussions.

To effectively govern the international financial system, we need to start from why, what and how to govern, among which a consensus has been basically reached on why to govern. What to govern mainly explains the objects to govern and the objectives of governance to achieve, that is, what are the objects of international financial governance. How to govern mainly covers who will govern and how to govern in a manner upon a mechanism which involves a series of rules and orders and coordination methods, for the cooperation and negotiation among its participants. Another core issue of how to govern is who will lead the governance of the global financial system, that is, what are the subjects of international financial governance.

In the above dimensions, the ability of countries in participating in international financial governance is reflected in the status of countries in the subject of international financial governance and the ability to determine the governance object, that is, the seats and says in participating in the formulation and coordination of rules on matters related to the international financial system. The research group will determine the secondary indicators according to the scope of the subjects and objects of global financial governance, and the tertiary indicators upon selected data indicators reflecting the seats and say.

ii Rating samples

Table 1 List of Economies

Economy	Code	Economy	Code	Economy	Code	Economy	Code
The United Arab Emirates	ARE	Chinese Mainland	CHN	Indonesia	IDN	Netherlands	NLD
Argentina	ARG	Germany	DEU	India	IND	Portugal	PRT
Australia	AUS	Spain	ESP	Ireland	IRL	Russia	RUS
Austria	AUT	Finland	FIN	Italy	ITA	Saudi Arabia	SAU
Belgium	BEL	France	FRA	Japan	JPN	Singapore	SGP
Brazil	BRA	Britain	GBR	Korea	KOR	Turkey	TUR
Canada	CAN	Greece	GRC	Luxembourg	LUX	USA	USA
Switzerland	CHE	Hong Kong, China	HKG	Mexico	MEX	South Africa	ZAF

Thirty-two economies were selected as rating samples in the report (see

Table 1), covering the member states of G20, BRICS countries, most member states of the Eurozone, and other countries or regions, including most developed countries and a few developing countries with large economies. Most of these economies are highly representative, considering their sound economic development, their financial activities of great global influence and the global status of their financial centers.

IV Construction of Indicators for Global Financial Competitiveness

This report adopts 35%, 35%, 10%, 10%, and 10% respectively for the weights of five primary indicators, namely, the competitiveness of the financial industry, the competitiveness of the currency, the competitiveness of the financial infrastructure, the competitiveness of the financial technology and the competitiveness in international financial governance. The construction of the five indicators will be elaborated as below.

i Construction of the indicators for the competitiveness of financial industry

1. Selection of indicators

The report evaluates the competitiveness of the financial industry through six secondary indicators, namely, the size of the financial system, the activity of the financial system, the efficiency of the financial system, the stability of the financial system, the availability of the financial services and the status of the international financial center owned by the economy. In addition to the measures suggested by the literature like that of Beck et al. (1999) to evaluate the financial system from the three dimensions of size, activity and efficiency of the financial system, the system of this report further includes the stability of the financial system, the difficulty in obtaining financial services and the status of international financial center into the scope of the system of indicators. (See Table 2)

Indicator 1.1: Size of financial system

The size of financial system measures the development of a country's financial system from the size level. The larger size of financial system, the greater capacity to serve the real economy. Morton (1995) summarizes the six basic functions of the financial system from the perspective of financial function. Different financial institutions can provide different financial services for the real economy. For example, as a typical representative of financial intermediaries, commercial banks can circulate necessary funds, realize the transfer of resources across time, regions and industries, in addition to the strength in screening projects, supervising enterprises and risk management (Diamond, 1984; Rajan and Zingales, 1999); While the stock market, as the representative of direct financing, can raise funds and has advantages in information disclosure, enterprise M & A, technological progress and risk diversification (Allen and gale, 2000; Levine, 2005). This model not only measures the size of financial system regarding financial sectors like banking, stocks, central bank assets, mutual funds, insurance, and pensions, but includes liquidity liabilities as an overall indicator for the evaluation. The model takes the proportion of the size of each department in GDP in the evaluation, which represents the size of financial system of a country or region in comparison to the whole economic scale. Relative indicators can avoid the problem of incompatibility caused by too large gaps in the economic volume of countries when absolute indicators are used. Therefore, the size of financial system is measured by three tertiary indicators, namely, the ratio of deposit bank assets to GDP, the ratio of stock market value to GDP, and the ratio of assets of other departments to GDP (including the assets of the central bank, mutual fund, insurance company and pension).

The larger the value of these indicators, the larger the relativesize of these sectors, that is, the larger the size of financial system. The data of these seven indicators are from the Global Financial Development Database (GFDD) of the World Bank (WB).

Indicator 1.2: Activity of financial system

The activity of financial system measures the dynamic of financial system in serving the real economy from the activity level. The stronger the activity of financial system, the more dynamic it is to serve the real economy. Credit to the private sector is usually the most comprehensive indicator to measure the activity of financial intermediaries, and a large number of literatures have confirmed that private sector credit has a significant, positive and stable impact on economic growth (Levine et al., 2000; Beck et al., 2000). As revealed in other literatures, the trading value of stock market is a reasonable indicator in measuring the activity of the stock market, which indicates the liquidity provided by the stock market to the real economy, and the trading value of stock market is a robust indicator of long-term economic growth (Levine and Zervos, 1998). Due to the limited data, this model only takes banks and stock markets, and uses the ratio of private sector credit to GDP, the ratio of bank loans to bank deposits to measure the activity of the banking sector, and the ratio of stock trading value to GDP to measure the activity of the stock market.

The greater the value of these indicators, the stronger the activity of these sectors, that is, the stronger the activity of financial system. The data of these three indicators are from the GFDD of WB.

Indicator 1.3: Efficiency of financial system

The efficiency of financial system measures the cost of financial services to the real economy from the perspective of operational efficiency. The higher the efficiency of the financial system, the lower the cost in serving the real economy. High efficiency of the financial market usually means better liquidity and greater efficiency in raising and converting funds for the real economy. This report selects two sectors: banking and the stock market. For the banking sector, it selects the ratio of bank non-interest income to total income, the ratio of bank operating expenses to total assets and the return on assets of the banking industry to measure the bank's operating costs and profitability. For the stock market, it selects the stock market turnover rate to measure the strength of stock liquidity and the financing efficiency of the stock market.

If a bank's operating expenses constitute a bigger share of its total assets, the bank and even the financial system as a whole will become less efficient. The larger the value of other indicators, the higher the efficiency of the banks and stock markets, that is, the higher the efficiency of the financial system. The data of these four indicators are from the GFDD of WB.

Indicator 1.4: Stability of financial system

The stability of financial system measures the sustainability and volatility of financial system in serving the real economy. Schinasi G J (2004) defines financial stability as the performance of the financial system in promoting the economy and the elimination of financial imbalances caused by endogenous or major adverse and unexpected events. ECB (2016) believes that financial stability can be defined as the condition for the financial system to resist shocks and eliminate financial imbalances, which reduces the possibility of interruption of the financial intermediation process and reduces the adverse impact on real economic activities. IMF (2006) mentions in the *Guidelines for the Preparation of Financial Stability Indicators* that financial stability indicators can assess and monitor the strength and vulnerability of financial system, improve the stability of financial system and reduce the collapse possibility of financial system. Wu Nianlu and Yun Huimei (2005) believes that financial stability is conducive to creating a good environment to realize financial functions and improve financial efficiency, so as to promote economic and social development. The stronger the stability of the financial system, the stronger the sustainability of its service to the real economy. Compared with the economic instability caused by the fluctuation of the stock market, the crisis in the banking sector is usually more infectious and destructive. Therefore, this model selects bank Z-score, non-performing loan ratio, the ratio of the capital to the total assets of the bank, the ratio of the bank regulatory capital to risk-weighted assets, the ratio of liquid assets to deposits and short-term financing, the ratio of the bank's non-performing loan reserve and bank stability for the comprehensive evaluation of the stability of the banking system, in addition to the selection of the stock market volatility for the evaluation of the stability of the stock market.

The greater the bank's non-performing loan ratio and the stock market volatility, the weaker the stability of the banks/stock markets, that is, the less stable the financial system is. The larger the value of other indicators, the stronger the stability of the banks, that is, the higher the stability of the financial system. The data of bank robustness indicators are survey data from *The Global Competitiveness Report* by the World Economic Forum (WEF) annually. The data of the other seven indicators are from the GFDD of WB.

Indicator 1.5: Availability of financial services

In addition to the characteristics of financial system in evaluating the potential of financial system in serving the real economy, this model also takes the availability of financial services into consideration. Beck et al. (2009) believes that the lack of financing channels is the key to long-term income inequality and economic slowdown. Mookerjee and Kalipioni (2010) measures the availability of financial services upon the number of banking institutions per 100,000 people and finds out that the improvement of the availability of financial services can effectively reduce the income inequality among countries.

This model selects the number of commercial bank branches for every 100,000 adults to measure the availability of banking services, and selects the ratio of stock market trading volume to total trading volume outside the top ten listed companies, the ratio of market value to the total market value of companies outside the top ten listed, and the number of listed companies for every million people to measure the difficulty of financing in the stock market, the financing of small and medium-sized enterprises (SMEs) to measure the difficulty of obtaining funds for SMEs, and the availability of venture capital to measure the difficulty of financing for start-ups.

The larger the values of these six indicators, the easier access to financial services in the economy. Among the six indicators, four tertiary indicators, the number of commercial bank branches for every 100,000 adults, the ratio of stock market trading volume to total trading volume outside the top ten listed companies, the ratio of market value to the total market value of companies outside the top ten listed, and the number of listed companies for every million people are from the world bank's global financial development database. The data on the availability of financing and venture capital for SMEs are from *The Global Competitiveness Report* issued by the WEF annually.

Indicator 1.6: Status of the international financial center(s)

The indicator measures the comprehensive competitiveness of the international financial center. The higher the status of the international financial center of a country or region, the higher the degree of its financial development, and the stronger the ability to allocate financial resources and manage risks globally, so as to better serve the real economy. Ni Pengfei (2004) believes that the international financial center, with its favorable financial and business environment, can effectively attract multinational banks and multinational corporations, so as to achieve strong control over the global economy. Liu Yi (2010) believes that an international financial center, as a city providing convenient international financing services, an effective international payment and clearing system and an active international financial trading place, can be globally influential. Solovjova et al. (2018) believes that the establishment of an international financial center is related to the financial liberalization and the globalization of financial markets, and has contributed to the country's overall economic development and growth. Its status depends on the development of banking system, the development of securities market, a safe banking system, government support and well-established national policies. Upon the use of *The Global Financial Centers Index* (GFCI) jointly released by Z / Yen Group of Companies of the UK and China Development Institute, this paper takes the scores of the top 30% financial centers as the indicators of the countries or regions to which they belong. The number of the cities selected varied due to the different sizes of countries, and for the same country or region, only the financial center with the highest score is selected in this report to represent the degree of financial development of the country or region.

2. Data processing

(1) Weight assignment

Table 2 Overview of Construction of the Indicators for the Competitiveness of Financial Industry and the Weights of Each Indicator

Primary indicators	Secondary indicators and their weights		Tertiary indicators and their weights	
1. The competitiveness of financial industry	1.1 Size of financial system	16.66%	1.1.1 Ratio of deposit bank assets to GDP	33.33%
			1.1.2 Ratio of stock market value to GDP	33.33%
			1.1.3 Ratio of assets of other sectors to GDP	33.33%
	1.2 Activity of financial system	16.66%	1.2.1 Ratio of private sector credit to GDP	25.00%
			1.2.2 Ratio of bank loans to bank deposits	25.00%
			1.2.3 Ratio of stock market trading value to GDP	50.00%
	1.3 Efficiency of financial system	16.67%	1.3.1 Ratio of bank non-interest income to total income	16.66%
			1.3.2 Ratio of bank operating expenses to total assets	16.67%
			1.3.3 Return on banking assets	16.67%
			1.3.4 Stock market turnover	50.00%
	1.4 Stability of financial system	16.67%	1.4.1 Bank Z-score	7.15%
			1.4.2 Ratio of the bank non-performing loan	7.15%
			1.4.3 Ratio of bank capital to total assets	7.15%
			1.4.4 Ratio of bank regulatory capital to risk weighted assets	7.14%
			1.4.5 Ratio of current assets to deposits and short-term financing	7.14%
			1.4.6 Ratio of non-performing loan reserve	7.14%
			1.4.7 Stability of the bank	7.14%
			1.4.8 Stock market fluctuation	50.00%
	1.5 Availability of financial system	16.67%	1.5.1 Number of commercial bank branches for every 100,000 adults	25.00%
			1.5.2 Ratio of stock market trading volume to total trading volume outside the top ten listed companies	8.34%
			1.5.3 Ratio of market value to total market value of companies other than the top ten listed companies	8.33%
			1.5.4 Number of listed companies per million people	8.33%
			1.5.5 SME financing	25.00%
			1.5.6 Availability of venture capital	25.00%
	1.6 Status of international financial center(s)	16.67%	1.6.1 GFCI	100%

Six secondary indicators are set under the competitiveness of financial industry with the same weight of 16.67%. Due to the differences in the number of indicators among various departments, the weights of the tertiary indicators under the secondary indicators are distributed evenly within their departments in this paper. For example, three tertiary indicators, namely, 1.2.1 the ratio of the private sector credit to GDP, 1.2.2 the ratio of bank loan to bank deposit, and 1.2.3 the ratio of the stock market transaction value to GDP are set under the secondary indicator 1.2 financial system activity, among which, indicators 1.2.1 and 1.2.2 are set with weights of 25% respectively in the banking sector, while indicator 1.2.3 is set with the weight of 50% in the sector of the stock market. (See Table 2)

The indicators for the competitiveness of financial industry can be calculated as the aggregation of the weights of the secondary indicators multiplied by the sum of the multiplication of the value of the tertiary indicators by their respective weights. For example, the formula of secondary indicator 1.2, the activity of the financial system is: the value of indicator 1.2.1 × 25% + the value of indicator 1.2.2 × 25% + the value of indicator 1.2.3 × 50%, the formula of indicators for the f competitiveness of the financial industry is: the value of indicator 1.1 × 16.66% + the value of indicator 1.2 × 16.66% + the value of indicator 1.3 × 16.67% + the value of indicator 1.4 × 16.67% + the value of indicator 1.5 × 16.67% + the value of indicator 1.6 × 16.67%.

(2) Mode of standardization

Due to the different dimensions of different data, it is necessary to standardize the data to convert it into values in the [0,1] interval. This report takes the practice of WEF for reference and adopts the Min-max standardization method to standardize the tertiary indicators. Considering abnormal values may be there for some economic indicators, or the reasonable value ranges for some indicators should be there in the economic sense, the report adopts the reasonable extreme value X_{min}^*, X_{max}^* to replace the original data value X_{min}、X_{max}. The determination of the reasonable extreme value X_{min}^*, X_{max}^* will be mainly determined upon the following two principles: firstly, the reasonable value range of the indicator should be defined in the sense of economics, and secondly, from the statistical significance, the indicator should be winsorized at the 10% or 90% percentile to eliminate the abnormal value①. According to the attributes of each index, this paper selects different principles to determine the reasonable maximum value (see Table 3).

Table 3 Selection of the Reasonable Extreme Value

Tertiary indicators	Acceptable minimum X_{min}^*	Acceptable maximum X_{max}^*	Notes
1.1.1 Ratio of deposit bank assets to GDP	0	150	Minimum, 90% quantile winsorized
1.1.2 Ratio of stock market value to GDP	0	200	Minimum, 90% quantile winsorized
1.1.3 Ratio of assets of other sectors to GDP	0	400	Minimum, 90% quantile winsorized
1.2.1 Ratio of private sector credit to GDP	0	160	Minimum, 90% quantile winsorized
1.2.2 Ratio of bank loans to bank deposits	50	140	10% and 90% quantile winsorized
1.2.3 Ratio of stock market trading value to GDP	0	130	Minimum, 90% quantile winsorized
1.3.1 Ratio of bank non-interest income to total income	0	50	Minimum, 90% quantile winsorized
1.3.2 Ratio of bank operating expenses to total assets	0	4	Minimum, 90% quantile winsorized
1.3.3 Return on banking assets	0	2	Minimum, 90% quantile winsorized

---

① The indicators of some developing countries have obviously deviated from the scope of the reasonable value. For example, the market value of Chinese Mainland stock market accounted for only 65.5% of GDP, far lower than that of Japan's 113.1% and lower than most developed countries, while Chinese Mainland stock market value accounts for 144.7% of GDP, which is higher than Japan's 112.3%, and is higher than most developed countries. The higher the proportion of stock market transaction value in GDP, the more active the stock transaction and the better the liquidity, which has a positive incentive effect on the stock IPO in the primary market. However, the ratio of Chinese Mainland stock market to GDP is obviously too high, which is beyond the scope of reasonable value, and cannot reflect the real function of stock market correctly. Therefore, this model selects Australia, Canada, Germany, Switzerland and the United States as the benchmark countries, and takes the average value of "transaction value of the stock market / market value of the stock" as the reasonable upper limit for Chinese Mainland and other developing countries to revise the abnormal value of the "the ratio of the transaction value of the stock market transaction value to GDP" of the developing countries. The average of "stock market turnover rate" of the five benchmark countries is used to revise the abnormalities in the "stock market turnover rate" in the developing countries.

Tertiary indicators	Acceptable minimum X^*_{min}	Acceptable maximum X^*_{max}	Notes
1.3.4 Stock market turnover	0	130	Minimum, 90% quantile winsorized
1.4.1 Bank Z-score	0	30	Minimum, 90% quantile winsorized
1.4.2 Bank non-performing loan ratio	0	15	Minimum, 90% quantile winsorized
1.4.3 Ratio of bank capital to total assets	5	15	10% and 90% quantile winsorized
1.4.4 Ratio of bank regulatory capital to risk weighted assets	10	25	10% and 90% quantile winsorized
1.4.5 Ratio of current assets to deposits and short-term financing	10	60	10% and 90% quantile winsorized
1.4.6 Non-performing loan reserve ratio	30	150	10% and 90% quantile winsorized
1.4.7 The stability of the bank	1	7	Minimum, Maximum
1.4.8 The fluctuations of the stock market	10	25	10% and 90% quantile winsorized
1.5.1 Number of commercial bank branches for every 100,000 adults	0	50	Minimum, 90% quantile winsorized
1.5.2 Ratio of stock market trading volume to total trading volume outside the top ten listed companies	0	80	Minimum, 90% quantile winsorized
1.5.3 Ratio of market value to total market value of companies other than the top ten listed companies	0	80	Minimum, 90% quantile winsorized
1.5.4 Number of listed companies per million people	0	80	Minimum, 90% quantile winsorized
1.5.5 SME financing	1	7	Minimum, Maximum
1.5.6 Availability of venture capital	1	7	Minimum, Maximum
1.6.1 GFCI	770	0	Minimum, Maximum

Most indicators are positively related to the competitiveness of the financial industry. The formula for the standardization of them is as follows, where X' stands for the value after winsorization:

$$Z = \frac{X' - X^*_{min}}{X^*_{max} - X^*_{min}}$$

Three tertiary indicators are negatively related to the competitiveness of financial industry, namely, indicator 1.3.2 the proportion of bank operating expenses in total assets, 1.4.2 the bank non-performing loan ratio and 1.4.8 the stock market volatility. The formula for the standardization of them is:

$$Z = 1 - \frac{X' - X^*_{min}}{X^*_{max} - X^*_{min}}$$

The same standardized data processing method is adopted for the calculation of the remaining four primary indicators in this report.

(3) Measures for the missing values

Table 4　　　List of Reference Indicators for Missing Indicators

Missing indicator A	Reference indicator B
1.1.1 Ratio of deposit bank assets to GDP	Ratio of current liabilities to GDP
1.1.2 Ratio of stock market value to GDP	Ratio of current liabilities to GDP
1.1.3 Ratio of assets of other sectors to GDP	Ratio of current liabilities to GDP
1.2.1 Ratio of private sector credit to GDP	Ratio of current liabilities to GDP
1.2.2 Ratio of bank loans to bank deposits	Ratio of current liabilities to GDP
1.2.3 Ratio of stock market trading value to GDP	Ratio of current liabilities to GDP
1.3.4 Stock market turnover	Ratio of current liabilities to GDP
1.4.2 Bank non-performing loan ratio	1.4.1 Bank Z-score
1.4.3 Ratio of bank capital to total assets	1.4.1 Bank Z-score
1.4.4 Ratio of bank regulatory capital to risk-weighted assets	1.4.1 Bank Z-score
1.4.6 Non-performing loan reserve ratio	1.4.1 Bank Z-score
1.5.1 Number of commercial bank branches for every 100,000 adults	1.2.2 Ratio of bank loans to bank deposits
1.5.2 Ratio of stock market trading volume to total trading volume outside the top ten listed companies	1.1.2 Ratio of stock market value to GDP
1.5.3 Ratio of market value to total market value of companies other than the top ten listed companies	1.1.2 Ratio of stock market value to GDP
1.5.4 Number of listed companies per million people	1.1.2 Ratio of stock market value to GDP

There are missing values in indicators of some countries or regions. In this case, two main methods can be adopted: 1) substitution. the data of the previous year can be directly used for substitution upon the assumption that the situation of this year is similar to that of the previous year, if there are the data of indicator A for the previous year of this country or region; 2) ranking: if the data of indicator A of the country or region in the previous year does not exist for possible exclusion in the statistics of the country or region, other indicators can be adopted for the ranking, specifically, the indicator with similar meaning to the missing indicator A will be taken as the reference indicator B for the ranking. If the ranking of the country is n, then select the average value of the corresponding indicator A of the two countries with the ranking of $n - 1$ and $n + 1$ as the missing value of the indicator A of the country. The list of reference sorting is shown in Table 4.

The same method will be adopted for the calculation of the missing value of the remaining four primary indicators in this report adopts unless otherwise specified.

ii Construction of the currency competitiveness indicators

1. Selection of indicators

```
2. Competitiveness of currency
├── 2.1 Store of Value (1/3)
│   ├── 2.1.1 proportion of foreign exchange reserve currencies (1 / 2)
│   └── 2.1.2 currency weights in the SDR basket (1 / 2)
├── 2.2 Medium of Exchange (1/3)
│   ├── 2.2.1 proportion of cross-border payment currencies (1 / 2)
│   └── 2.2.2 proportion of currencies of foreign exchange market turnover (1/2)
└── 2.3 Unit of Account(1/3)
    ├── 2.3.1 exchange rate anchor (1 / 4)
    ├── 2.3.2 basket currencies (1 / 4)
    ├── 2.3.3 proportion of currencies for international banking liabilities (1 / 4)
    └── 2.3.4 proportion of currencies for international debt securities (1 / 4)
```

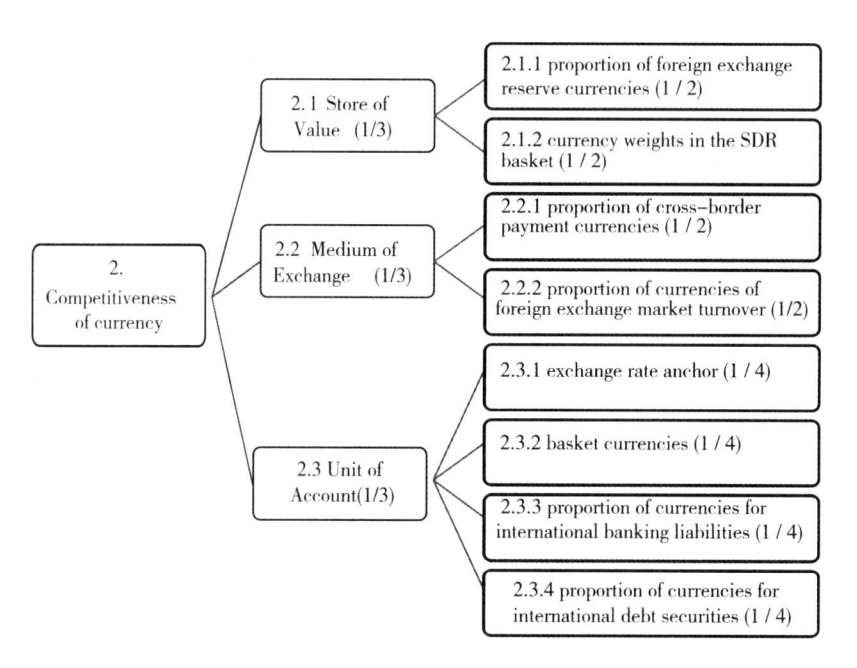

Figure 1 Overview of Construction of the Indicators for the Competitiveness of Currency and the Weight of Each Indicator

Upon thorough consideration on the availability of data and relevant research literature, three secondary indicators for the competitiveness of the currency are constructed in this report, namely "store of value", "medium of exchange" and "unit of account" (Figure 1), with same weighting. The setting of the three secondary indicators is consistent with the division of international monetary functions in the literature. In terms of the selection of sub-indicators under the secondary indicators, this report refers to the review of the basket share of special drawing rights (SDR) conducted by the IMF every five years (IMF, 2015), and creates the currency anchor indicator based on our own research, so as to more comprehensively reflect the currency competitiveness and make the indicators more policy-relevant. Table 5 summarizes the different functions of the currency measured by each sub-indicator in the public and private sectors.

Table 5   Correspondence Between Sub-Indicators for the Competitiveness of Currency and International Functions of Currency

The functions of the currency	Government	Private sectors
Store of value	Foreign exchange reserve	Currency substitution in private sectors
Corresponding sub-indicators	Proportion of foreign exchange reserve currency and SDR weight	n. a. *
Medium of exchange	Medium currency of foreign exchange market intervention	Currency for trade and financial transactions
Corresponding sub-indicators	n. a. *	Proportion of cross-border payment currencies and foreign exchange market turnover
Unit of account	The anchor currency chosen when a country determines its exchange rate system	Pricing currency for trade and finance
Corresponding sub-indicators	Exchange rate anchor and basket currencies	Proportion of currencies for international banking liabilities and proportion of currencies for international debt securities

Notes:

1. The 3 × 2 matrix diagram of the international monetary function was proposed by Kenen (1983) when discussing the international monetary status of the US Dollar. The version adopted in this paper originates from Chinn and Frankel (2007).

2. Indicators marked with * indicate that it is difficult to find internationally comparable indicators for the corresponding monetary functions.

The report calculates the competitiveness of currency from the perspective of currency rather than sovereignty, so RMB and HKD will be used to reflect respectively the currency competitiveness of Chinese Mainland and Hong Kong SAR. Since it is difficult to seperate indicators at the country level, the Eurozone will be taken as a whole as well. When aggregated to generate the indicators for the global financial competitiveness, the score will be given upon the export proportion of each member state to construct the competitiveness of currency of the Eurozone. The export proportion will take both trade in goods and trade in services into consideration with equal weights for the average exports over the past five years. Specifically, the final score of the competitiveness of the currency of each sample country in the Eurozone is to be obtained by splitting the score of the competitiveness of the currency of the Eurozone upon the proportion of the exports of the countries in the Eurozone.

"Store of value" includes two equally-weighted tertiary indicators, namely, the "proportion of foreign exchange reserve currencies" and "currency weights in the SDR basket". Theoretically, the function of international currency as store of value will be reflected in both government and private sectors. However, the private sector pays more attention on the substitution of an international currency for its own currency, which is hard to obtain continuous quantitative data. Therefore, in measuring the function of the currency as store of value, this report focuses on the public sector. "The proportion of foreign exchange reserve currencies" reflects the currency as the store of value at the international level and is the currency choice of official reserve. SDR is an international reserve asset used to supplement the official reserves of member states (IMF, 2021). Therefore, the five currencies in the SDR currency basket can play the function as store of value, and their scale depends on the weights in the SDR currency basket.

For the function as the "medium of exchange", there are two tertiary indicators with equal weight, namely, "proportion of cross-border payment currencies" and "proportion of currencies of foreign exchange market turnover". The two tertiary indicators depict the role of the currency as the medium of exchange among the private sectors to better reflect the role of trading currency in the international financial market and international business activities. The function of a currency as the medium of exchange in the public sectors focuses on the vehicle currency of foreign exchange market intervention. However, since the currency structure of government foreign exchange market intervention is not available, it is difficult to describe this function by indicators.

The function of the currency as "unit of account" comes with four tertiary indicators with even weights, namely, "exchange rate anchor", "basket currencies", "proportion of currencies for international banking liabilities" and "proportion of currencies for international debt securities". Among these four indicators, "exchange rate anchor" and "basket currencies" can reflect the anchor currency when a country's exchange rate system is selected. For "exchange rate anchor", this report refers to the annual report of IMF's *De Facto Classification of Exchange Rate Regimes and Monetary Policy Framework* (IMF, 2019). Currency anchor is an important part of the formulation and implementation of the exchange rate policy for countries with non-free floating exchange rate regimes. The indicator for the "basket currencies" is calculated by the author of this report, with the research of Frankel and Wei (1994) as the benchmark framework and the extended research of Xu Qiyuan and Yang Panpan (2015) as the basis. The weight of each currency in the anchor basket of a country is calculated, the weight of the anchor currency is obtained based on the situation of all sample countries as the score of the indicators. The "proportion of currencies for international banking libabilities" and "proportion of currencies for international debt securities" reflect that the function of the currency as a unit of account in the private sectors.

2. Data processing

The sources and processing of the data of each sub-indicator are introduced below.

Indicator 2.1: Store of value

2.1.1 Proportion of foreign exchange reserve currencies

The data of the proportion of foreign exchange reserves come from the database of the Currency Composition of Official Foreign Exchange Reserves survey (COFER) by IMF, with the latest value available at the time of report compilation (Q4, 2020) chosen as the samples. In terms of data availability, the COFER database only provides allocated reserves data of 8 identifiable currencies, namely, US Dollar, Euro, Japanese Yen, British Pound, RMB, Canadian Dollar, Australian Dollar and Swiss Franc. In this report, the sum of the eight currencies is standardized to 100% before being adjusted to the percentage score; the indicator will be scored as 0 for countries with no data.

2.1.2 Currency weights in the SDR basket

The data of Currency weights in the SDR basket come from IMF SDR Weights allocated in the 2016 SDR adjustment. Since SDR only includes five currencies: US Dollar, Euro, RMB, Japanese Yen and British Pound, only these five currencies have scores for this indicator, with their total scores adjusted to 100 percent. There is no scores for other currencies.

Indicator 2.2: Medium of exchange

2.2.1 Proportion of cross-border payment currencies

The data for the proportion of currencies for cross-border payments come from SWIFT (Society for Worldwide Interbank Financial Telecommunications). The indicators measure the currency selection of cross-border payments with the data selected as the latest available at the time of the compilation of this report (December 2020). There are no data for India, Korea, Brazil, Indonesia, Saudi Arabia, Argentina and the United Arab Emirates, so the proportions of these currencies are set to 0. The total proportion for all the available currencies has been normalized to 100 percent.

2.2.2 Proportion of currencies of foreign exchange market turnover

The data for the proportion of currencies of foreign exchange market turnover come from the Triennial Central Bank Survey of BIS (Bank for International Settlement), which provides transaction data in global foreign exchange markets, including information of transaction currencies. The data is selected as the latest available in 2019. Since the foreign exchange turnover data contains two-way trading information, the value after summing up the proportion of all countries is 200%. In this report, the value is standardized to sum up to 100%. In terms of data availability, this report has data on the currencies of the sample countries except for the Argentine Peso.

Indicator 2.3: Unit of account

2.3.1 Exchange rate anchor

The data of the exchange rate anchor come from the *Annual Report on Exchange Arrangements and Exchange Restrictions* (2019) by IMF, in which the exchange rate system of each country is the de facto exchange rate system identified by IMF staff, rather than the de jure exchange rate system. For countries other than floating exchange rate system arrangements, some monetary authorities will buy or sell foreign exchange to keep their currency at a predetermined level or a certain range. For these countries, the exchange rate has become a nominal anchor or intermediate target of monetary policy (IMF, 2020). IMF identifies and makes statistics on the exchange rate anchors. The major anchor currencies are the US Dollar and the Euro. The Australian Dollar, Singapore Dollar, South African Rand, Indian Rupee are also anchor currencies for some countries. The data are as of April 30, 2019. The calculation method is to assign scores according to the number of anchor countries, and then adjust them to 100 percentage point as a whole.

2.3.2 Basket currencies

The indicators for basket currencies measure the composition of the currency basket that a currency is actually anchored. The measurement of indicators is based on the benchmark framework of Frankel and Wei (1994) and the extended research of Xu Qiyuan and Yang Panpan (2015). Among them, the currencies of the currency basket are consistent with the SDR, including US Dollar, Euro, Japanese Yen, British Pound and RMB. Therefore, the currency basket index can only reflect the ranking of these five currencies. We have included 26 reference currencies to calculate the weight[①]. The specific steps are as follows: (1) standardize the data of the daily exchange rate of all currencies into bilateral exchange rate against Swiss Franc; (2) Since the US Dollar still remains an important reference currency of RMB, the other main reference currencies (US Dollar, Euro, Japanese Yen and British Pound) are adopted to regress against RMB to eliminate the non-autonomous components of RMB. Then, take the regressed residual term as the independent fluctuations of RMB, and use this data to replace the exchange rate of RMB; (3) Using the differentiated exchange rate data of the reference currency as the explained variable and the exchange rates of five basket currencies as the explanatory variables. The time-varying parameter estimation based on the state-space model is applied to obtain the currency basket weight of each currency over time. And the weights are standardized and take the average value in 2020; (4) The five basket currencies have a weight corresponding to each reference currency. The ranking of the basket currencies of US dollar, Euro, Japanese Yen, British Pound and RMB can be obtained by simply averaging these weights before being adjusted to the percentage system.

2.3.3 Proportion of currencies for international banking liabilities

The data of the proportion of currencies for international banking liabilities come from the Local Banking Statistics (LBS) by the Bank for International Settlements (BIS). LBS reflect the cross-border international banking business, which lays its focus on the international banking business from the perspective of residence rather than the nationality of the parent companies. LBS cover about 95% of cross-border banking business. This indicator adopts the latest data (the fourth quarter of 2020) from the statistics of different types of moneys of account used in international banking liabilities. The database contains data of five currencies, namely the currency of the United States, the Eurozone, the United Kingdom, Japan and

---

[①] Reference currencies come from the countries and areas of East Asia: 10 ASEAN countries, South Korea, Taiwan, China, Hong Kong, China; Other G10 Economies: Australia, New Zealand, Canada, Norway, Sweden; Other G20 developing countries: Argentina, Brazil, India, Mexico, South Africa, Russia, Saudi Arabia, Turkey.

Switzerland. For the data of other countries, the following methods are adopted: (1) For RMB, based on the global proportion of RMB international banking liabilities in the second quarter of 2015 at 1.8% (Table 4) released in the SDR share evaluation report by IMF (2015), assuming that this proportion changes at the same rate as China's GDP in the world, the proportion in 2020 will be 2.11%, which will be used in this report; (2) The other currencies are allocated according to the corresponding scale of foreign exchange market trading volume in 2.2.2, and the corresponding indicators has been described as above; (3) Assuming that the sum of the shares for all sample currencies is 100%, the proportion of other currencies is 5.08% except for the shares of the five known currencies and the share of RMB upon calculations, will be distributed following the method in (2) before adjusted to the percentage system finally.

2.3.4 Proportion of currencies for international debt securities

The data of the proportion of currencies for international debt securities come from the International Debt Securities from the Debt Securities Statistics by BIS, which adopts the following table for the explanation of the difference between international debt securities (IDS) and domestic debt securities (DDS). This indicator adopts the currency information of bond issuance stock data, with the latest data (the fourth quarter of 2020) when the indicator is prepared. Of all the sample countries, the data are available for all but South African Rand, whose data are thus set to 0, along with the rest adjusted to a percentage system after standardization.

Table 6　　　　　　　　　　Categories of IDS and DDS

National of country A issuing in	National of country A residing in	
	Country A	Country B
Country A	DDS	IDS
Country B	IDS	DDS
Country C	IDS	IDS

iii. Construction of indicators for the competitiveness of financial infrastructure

1. Selection of indicators

In terms of financial infrastructure hardware, our data mainly come from the statistical indicators on payment and financial market infrastructure (Red Book of Statistical Indicators) by the Bank for International Settlements (BIS). Specific indicators include: the number of institutions providing payment services (per million residents), the proportion of cashless payment amount in GDP, the number of terminals (per resident), the proportion of payment transactions processed by the selected payment system in GDP, the number of institutions using SWIFT in the country, the proportion of clearing amount of the selected central counterparty and clearing house in GDP, the proportion of the number of instructions delivered by the selected central securities depository in GDP. These indicators are selected mainly based on the consideration of the facilities of the financial infrastructure concerning payment, clearing and registration defined by CPMI (The Committee on Payments and Market Infrastructures).

The indicators for the institutional software related to financial infrastructure mainly come from the sub-indicators of the World Business Environment Survey by the World Bank. These sub-indicators include: (1) indicators for access to credit, which are mainly used to measure the strength of a country's credit system and the effectiveness of guarantee and bankruptcy laws in promoting lending; (2) indicators for the protection of the investors, which are applied in measuring the protection of minority shareholders' rights when directors abuse corporate finance for private interests, as well as various measures to the risks of damage to shareholders' interests, including equity, governance guarantee and the openness and transparency of the company; (3) indicators for the enforcement of contracts, which are employed to measure the time and cost for a local primary court in resolving a commercial dispute, as well as the quality of judicial procedures, among which, the indicator for judicial procedure quality measures whether a series of good measures are taken in each economy to improve the quality and efficiency of the court system. The scoring of the above three sub-indicators are handled in full accordance with the methods stated in the methodology of the World Business Environment Survey by the World Bank.

In addition, this report also adds the application scope indicator of the *International Financial Reporting Standards (IFRS)* as a measure of the quality of accounting standards. According to the standards for the use of IFRS, the accounting standards implemented by various countries and jurisdictions can be divided into: non-adoption of the IFRS standards (0 points), compulsory adoption of the IFRS standards for domestic public companies (2 points), non-mandatory adoption of the IFRS standards for domestic public companies (1 point), compulsory adoption of the IFRS standards or allowance of the adoption of the IFRS standards for foreign companies must or are allowed to adopt IFRS standards for listed in some countries (2 points) compulsory adoption of the IFRS standards or allowance of the adoption of the IFRS standards for small and micro enterprises (2 points), and consideration on applying IFRS standards for small and micro-enterprises within the jurisdiction (1 point). Then the application of IFRS standards in a country will be scored and ranked as the comparison and measurement of accounting standards infrastructure. The specific construction and weights for the indicators are shown in Figure 2.

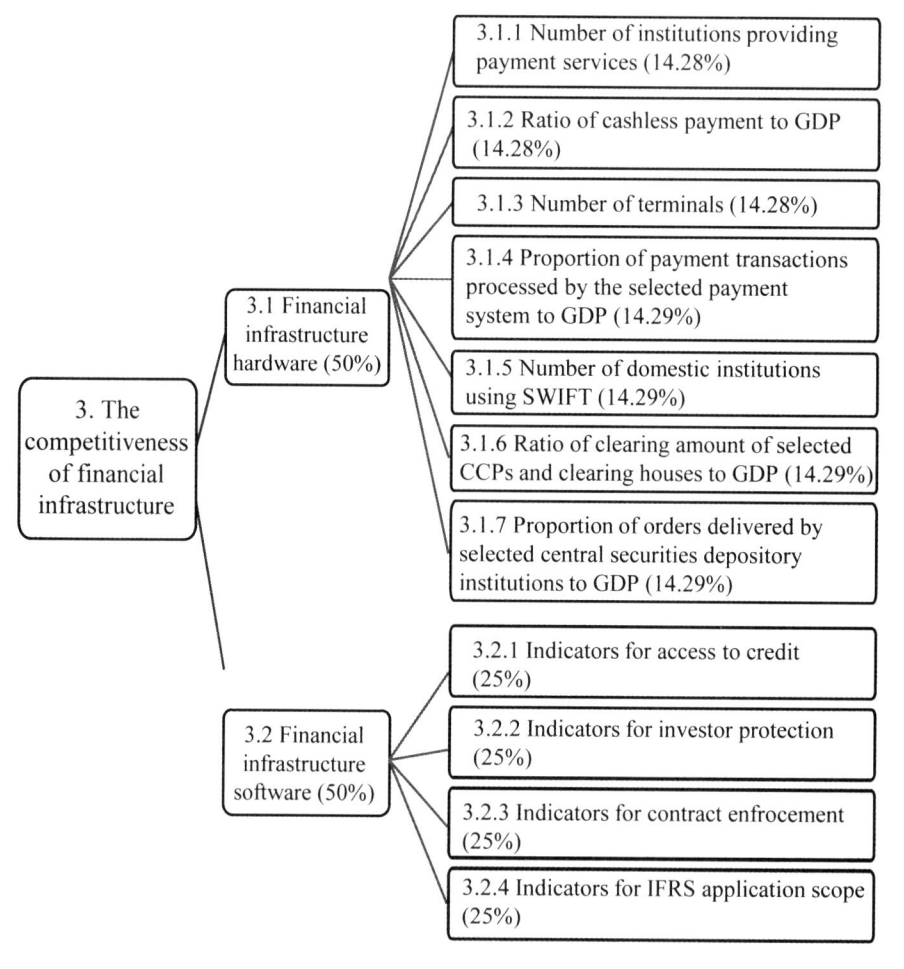

- 3. The competitiveness of financial infrastructure
  - 3.1 Financial infrastructure hardware (50%)
    - 3.1.1 Number of institutions providing payment services (14.28%)
    - 3.1.2 Ratio of cashless payment to GDP (14.28%)
    - 3.1.3 Number of terminals (14.28%)
    - 3.1.4 Proportion of payment transactions processed by the selected payment system to GDP (14.29%)
    - 3.1.5 Number of domestic institutions using SWIFT (14.29%)
    - 3.1.6 Ratio of clearing amount of selected CCPs and clearing houses to GDP (14.29%)
    - 3.1.7 Proportion of orders delivered by selected central securities depository institutions to GDP (14.29%)
  - 3.2 Financial infrastructure software (50%)
    - 3.2.1 Indicators for access to credit (25%)
    - 3.2.2 Indicators for investor protection (25%)
    - 3.2.3 Indicators for contract enfrocement (25%)
    - 3.2.4 Indicators for IFRS application scope (25%)

Figure 2 Overview of the Construction of the Indicators for the Competitiveness of the Financial Infrastructure and the Weight of Each Indicator

2. Date Processing

Many missing values can be encountered when it comes to the indicators for the hardware of financial infrastructure. To solve this problem, the following solution is adopted: if a single indicator in a country or region is missing, an equal weight of the values will be used for the remaining indicators for the ranking of the country or region. If no indicators can be used in a certain country or region, the average value of each indicator will be used, with the average of the equal weight for ranking. The reason why this method is taken, instead of the method for the processing of the missing value of similar indicators related to the competitiveness of the financial industry, is that there are large differences between various indicators of countries. If the average value of the front and rear ranking is taken after ranking according to an indicator (such as the software for the financial infrastructure), it is possible that the value of the indicators to be filled will be significantly overestimated or underestimated. Comparatively, it is smoother to take the overall average value.

Then we move on to the weighted average of the scores of standardized financial infrastructure software and hardware.

iv. Construction of the indicators for the competitiveness of the financial technology

1. Selection of indicators

The underlying technology determines the development potentials of financial technology, while the degree of market development reflects the application prospect of financial technology. In addition to the underlying technology, the application field of financial technology is further divided into consumer end and industrial end, which are measured by user access and industrial development potential respectively. The ratio of the final weight of the three secondary indicators is 50 : 25 : 25.

The "indicators for the computing power" measures the computing power of the financial technology industry in various countries and shows the strength of its technical foundation. This book cites the computing power index in the *Global Computing Index Report* 2020 released by IDC as the original data for the calculation of the "indicator for the computing power". The computing

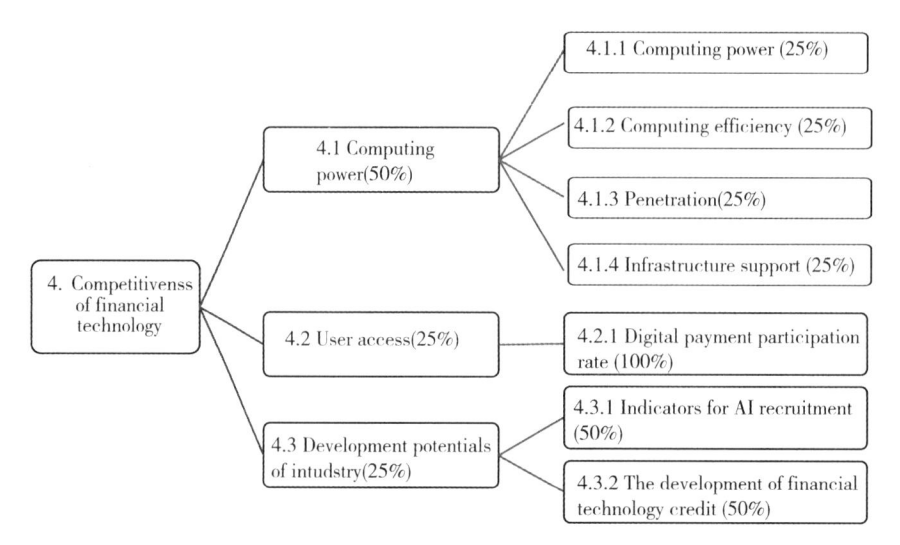

```
4. Competitivenss          ┌─ 4.1.1 Computing power (25%)
   of financial            │
   technology  ─┬─ 4.1 Computing ─┼─ 4.1.2 Computing efficiency (25%)
               │   power(50%)    │
               │                 ├─ 4.1.3 Penetration(25%)
               │                 │
               │                 └─ 4.1.4 Infrastructure support (25%)
               │
               ├─ 4.2 User access(25%) ── 4.2.1 Digital payment participation
               │                          rate (100%)
               │
               └─ 4.3 Development potentials ─┬─ 4.3.1 Indicators for AI recruitment
                  of intudstry(25%)           │   (50%)
                                              └─ 4.3.2 The development of financial
                                                  technology credit (50%)
```

Figure 3　Overview of the Indicator Construction and the Weights of Financial Technology Competitiveness

power indicator covers four dimensions of the computing power, computing efficiency, application and infrastructure support to evaluate the computing power development and development potential of key countries in the world in 2020. However, the original report only offers data from 10 countries and regions, including the United States, Chinese Mainland, Japan, Germany, the United Kingdom, France, Australia, Brazil, South Africa and Russia. In this report, the method of substitution and the method for the missing values are employed to supplement the indicators of the other 24 main countries or regions in the world. When making up the missing values for the data of the "computing power", the number and ranking of the world's top 500 supercomputers and the ranking of smartphone penetration in various countries are used for reference. When making up the last three indicators, such as "computing efficiency", the ranking of the indicator for the "computing power" is borrowed for reference. In this report, the standardized method is adopted in processing the original data, and the weighted sum of each data is used to obtain the indicators for the computing power of various countries. Therefore, the indicators for the computing power stay between 0 – 1, with the indicators of the countries topping in the comprehensive ranking at 1, and the last country at 0. The higher the value of the indicator for a country's computing power, the stronger the country's computing power and the greater its strength in international computing power.

"The indicator for user access" measures the penetration and user base of the financial technology industry in various countries, and the ratio of the number of people connected to the financial technology industry in various countries to all potential users in the financial technology industry is employed to show the current user access of the financial technology industry in various countries. This paper quotes the 2017 data(latest data) of "the ratio of people aged 15 and over using or receiving digital payment in the previous year" published in the Findex database by the World Bank. The original data consists of 32 countries required in this paper. Therefore, the indicator for user access can be easily obtained merely by standardizing the original data. The indicators for user access stay between 0 – 1, with the indicators for the country topping the comprehensive ranking at 1, and the indicators for the last country at 0. The higher the indicators for the user access of a country, the deeper the penetration of its financial technology industry, the stronger its ability to "liquidate" its potential users, and the larger the number of user groups relative to its population.

The "indicators for the development potential" take the development of the terminal industry in the financial technology industry to measure the potential of the future development of the financial technology industry in various countries, and the two key factors determining the development potential of an industry are the input of labor force and capital. Based on this acknowledgment, this report employs the recruitment and reserve of AI professionals in various countries as a showcase of the labor input in the financial technology industry, and the development of financial technology credit in various countries as a display of the capital input in the financial technology industry. As for AI professionals, upon the National AI Recruitment Index 2020 released by Stanford University and the National AI Preparation Index 2019 released by Oxford Insights and the Center of International Studies, this report obtains the scores and rankings of 32 countries; For the development of credit in the financial technology, this report takes the date concerning the per capital scale (the latest data) of fintech credit in 2018 from Fintech Credit Data released by G. Cornelli et al as the original data. In this report, the indicator for the industrial potential of each country is obtained as the weighted aggregations of the standardized scores of the two tertiary indicators. The indicators for the potential of the industrial development stay between 0 – 1. The higher the industrial potential of a country, the sounder the development of the country's financial technology terminal industry, the greater the potential in the future market, and the higher the possibility of profit.

2. Date processing

The data of this section will be processed following the same method as that for the competitiveness of financial industry.

v. Construction of the indicators for the competitiveness in international financial governance

1. Selection of indicators

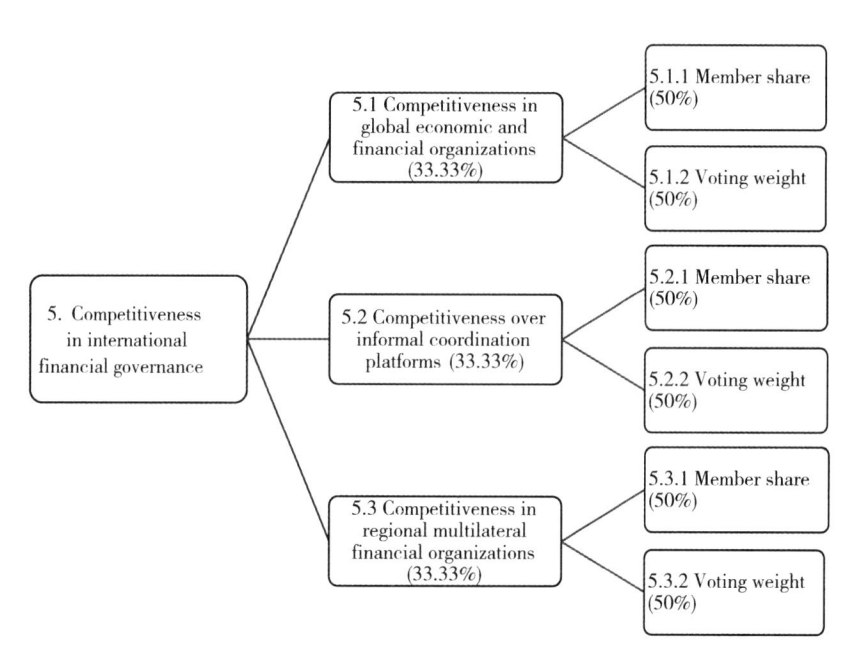

Figure 4 Overview of the Construction of the Indicator for the Competitiveness in International Financial Governance and the Weight of Each Indicator

(1) Secondary indicators

According to the definition by the Commission on Global Governance of the United Nations, governance is the sum of many ways in which individuals and various public or private institutions manage common affairs. James N. Rosenau, one of the main founders of the theory of global governance, believes that compared with the ruling by government, governance has a lot to do with not only government mechanisms, but informal and non-governmental mechanisms. Global governance includes the formulation and implementation of rules at levels beyond the national and international ones while recognizing the roles of the countries in the international system[1]. It can be seen that although sovereign states were, are, and will be the protagonists of international governance, their roles and effects in the framework of the international governance system are declining day by day, while international organizations, breaking through the geographical and field restrictions in the initial period, are playing a greater role in today's international political, economic, financial and even social fields.

So, the subjects participating in international financial governance at least fall into the following groups. First, governments and relevant government departments, especially ministries of finance, central banking departments, and financial supervision departments of various countries, participate most widely. Second, formal international organizations, especially the International Monetary Fund (IMF) and the Bank for International Settlements (BIS), have the most extensive and important participation. Third, informal organizations and social groups, such as the G20 and the Financial Stability Board (FSB), are engaging in international financial governance most extensively. Furthermore, transnational corporations, transnational events, and many non-governmental institutions are also exerting influence on international financial governance.

The formal or informal international organizations, meeting the needs of financial globalization, are gaining increasing importance as the subjects of global governance and financial governance, through the consultation of which governments and relevant government departments of various countries are solving international problems. Upon the consideration of this, the research group takes international organizations as the subjects of international financial governance.

Next, we determine which formal or informal organizations should be included in the framework of the analysis according to the objects of the international financial governance. According to the understanding of international financial governance in the courses of the U. N. Institute for Training and Research (UNITAR), international financial governance means to maintain an international monetary system that is predictable, stable and conducive to the payment of international economic transactions; besides, international financial governance aims to supervise the international financial

---

[1] See James N. Rosenau, "Governance in the Twenty First Century", *Global Governance*, Vol. 1, pp. 13 – 43.

system, protect the interests of depositors and investors around the world, and distribute credit effectively and fairly among all potential borrowers[①]. Some scholars believe that, besides international monetary system and international financial regulatory system, international financial governance should at least include the reform of international financial governance mechanism, including the reform of international monetary and financial institutions, as well as the reform of decision-makers of international financial governance and reform, such as how to better play the role of G20. Other scholars pointed out that in addition to the reform of the international monetary system, global financial supervision and the reform of international financial governance institutions, international financial governance should cover the following issues: international macroeconomic policy coordination, regional financial cooperation, the construction of global financial safety network and international capital flow[②].

Accordingly, some scholars pointed out that the International Monetary Fund (IMF) and the World Bank (WB) established by the Bretton Woods system after World War II, the Bank for International Settlements (BIS) established after World War I, and the Financial Stability Forum (FSF) established by the Group of Seven (G7) and regional development banks established in various regions, such as the European Bank for Reconstruction and Development (EBRD), the Asian Development Bank (ADB), the African Development Bank (AfDB), and the Inter-American Development Bank (IDB) collectively constitute the contemporary international financial organization system, which falls into three categories concerning macro stability, multilateral development, financial supervision and standard-setting[③]. Xiong Beichen (2021) believes that international organizations participating in international financial governance should include the International Monetary Fund (IMF), the European Financial Stability Facility (EFSF), the Arab Monetary Fund (AMF), the Executives' Meeting of East Asia and Pacific Central Banks (EMEAP), the Eastern Caribbean Central Bank (ECCB), the Bank for International Settlements (BIS), the Financial

---

① See Daniel Bradlow, Materials for A 4-Part On-Line Course on Global Financial Governance, offered by United Nations Institute on Training and Research (UNITAR), UNITAR, On-Line Training Courses in Public Finance and Trade, 2009, available at: http://papers.ssrn.com/sol3/papers.cfm?abstract_id=1488020.

② Zhang Liqing, "Eight Issues in Global Financial Governance", *China Forex*, 2021 (4).

③ Global financial governance research group of Shanghai Development Research Foundation. Global financial governance: Challenges, Objectives and Reforms—A Research Report on the Topics of the G20 Summit in 2016 [J]. International Economic Review, 2016 (3): pp. 26–40

Stability Board (FSB), the International Association of Insurance Supervisors (IAIS), the International Organization of Securities Commissions (IOSCO), African Development Bank (AfDB), Inter-American Development Bank (IDB) and Asian Infrastructure Investment Bank (AIIB). In addition, international organizations such as the Organization for Economic Co-operation and Development (OECD)[1], Paris Club[2], Chiang Mai Initiative (CMI)[3], New Development Bank (NDB)[4] and Asian Infrastructure Investment Bank (AIIB)[5] are often included in the framework of the analysis.

To sum up, this report takes the following international formal or informal institutions as the subjects of international financial governance, including the International Monetary Fund (IMF), the World Bank (WB), the Bank for International Settlements (BIS), the Organization for Economic Cooperation and Development (OECD), the Group of 20 (G20), the Financial Stability Board (FSB), the Paris Club, the Inter-American Development Bank (IDB), African Development Bank (AfDB), European Bank for Reconstruction and Development (EBRD), European Investment Bank (EIB), Asian Development Bank (ADB), Asian Infrastructure Investment Bank (AIIB) and New Development Bank (NDB).

Different from previous studies that classify international financial organizations according to the object of international financial governance (i.e. what "issues" to govern), this report classifies international financial governance according to the level of international financial governance. Firstly, international financial governance is divided into the global level and regional level; Then, according to the international organization mechanism, that is, whether there is a formal consultation mechanism, the global level is divided into global financial organizations and informal coordination platforms; Finally, the competitiveness of international financial governance is divided into three secondary indicators: the competitiveness of global economic and

---

[1] Zhang Qinglin, Liu Tianzi, "Summary of Some Prominent Issues in Global Financial Governance", *Financial Jurists* (Volume IV). 2012.

[2] Tsingou E., "The Club Rules in Global Financial Governance", *The Political Quarterly*, 2014, 85 (4).

[3] Hong Xiaozhi, "Literature Review of Global Financial Governance Reform", *Southwest Finance*, 2012, (3).

[4] Pan Qingzhong, Li Daokui, Feng Ming, "Where is the 'New Development Bank (NDB)' — the Background, Significance and Challenges of the Establishment of NDB", *International Economic Review*, 2015 (02): 10 + 136 – 149.

[5] Zhang Mo Nan, "AIIB's Effects in Three Dimensions of the Pattern of the Global Financial Governance", *Financial Expo*, 2016 (02): 56 – 57.

financial organizations, the competitiveness of informal coordination platforms and the competitiveness of regional multilateral financial organizations.

Table 7 Secondary Indicators for the Competitiveness in International Financial Governance

Secondary indicators	Organizations covered	Number
Competitiveness among global economic and financial organizations	International Monetary Fund (IMF), World Bank (WB), Bank for International Settlements (BIS), Organization for Economic Cooperation and Development (OECD)	4
Competitiveness over informal coordination platforms	Group of 20 (G20), Financial Stability Board (FSB), Paris Club	3
Competitiveness in regional multilateral financial organizations	Inter-American Development Bank (IDB), African Development Bank (AfDB), European Bank for Reconstruction and Development (EBRD) European Investment Bank (EIB), Asian Development Bank (ADB) Asian Infrastructure Investment Bank (AIIB), New Development Bank (NDB)	7

In the era of globalization, no country or institution possesses sufficient resources and knowledge to solve all problems alone. Global governance requires communication and consultation among various actors, sharing various resources and information, and taking concerted action. If an organization covers major countries in the world, the decisions, opinions, guidelines and other documents formed under the relevant mechanisms of the organization may be implemented and promoted worldwide, while regional financial institutions can probably only be functioning in a regional scope. This is the reason why this report adopts hierarchical classification of international financial governance.

Furthermore, international mechanisms can be divided into formal and informal types: formal international mechanisms refer to international mechanisms established by international organizations through the law, maintained by councils, conferences and other entities, and guaranteed by international bureaucrats, such as the International Monetary Fund (IMF) and the World Bank (WB), while the informal international mechanism refers to the international mechanism established among member states according to the consensus reached upon the goals pursued by each other, and the implementation of the agreement is guaranteed according to their common interests or "gentleman's agreement" and mutual supervision, such as CSCE, G8, etc. Under the two mechanisms, there are great differences in how member states reach consensus and the ways to ensure the implementation of consensus. Therefore, this report divides global institutions into formal global financial organizations and informal coordination platforms.

(2) Tertiary indicators

After determining the subject (international organizations) and object (scope of discussion) of international financial governance, the indicators to measure the representation and discourse power of countries concerning the subjects and objects of international financial governance are to be decided.

The "reality" of international finance, to a great extent, is "established". Whoever enjoys the right to establish the "reality" of international finance will be the implementer (or disseminator) of the discourse. In this sense, the main content of the discourse power of international financial governance reflects the views and positions related to the own financial interests or the international responsibilities and obligations of a sovereign state. Therefore, the international financial discourse power is reflected in the carrier, channel or way by which the discourse implementer expresses and affects the objects of the discourse, among which the international agenda-setting is either regarded as part of the defining elements of the international financial discourse power or as means to acquire it. Under the existing international financial system, a country can highlight its international financial discourse right with the help of a multi-level discourse platform. The bilateral discourse platform mainly includes direct contacts between the two countries, such as economic and trade exchanges, regulatory cooperation, financial forums, strategic dialogues, capital transactions, aid exchanges and so on. Multilateral discourses are mainly conducted through platforms like formal international financial institutions or certain international financial mechanisms.

According to the previous definition of the subjects and objects of international financial governance, the research group measures a country's representation and voice in international organizations, that is, the country's competitiveness in international financial governance, by seeing whether a country participates in decision-making in international organizations and to what extent it can push opinions into decisions.

Taking the International Monetary Fund (IMF) as an example, this report analyzes the expression of a country's representation and voice. If a country wants to be a member (representative) of the IMF, it needs to submit an application. After the board of directors of the fund considers and approves it, it will submit a report on the "membership resolution" to the governance committee to suggest the quota the applicant country can allocate in the fund. After the governance committee approves the application, the applicant country will become a full member upon signing the membership document. The "quota" of member states determines a country's dues payable, voting power, the share of financial assistance received, and the number of SDRs. This shows that the member share is a certain amount of funds subscribed by the member states to the IMF, which is equivalent to the shares owned by the member states in the IMF. It is the most important indicator to measure the relative position of member states in the IMF. So, the member share can be used as an indicator tomeasure a country's representation in the IMF.

In the decision-making mechanism, consensus and voting are the two rules of procedures of the IMF. Although consensus is a principle widely adopted by the IMF executive board, it is not a manifestation of consensus. It usually takes place in informal meetings and is dominated by developed countries. When making resolutions on major issues, the IMF usually adopts voting and is based on the principle of majority vote. The voting rights of each member state consist of basic voting rights and share-based voting rights. Both the weighted voting system and majority voting system help to lead to a quick decision. So, the voting weight can be used as an indicator to measure a country's voice in the IMF.

Therefore, this report selects the member share and voting weight as the tertiary indicators for competitiveness in international financial governance.

2. Data processing

The data will be standardized following the same method as that for the competitiveness of the financial industry. Some data are specially processed methods in this section, as follows.

Firstly, some formal and informal international organizations with no data on the proportion of member shares or voting rights of, average rights are assumed to them according to their membership. For example, the African Development Bank has only the proportion of voting rights but no proportion of member subscribed shares, so it is assumed that the subscribed member shares are evenly distributed among members, the value of member countries is 100, and the value of non-member countries is 0.

Secondly, the indicators for the proportion of member share and the indicators for the proportion of the voting right in the secondary indicators are weighted by 50% respectively to obtain the competitiveness in international financial governance of sample countries in a single institution or platform.

Then, the individual institutions or platforms in each type of institution are weighted equally to obtain the classified indicators for competitiveness. For example, the International Monetary Fund (IMF), the World Bank (WB), the Bank for International Settlements (BIS) and the Organization for Economic Cooperation and Development (OECD) are equally weighted to obtain the competitiveness of global financial organizations; average weight is respectively given to the Group of 20 (G20), the Financial Stability Board (FSB) and the Paris Club to obtain the competitiveness of the informal coordination platform; the Inter-American Development Bank (IDB), the African Development Bank (AfDB), the European Bank for Reconstruction and Development (EBRD), the European Investment Bank (EIB), the Asian Development Bank (ADB), the Asian Infrastructure Investment Bank (AIIB) and the New Development Bank (NDB) are weighted on average to obtain regional multilateral financial competitiveness.

Finally, the three secondary indicators are weighted equally to obtain the indicators for international financial governance competitiveness (IFGC).

V Evaluation of the global financial competitiveness

i. General indicators

Table 8 Rating of the General Indicators for Global Financial Competitiveness

Ranking	Economy	Rating	Ranking	Economy	Rating
1	USA	85.1	17	Luxembourg	28.9
2	Britain	51.3	17	Italy	28.9
3	Japan	44.8	19	The United Arab Emirates	28.5
4	Germany	43.9	20	South Africa	27.2
5	Canada	42.2	21	Brazil	25.4
6	Australia	41.3	22	Saudi Arabia	25.3
6	France	41.3	23	Ireland	25.2
8	Chinese Mainland	41.2	24	Austria	24.6
9	Korea	40.7	25	Russia	22.9
10	Switzerland	40.6	26	India	22.4
11	Netherlands	39.8	27	Portugal	22.2
12	Singapore	38.7	28	Turkey	21.5
13	Hong Kong, China	38.4	29	Mexico	19.1
14	Spain	34.9	30	Indonesia	17.6
15	Belgium	32.3	31	Greece	15.8
16	Finland	31.6	32	Argentina	15.0

Table 8 shows the ranking of the global financial competitiveness of 32 economies in the world, in which European and American countries occupy 7 positions of the top 10, including the United States and Britain occupying the top 2 positions; 3 of the Asian economies entered the world's top 10, with

Japan ranking the 3rd, Chinese Mainland the 8th, and Korea the 9th.

The global financial competitiveness of the United States ranks 1st in the world, with its score 33.8 points higher than that of the United Kingdom, which ranks 2nd. This is the group with the largest gap between scores of the two adjacent economies, indicating the prominent competitive strength of the United States in the global financial field. Judged by five primary indicators, the United States tops the world concerning four indicators, including the competitiveness of financial industry, the competitiveness of currency, the competitiveness of financial technology and the competitiveness in international financial governance, with only the competitiveness of the financial infrastructure ranking the 5th, which can be clear evidence that the United States boasts relatively stable foundation as support for the financial competitiveness. In addition, among the four leading primary indicators of the United States, the strength of the competitiveness of currency comes as the most prominent, 38.8 points higher than that of the Euro at the 2nd place, which clearly manifests that the international status of the US Dollar generates the most powerful force for the United States in maintaining its global financial competitiveness.

Britain ranks 2nd globally in terms of global financial competitiveness, with its competitive advantage mainly manifested through two primary indicators, namely, the competitiveness of financial infrastructure and the competitiveness of financial industry. Britain tops the world concerning the competitiveness of its financial infrastructure at 13.7 points higher than that of Singapore, which ranks 2nd. This is also the group with the largest gap in the scores between the two adjacent economies concerning the competitiveness in the financial infrastructure, which fully demonstrates the accumulated strength of Britain as a classic capitalist country in this field. In addition, globally, the competitiveness of Britain's financial industry is 2nd only to that of the United States, which also represents a key factor supporting Britain as a world financial power.

Chinese Mainland ranks 8th in the world in terms of global financial competitiveness, following France at a distance of 0.1 points and 0.5 points ahead of Korea. Among the 5 first primary indicators, Chinese Mainland stays the nearest to the world's leaders in terms of the competitiveness of the financial industry at 16.2 points lower than that of the US who ranks 1st. The past two decades witnessed the sustainable and rapid growth of China's financial industry when the world's largest and most profitable banking system cultivated and the world's second-largest stock market and bond market established. In addition to the scale, the efficiency and activity of China's financial system and the influence of its international financial centers have been significantly improved, with the three sub-indicators for them ranking among the top 10 in the world. In terms of the competitiveness of currency, one of the primary indicators, China sees the largest gap between itself and the world's leaders, at 90.2 points lower than that of the United States. Since 2009, China has gradually promoted the internationalization of RMB, and RMB was included in the SDR currency basket in 2016. It can be seen that the internationalization of RMB has also made significant progress in the past 10 years, though the international status of RMB still does not match China's economic volume. Compared with the US Dollar and the Euro, there is still big room for the internationalization of RMB.

ii Primary indicators

1. The competitiveness of financial industry

Table 9   Rating of the Competitiveness of Financial Industry

Ranking	Economy	Rating	Ranking	Economy	Rating
1	USA	78.0	17	Finland	53.4
2	Britain	75.4	18	The United Arab Emirates	51.3
2	Hong Kong, China	75.4	19	South Africa	46.6
4	Switzerland	75.1	20	Saudi Arabia	38.6
5	Singapore	71.4	21	Portugal	36.7
6	Korea	69.4	22	India	35.2
7	Canada	68.8	23	Brazil	33.9
8	Australia	68.5	24	Turkey	33.3
9	Japan	67.9	25	Austria	32.1
10	Netherlands	63.5	26	Indonesia	31.7
11	Chinese Mainland	61.8	27	Mexico	30.3

					Continued
Ranking	Economy	Rating	Ranking	Economy	Rating
12	France	59.6	28	Ireland	29.3
13	Luxembourg	57.3	29	Italy	28.3
13	Spain	57.3	30	Russia	27.2
15	Germany	56.1	31	Greece	24.2
16	Belgium	55.1	32	Argentina	18.8

Table 9 shows the competitiveness of financial industry in terms of rating and ranking. Among the 32 economies selected, the United States, Britain and Hong Kong, China ranked the top three, followed by Singapore and Japan at the 5th and 9th respectively, and Chinese Mainland, France and Germany at the 11th, 12th and 15th respectively.

The United States comes as the 1st in the world when referring to the indicator for the competitiveness of financial industry thanks to the most developed financial system in the world of the U.S. Moreover, with attentions to the comprehensive and in-depth development of its financial system, the United States sees all the indicators of its financial industry ranking relatively high. Based on the specific indicators, the relative size of the U.S. financial system ranks 10th, the activity of the financial system ranks 6th, the efficiency of the financial system ranks 2nd, the financial stability ranks 2nd, the availability of financial services ranks 2nd, and the status of its international financial centers tops the world.

The UK's ranks 2nd when related to the competitiveness of its financial industry. As an established capitalist country, British Pound still remains an important international currency, as Britain's financial system plays a significant role in the world. Based on the specific indicators, the relative size of the British financial system ranks 4th, the activity of the financial system ranks 4th, the efficiency of the financial system ranks 5th, the financial stability ranks 7th, the availability of financial services ranks 8th, and the status of its international financial centers comes 2nd only to that of the United States.

Concerning the indicator for the competitiveness of the financial industry, Chinese Mainland ranks 7th globally. Specific indicators show that Chinese Mainland's financial system stays at the 16th position in scale, with the activity of the financial system at 10th, the efficiency of its financial system at 6th, the financial stability at 24th, the availability of financial services at

18th, and the status of its international financial centers at 3rd. The financial system of Chinese Mainland comes comparatively backward in size, partly for its large economic volume. On the other hand, although the banking and stock market in Chinese Mainland has enjoyed sound development, yet the advancement of mutual funds, insurance companies and pension departments still lags behind. Chinese Mainland's financial system stays in the middle, showing that the credit of the commercial banks and the trading among the stock markets are robust in China when its financial system enjoys a great activity. The efficiency of the financial system of Chinese Mainland ranks relatively high, reflecting the high return on assets and the high turnover rate of the stock markets, and the relatively efficient operation of the financial system. The financial stability of Chinese Mainland stays relatively backward. First, the fluctuation of the stock market remains too high and the stability of the capital market stays poor. Second, the proportion of indirect financing is high, and there is great pressure on bank risk control. Chinese Mainland's financial services availability ranks moderately, showing the obvious progress made by China's financial system in financing the real economy. The status of the international financial centers of Chinese Mainland ranks relatively high, mainly because Shanghai, Beijing and Shenzhen have already served as the important international financial center cities for their high comprehensive competitiveness.

2. The competitiveness of currency

Table 10 indicates the competitiveness of currency by country (or region). Based on the standardized scoring of the three secondary indicators of "store of value", "medium of exchange" and "unit of account", the score of the competitiveness of the currency of the United States comes out at 100 as the 1st, followed by score of the Eurozone at 61.2 as the 2nd. Britain, Japan and Chinese Mainland come close concerning the score of the competitiveness of currency, holding the 3rd to the 5th positions, evidence that the competitiveness of RMB is nearing that of the Japanese Yen and British Pound. Australia, Canada and Switzerland rank 6th to 8th in relation to the competitiveness of their currencies, with a large gap comparing to the scores of the top five currencies. Hong Kong, China ranked 9th with a score of 1.475.

Table 10   Rating of the Competitiveness of Currency

Ranking	Economy	Rating	Ranking	Economy	Rating
1	USA	100	12	India	0.8
2	Eurozone	61.2	13	Mexico	0.5
3	Britain	13.6	14	Korea	0.4
4	Japan	10.6	14	Turkey	0.4
5	Chinese Mainland	9.8	14	Russia	0.4
6	Australia	3.5	17	Brazil	0.3
7	Canada	2.6	18	Indonesia	0.1
8	Switzerland	1.7	19	The United Arab Emirates	0.0
9	Hong Kong, China	1.5	19	Saudi Arabia	0.0
10	Singapore	1.1	19	Argentina	0.0
11	South Africa	1.0			

The United States ranks 1st with an absolute advantage concerning the competitiveness of currency. The scores for the competitiveness of currency are based on the centesimal system with reference to the highest value of the secondary indicators. Since the US Dollar ranks 1st globally in terms of "store of value", "media of exchange" and "unit of account", its score of the competitiveness of currency gets 100. With the establishment of Bretton Woods system, the US Dollar has established its core position in the international monetary system and has been playing the role as the dominant international currency in the last half century and has been widely used in international reserves and transaction settlement even after the disintegration of the Bretton Woods system. A complete US Dollar system has been established in the world, which enables the US Dollar to give full play to the three basic functions of currency globally.

After the United States comes the Eurozone. Since the competitiveness of currency is measured upon currencies rather than sovereignty, the Eurozone will not be further divided in this section. Since the adoption of the single currency Euro and the unified monetary policy among the EU countries from 1999, 19 member states have joined the Eurozone so far. The uniform currency not only facilitates the international trade among countries in the

Eurozone, but also helps maintain the extensive trade relations with countries outside the area. Since its adoption, the international status of Euro has enjoyed continuous growth, ranking 2nd only to the US Dollar concerning various secondary indicators.

The competitiveness of British Pound, Japanese Yen and RMB ranks 3rd to 5th as the 2nd echelon of international currencies. Britain has once been the central country of the international monetary system in the 19th century, and British Pound still plays the role of international currency to a certain extent, ranking 3rd under the two secondary indicators of "medium of exchange" and "unit of account", and 5th under "store of value". Japan quickly caught up in the 1960s and 1980s, which helped the Yen gain its international status today, ranking 3rd, 4th and 6th respectively under the three secondary indicators of "store value", "medium of exchange" and "unit of account". Newly uprising, with the internationalization of RMB since 2009, Chinese Mainland has gradually narrowed the gap between its currency and that of Britain and Japan. In terms of secondary indicators, RMB ranks 4th under "store of value" and "unit of account", and 7th under "medium of exchange".

3. The competitiveness of financial infrastructure

Table 11 shows the competitiveness of financial infrastructure by country (or region), with Britain on top of the list, the United States at the 5th and 10th for Chinese Mainland.

The standardized score of the UK, which ranks 1st, is much higher than that of Singapore, which ranks 2nd, showing that as a traditional financial empire, the UK maintains a great strength in financial infrastructure, with both of its software and hardware ranking at the top (See the ranking of the sub-indicator in the appendix for details).

Due to the large turbulence in the business environment in recent years, the score for the software of the U.S. financial infrastructure ranks comparatively low, which injures the overall performance of the U.S. financial infrastructure, is resulting in its ranking at the 5th.

Chinese Mainland and Hong Kong, China ranks 3rd and 11th respectively, among which Hong Kong, China ranks 2nd in financial infrastructure software, second only to that of Singapore and 3rd in financial infrastructure hardware, indicating that Hong Kong has strong international competitiveness in both financial system environment and financial infrastructure hardware. Chinese Mainland shows its strength in the hardware of the financial infrastructure, ranking 2nd after Britain, highlighting the achievements of Chinese Mainland in the construction of its financial infrastructure in recent years. However, Chinese Mainland ranks 24th in terms of the software of the financial infrastructure, indicating that there is still room for the development of the software of its financial infrastructure in the future.

Table 11　　　Rating of the Competitiveness of Financial Infrastructure

Ranking	Economy	Rating	Ranking	Economy	Rating
1	Britain	72.6	17	Saudi Arabia	40.1
2	Singapore	58.9	18	Spain	39.5
3	Hong Kong, China	58.4	19	Switzerland	39.2
4	Korea	50.2	20	Brazil	38.9
5	USA	49.7	21	South Africa	37.8
6	Australia	47.7	22	Finland	36.8
7	Ireland	46.3	23	Mexico	35.3
8	Belgium	44.8	24	Portugal	34.9
9	Canada	44.5	25	Japan	34.0
10	Chinese Mainland	43.4	26	Netherlands	33.2
11	Germany	43.0	27	Italy	32.7
12	The United Arab Emirates	41.5	28	Greece	32.0
13	Austria	41.4	29	Argentina	29.5
14	France	41.1	30	Luxembourg	29.0
15	Turkey	40.9	31	India	21.6
16	Russia	40.7	32	Indonesia	18.3

4. The competitiveness of financial technology

Table 12 reflects the competitiveness of financial technology by country (or region), with the United States ranks 1st all over the world, followed by Germany at the 2nd place, and Chinese Mainland at the 10th.

It can be easily seen that among the 32 samples, the United States is far ahead of other countries, while the indicators for the overall competitiveness of other countries are evenly distributed between 0 – 70. As the only superpower in the world, the United States boasts a very advanced financial industry and high-tech industry. Its rich resources of professionals for the financial technology, well-structured and dynamic mechanism for the development of the financial technology and huge capital base have served as the source of its strong competitiveness of the financial technology.

Table 12   Rating of the competitiveness of Financial Technology

Ranking	Economy	Rating	Ranking	Economy	Rating
1	USA	93.1	17	Austria	45.3
2	Germany	69.2	17	Hong Kong, China	45.3
3	Italy	68.7	19	Saudi Arabia	41.6
4	Japan	67.4	20	Luxembourg	40.0
5	Canada	65.7	20	Brazil	40.0
6	Netherlands	64.8	22	Spain	38.9
7	Britain	64.6	23	Russia	38.1
8	France	62.5	24	South Africa	35.9
9	Australia	61.0	25	Belgium	30.7
10	Chinese Mainland	60.3	26	India	30.4
11	Ireland	57.6	27	Portugal	29.4
12	Singapore	54.2	28	Greece	22.2
13	The United Arab Emirates	53.2	29	Turkey	17.3
14	Finland	51.9	30	Argentina	15.6
15	Korea	51.6	31	Indonesia	12.4
16	Switzerland	50.6	32	Mexico	3.8

In terms of the degree of dispersion, the variance of the 32 samples is 377.41, and the greater the degree of dispersion, the larger the gap in the overall competitiveness of financial technology in various countries. Thirty-two sample countries cover developed countries and developing countries of various economic strength upon different pillar industries. Specifically, the great differences in the emphasis and development capability of countries for the industry of the financial technology result in the significant differences in the indicators for the competitiveness of the financial technology.

From the perspective of central tendency, the median of 32 samples is 45.3, while the average is 45.6. It can be seen from the median and average that financial technology belongs to an emerging financial service model, the industry of the financial technology is still an emerging industry for most countries, with the construction of industrial system and industrial scale still in the primary stage. The development of the industry of the financial technology calls for strong computing power as the technical basis. However, most technologies belong to slow parameters with long profit cycles, which call for large investments of talents and capital in the early stage. At present, the agglomeration effect of global financial industry and high-tech industry is prominent with enterprises of sufficient strength to invest in the industry of the financial technology only found in few countries. With the development of the industry of financial technology, an increasing number of users access the industry, and the possibility of "realizing" the potential users determines the application width of underlying technology, which can, to some extent, be used to measure the current development of the financial technology industry in various countries. Stable computing power and high user access support the development of financial technology industry, while the industrial development shows the potentials of this industry. For most countries, traditional financial institutions still need to enhance the application of big data, artificial intelligence and other technologies due to the lack of sufficiently advanced technical means, while scientific and technological innovation enterprises cry out for the strong support of funds needed to develop financial technology products, in addition to the users' lack of confidence in the profitability and reliability of their products. Generally speaking, users have narrow contact with financial technology products, and their recognition of financial technology products still needs to be improved. How to realize the effective interconnection between the financial industry and the high-tech industry and improve the application efficiency of high technology in the financial industry still remains a problem.

Among 32 sample countries or regions, the top ten, concerning the indicators for the overall competitiveness, are the United States (93.1), Germany (69.2), Italy (68.7), Japan (67.4), Canada (65.7), Holland (64.8), Britain (64.6), France (62.5), Australia (61.0), and Chinese Mainland (60.3). Among them, the first echelon is of all developed countries but China, and most of them are European countries. The second echelon is also dominated by developed countries and regions. So, it can be easily seen that developed countries have obvious advantages in the financial technology. It is worth noting that Italy ranks 3rd, higher than Britain and France, thanks to its strong industrial development potential with its financial technology credit level being 2nd only to the United States.

Compared with the leading countries from Europe and America, China has advantages in computing power, with its computing power and efficiency staying in the forefront of the world. This will support the financial industry in carrying out technological innovation, achieving agile changes in financial products, service modes, business processes and organizational forms, and enhancing the overall efficiency and profitability of the financial industry. The gap between China and advanced countries in Europe and America mainly lies in user access and industrial development potential for two reasons. Firstly, the financial technology in China is still experiencing development and the inclusiveness and regulatory flexibility of it are relatively low, which hinders the expansion of the financial technology industry market. Secondly, the lack of data on the consumer side of the financial technology in China is likely to lead to the significant underestimation of the development of the financial technology in China.

5. The competitiveness in international financial governance

Table 13 shows the competitiveness in international financial governance by country (or region), with the U.S. at the 1st position, followed by Japan at the 3rd, and Chinese Mainland at the 9th.

Table 13   Rating of the Competitiveness in International Financial Governance

Ranking	Economy	Rating	Ranking	Economy	Rating
1	USA	85.1	17	Mexico	44.2
2	Germany	73.0	18	Turkey	39.5
3	Japan	72.5	19	Belgium	38.9
4	France	69.5	20	Argentina	38.8
5	Italy	67.5	21	Austria	37.8
6	Britain	64.1	22	Finland	37.1
7	Canada	62.2	23	Saudi Arabia	35.8
8	Korea	60.3	24	Indonesia	33.8

Continued

Ranking	Economy	Rating	Ranking	Economy	Rating
9	Chinese Mainland	57.7	25	South Africa	31.4
10	Brazil	55.9	26	Ireland	29.6
11	Russia	53.5	27	Portugal	25.5
12	Australia	52.9	28	Singapore	20.2
13	Spain	52.2	29	Greece	15.6
14	Netherlands	50.8	30	Luxembourg	12.0
15	Switzerland	47.3	31	Hong Kong, China	11.5
16	India	46.4	32	The United Arab Emirates	0.6

It can be seen that the developed countries and especially the United States still occupy an absolute advantage concerning the competitiveness in international financial governance. Among them, the United States, which is the most competitive in international financial governance, has a score of 85.1. Among the top 10 countries, the developed countries occupy 8 seats, with the G7 countries taking the first 7 in the world.

Comparatively, developing countries have not developed the competitiveness in international financial governance in line with its strength, with only two developing countries, Chinese Mainland and Brazil ranking 9th and 10th in the top ten countries.

The ranking better confirms the United States' dominant voice in international financial governance. The western developed countries led by the United States show a strong presence as a whole, while the non-western world, including the majority of emerging market countries, countries experiencing economic transitions and developing countries, stays in a disadvantageous position.

Appendix

i Sub-indicators for the competitiveness of financial industry

Indicator 1.1: Size of financial system

Table 14 Ranking of Secondary Indicator for the Competitiveness of Financial Industry: The Size of Financial System

Ranking	Economy	Rating	ranking	Economy	Rating
1	Hong Kong, China	100.0	17	Spain	45.7
1	Singapore	100.0	18	Belgium	42.6
3	Switzerland	91.8	19	Brazil	40.0
4	Britain	81.5	20	Germany	39.7
5	Netherlands	79.4	21	The United Arab Emirates	38.9
6	Luxembourg	75.1	22	Italy	38.7
7	Australia	74.6	23	Portugal	37.8
8	Canada	74.1	24	Austria	35.0
9	Japan	70.0	25	India	30.4
10	USA	65.7	26	Greece	30.3
11	South Africa	60.8	27	Saudi Arabia	26.4
12	France	59.4	28	Russia	20.8
13	Korea	58.6	29	Turkey	20.6
14	Ireland	51.4	30	Indonesia	19.5

Continued

Ranking	Economy	Rating	ranking	Economy	Rating
15	Finland	50.9	31	Mexico	18.0
16	Chinese Mainland	47.4	32	Argentina	10.0

Table 14 shows the specific scores of the size of the financial system of each economy, where the scale is referred to in a "relative" sense. The higher the score for the indicator, the more financial resources the financial system can allocate, and the stronger its ability to provide financial services to the citizen of the country. It can be found that the most advanced economies are basically developed economies, of which both Hong Kong, China and Singapore rank 1st, 8.2 points higher than Switzerland, which ranks 3rd; the financial system of Chinese Mainland ranks 16th considering its scale. In terms of the sub-indicators, Chinese Mainland ranks 1st in terms of the ratio of the deposit bank assets to the GDP, and 18th in terms of the ratio of the stock market value to the GDP, and 26th in terms of the ratio of the assets of other sectors to the GDP. It can be seen that the ratio of the banking assets to the GDP in Chinese Mainland is higher than those of the developed countries such as Britain and the United States, while the size of the development of the mutual funds, pension and insurance companies in Chinese Mainland is lagging behind.

1.1.1 Ratio of deposit bank assets to GDP

Table 15 Ranking of Tertiary Indicator for the Competitiveness of Financial Industry: Ratio of Deposit bank Assets to GDP

Ranking	Economy	Rating	Ranking	Economy	Rating
1	Hong Kong, China	100.0	17	Luxembourg	72.7
1	Japan	100.0	18	Brazil	70.2
1	Chinese Mainland	100.0	19	Finland	66.9
1	Switzerland	100.0	20	Austria	64.8
1	Singapore	100.0	21	Germany	60.7
6	Korea	94.3	22	Belgium	53.9
7	Australia	93.6	23	South Africa	52.0
8	Britain	87.8	24	Turkey	48.6

					Continued
Ranking	Economy	Rating	Ranking	Economy	Rating
9	Spain	86.6	25	India	45.6
10	Canada	85.2	26	Saudi Arabia	43.6
11	Portugal	83.9	27	USA	41.6
12	Netherlands	82.2	28	Russia	38.7
13	Italy	78.7	29	Ireland	33.9
14	France	75.3	30	Mexico	27.5
15	Greece	74.8	31	Indonesia	25.4
16	The United Arab Emirates	73.1	32	Argentina	13.9

1.1.2 Ratio of stock market value to GDP

Table 16 Ranking of Tertiary Indicator for the Competitiveness of the Financial Industry: Ratio of Stock Market Value to GDP

Ranking	Economy	Rating	Ranking	Economy	Rating
1	Hong Kong, China	100.0	17	Saudi Arabia	32.8
1	Switzerland	100.0	18	Chinese Mainland	32.7
1	Singapore	100.0	19	Spain	30.3
1	South Africa	100.0	20	The United Arab Emirates	30.1
5	Britain	82.2	21	Germany	27.1
6	USA	76.6	22	Indonesia	23.3
7	Canada	67.2	23	Brazil	21.7
8	Netherlands	58.0	24	Russia	21.3
9	Japan	56.5	25	Ireland	20.4
10	Australia	53.1	26	Mexico	16.5
11	Luxembourg	52.6	27	Austria	16.4
12	Korea	50.2	28	Portugal	15.3
13	Finland	49.2	29	Italy	13.6
14	France	47.8	30	Greece	10.9
15	Belgium	41.7	31	Turkey	10.8
16	India	37.3	32	Argentina	6.4

1.1.3 Ratio of assets of other sectors to GDP

Table 17　Ranking of Tertiary Indicator for the Competitiveness of the Financial Industry: Ratio of Assets of Other Sectors to GDP

Ranking	Economy	Rating	Ranking	Economy	Rating
1	Hong Kong, China	100.0	17	South Africa	30.3
1	Ireland	100.0	18	Brazil	28.0
1	Luxembourg	100.0	19	Italy	23.8
1	Singapore	100.0	20	Austria	23.7
5	Netherlands	98.1	21	Spain	20.2
6	USA	79.0	22	Portugal	14.2
7	Australia	77.1	23	The United Arab Emirates	13.6
8	Switzerland	75.5	24	Indonesia	10.0
9	Britain	74.4	24	Mexico	10.0
10	Canada	69.9	26	Argentina	9.8
11	France	55.1	27	Chinese Mainland	9.4
12	Japan	53.5	28	India	8.2
13	Finland	36.7	29	Greece	5.2
14	Belgium	32.1	30	Saudi Arabia	2.9
15	Germany	31.2	31	Russia	2.4
15	Korea	31.2	32	Turkey	2.3

Indicator 1.2: Activity of financial system

Table 18 shows the specific score of the activity of financial system of each economy. The larger the indicator, the more dynamic the accumulation of financial resources in the financial system. Switzerland ranked 1st, Britain 4th, the United States 6th, and Chinese Mainland 10th. In terms of sub-indicators, Chinese Mainland financial intermediaries dived a little deeper. The ratio of the private sector credit issued by the deposit banks and other financial institutions to GDP ranked 6th, and the ratio of bank loans to bank deposit ranked 1st. The ratio of the stock market transaction value to GDP ranked 15th.

Table 18 Ranking of Secondary Indicator for the Competitiveness of Financial Industry: Activity of Financial System

Ranking	Economy	Rating	Ranking	Economy	Rating
1	Switzerland	89.0	17	Greece	43.5
2	South Africa	86.6	18	France	42.8
3	Finland	85.4	19	Turkey	38.8
4	Britain	84.0	20	Germany	37.5
5	Korea	82.9	21	Belgium	35.4
6	USA	78.9	22	Brazil	33.7
7	Hong Kong, China	77.9	23	Austria	29.8
8	Australia	70.4	23	Italy	29.8
9	Japan	67.8	25	The United Arab Emirates	29.4
10	Chinese Mainland	65.2	26	Russia	29.2
11	Canada	63.7	27	India	28.5
12	Netherlands	58.6	28	Indonesia	20.9
13	Singapore	58.5	29	Mexico	18.3
14	Portugal	52.9	30	Luxembourg	16.1
15	Spain	52.1	31	Ireland	13.6
16	Saudi Arabia	49.7	32	Argentina	6.9

1.2.1 Ratio of private sector credit granted by deposit banks and other financial institutions to GDP

Table 19 Ranking of Tertiary Indicator for the Competitiveness of the Financial Industry: Ratio of Private Sector Credit Granted by Deposit Banks and Other Financial Institutions to GDP

Ranking	Economy	Rating	Ranking	Economy	Rating
1	Switzerland	100.0	17	France	60.5
1	USA	100.0	18	Finland	57.8
1	Hong Kong, China	100.0	19	The United Arab Emirates	51.3
1	Japan	100.0	20	Italy	51.2

Continued

Ranking	Economy	Rating	Ranking	Economy	Rating
5	Chinese Mainland	94.1	21	Austria	51.1
6	South Africa	88.7	22	Germany	47.2
7	Australia	87.8	23	Turkey	40.7
8	Korea	83.1	24	Saudi Arabia	40.3
9	Britain	82.3	25	Russia	40.0
10	Singapore	79.9	26	Brazil	39.9
11	Netherlands	69.3	27	Belgium	39.6
12	Portugal	65.7	28	India	29.7
12	Canada	65.7	29	Ireland	28.0
14	Spain	65.6	30	Indonesia	23.4
15	Luxembourg	64.0	31	Mexico	21.0
16	Greece	63.6	32	Argentina	8.4

1.2.2 Ratio of bank loans to bank deposits

Table 20　Ranking of Tertiary Indicator for the Competitiveness of Financial Industry: Ratio of Bank Loans to Bank Deposits

Ranking	Economy	Rating	Ranking	Economy	Rating
1	Chinese Mainland	100.0	17	Italy	56.5
1	Greece	100.0	18	Switzerland	56.1
1	Saudi Arabia	100.0	19	Austria	56.0
4	Australia	99.2	20	Brazil	50.7
5	Finland	98.0	21	The United Arab Emirates	47.9
6	Turkey	92.3	22	Germany	46.5
7	Portugal	82.2	23	Indonesia	46.2
8	France	76.5	24	Mexico	37.4
9	Canada	73.5	25	India	25.7
10	Netherlands	71.5	26	Argentina	17.8
11	South Africa	67.9	27	USA	15.4

Continued

Ranking	Economy	Rating	Ranking	Economy	Rating
12	Spain	64.9	28	Ireland	14.5
13	Korea	63.8	29	Hong Kong, China	11.8
14	Russia	61.8	30	Belgium	8.6
15	Singapore	61.6	31	Japan	0.0
16	Britain	59.9	31	Luxembourg	0.0

1.2.3 Ratio of stock market trading value to GDP

Table 21　Ranking of Tertiary Indicator for the Competitiveness of Financial Industry: Ratio of Stock Market Transaction Value to GDP

Ranking	Economy	Rating	Ranking	Economy	Rating
1	Switzerland	100.0	17	Saudi Arabia	29.3
1	USA	100.0	17	India	29.3
1	Hong Kong, China	100.0	19	Germany	28.2
4	Britain	96.9	20	Brazil	22.1
5	South Africa	94.8	21	France	17.1
6	Finland	93.0	22	Turkey	11.0
7	Korea	92.4	23	The United Arab Emirates	9.2
8	Japan	85.6	24	Russia	7.5
9	Canada	57.7	25	Mexico	7.3
10	Australia	47.3	26	Indonesia	6.9
11	Netherlands	46.8	27	Austria	6.2
11	Belgium	46.8	28	Ireland	6.0
13	Singapore	46.3	29	Italy	5.7
14	Spain	38.9	30	Greece	5.2
15	Chinese Mainland	33.4	31	Argentina	0.6
16	Portugal	31.9	32	Luxembourg	0.1

Indicator 1.3: Efficiency of financial system

Table 22 shows the specific score of the efficiency of the financial system of each economy. The larger thescore of the indicator, the lower cost the financial system needed to operate efficiently and gather financial resources. In terms of this indicator, Korea ranked 1st, followed by the United States at the 2nd place, while Britain ranked 5th, and Chinese Mainland 6th. In terms of sub-indicators, Chinese Mainland ranked 31st concerning the ratio of non-interest income to total revenue of the bank, 2nd when related to the ratio of bank operating expenses to total assets, and 12th for return on banking assets, and 8th together with Turkey for stock market turnover.

Table 22 Ranking of Secondary Indicator for the Competitiveness of Financial Industry: Efficiency of Financial System

Ranking	Economy	Rating	Ranking	Economy	Rating
1	Korea	75.7	17	Belgium	46.7
2	USA	75.2	18	Singapore	45.9
3	Finland	74.0	19	Netherlands	45.6
4	Japan	70.4	20	Italy	43.7
5	Britain	60.1	20	The United Arab Emirates	43.7
6	Chinese Mainland	60.0	22	India	43.0
7	Turkey	58.8	23	South Africa	40.8
8	Germany	56.2	24	Austria	40.0
8	Hong Kong, China	56.2	25	Portugal	36.7
10	Spain	55.3	26	Argentina	36.4
10	Saudi Arabia	55.3	27	Indonesia	35.3
12	Brazil	54.9	28	Mexico	35.1
13	Canada	54.4	29	Ireland	32.8
14	Australia	50.1	30	Luxembourg	32.6
15	France	49.3	31	Greece	29.0
16	Switzerland	46.8	32	Russia	23.4

1.3.1 Ratio of non-interest income to the total income of the bank

Table 23 Ranking of Tertiary Indicator for the Competitiveness of Financial Industry: Ratio of Non-Interest Income to the Total income of the Bank

Ranking	Economy	Rating	Ranking	Economy	Rating
1	Switzerland	100.0	17	Netherlands	79.2
1	Finland	100.0	18	Britain	77.3
1	Belgium	100.0	19	The United Arab Emirates	75.9
1	Portugal	100.0	20	India	73.9
1	France	100.0	21	Spain	72.2
1	Argentina	100.0	22	Russia	71.8
1	Luxembourg	100.0	23	Korea	68.5
8	Italy	98.9	24	Ireland	67.7
9	Germany	96.3	25	USA	66.5
10	Canada	93.7	26	Turkey	60.4
11	Austria	90.3	27	Mexico	55.8
12	Brazil	88.4	28	Saudi Arabia	54.5
13	Japan	86.2	29	Chinese Mainland	53.2
14	South Africa	84.9	30	Australia	53.0
15	Hong Kong, China	82.9	31	Indonesia	52.4
16	Singapore	81.6	32	Greece	39.4

1.3.2 Ratio of operating expenses to total assets of the bank

Table 24 Ranking of Tertiary Indicator for the Competitiveness of Financial Industry: Ratio of Operating Expenses to Total Assets of the Bank

Ranking	Economy	Rating	Ranking	Economy	Rating
1	Japan	79.2	17	India	45.8
2	Chinese Mainland	78.4	18	Britain	40.8
3	Hong Kong, China	76.2	19	Austria	39.3
4	Australia	73.2	20	Belgium	37.6

Global Financial Competitiveness Report 2021   181

Continued

Ranking	Economy	Rating	Ranking	Economy	Rating
5	The United Arab Emirates	70.9	21	USA	36.8
6	Singapore	68.4	22	Spain	36.4
7	Luxembourg	67.6	23	Turkey	31.6
8	Saudi Arabia	66.3	24	Switzerland	30.8
9	France	61.0	25	Portugal	28.8
10	Finland	59.8	26	Ireland	21.3
11	Netherlands	55.8	27	Indonesia	18.6
12	Canada	55.1	28	South Africa	10.5
13	Italy	55.0	29	Argentina	0.0
14	Greece	54.9	29	Brazil	0.0
15	Korea	54.8	29	Russia	0.0
16	Germany	54.1	29	Mexico	0.0

1.3.3 Return on banking assets

Table 25   Ranking of Tertiary Indicator for the Competitiveness of Financial Industry: Return on Banking Assets

Ranking	Economy	Rating	Ranking	Economy	Rating
1	Argentina	100.0	17	Australia	42.0
2	Saudi Arabia	99.1	18	Belgium	41.1
3	Indonesia	95.5	19	Netherlands	37.0
4	Mexico	88.9	20	Italy	34.7
5	Turkey	81.8	21	Korea	31.1
6	Brazil	74.4	22	Luxembourg	27.8
7	The United Arab Emirates	72.1	23	France	20.6
8	South Africa	66.9	23	Britain	20.6
9	Ireland	58.5	25	Russia	18.8
10	Hong Kong, China	57.9	26	Japan	14.1

Continued

Ranking	Economy	Rating	Ranking	Economy	Rating
11	Singapore	54.4	27	Switzerland	9.1
12	Chinese Mainland	49.3	28	Spain	8.7
13	USA	48.2	29	Germany	7.7
14	Finland	47.4	30	Greece	0.0
15	Canada	44.3	30	India	0.0
16	Austria	43.0	30	Portugal	0.0

1.3.4 Stock market turnover

Table 26   Ranking of Tertiary Indicator for the Competitiveness of Financial Industry: Stock Market Turnover

Ranking	Economy	Rating	Ranking	Economy	Rating
1	USA	100.0	17	Saudi Arabia	37.2
1	Korea	100.0	18	Belgium	33.9
3	Japan	80.9	18	Netherlands	33.9
4	Finland	79.0	20	Portugal	30.5
5	Britain	73.9	21	South Africa	27.5
6	Spain	71.5	22	Greece	26.5
7	Germany	59.8	23	Italy	24.5
8	Turkey	59.6	24	Singapore	23.7
8	Chinese Mainland	59.6	25	Austria	22.5
10	Brazil	55.4	26	Mexico	21.9
11	Switzerland	47.1	27	Russia	16.6
12	India	46.1	28	Ireland	16.5
13	Canada	44.5	29	Indonesia	15.0
14	Australia	44.1	30	The United Arab Emirates	14.4
15	Hong Kong, China	40.0	31	Argentina	6.1
16	France	38.1	32	Luxembourg	0.1

Indicator 1.4: Stability of financial system

Table 27 shows the specific scores of theindicator for the stability of the financial system of each economy. The larger the score, the stronger the sustainability of the financial system in gathering the financial resources. The U. S. ranked 1st, Britain 6th, Hong Kong of China 12th, and Chinese Mainland 22th. In terms of sub-indicators, Chinese Mainland bank Z-score ranked 7th, the bank's non-performing loan ratio 12th, the ratio of bank capital to total assets 17th, the ratio of bank regulatory capital to risk-weighted assets 29th, the ratio of current assets to deposits and short-term financing 30th, the rate of non-performing loan reserve ratio 1st, bank robustness 27th, and the stock market volatility 21st. Although never experienced any banking crisis in its history, China still needs to be alert about the stability of its banking system.

Table 27   Ranking of Secondary Indicator for the Competitiveness of Financial Industry: Stability of the Financial System

Ranking	Economy	Rating	Ranking	Economy	Rating
1	U. S. A	75.8	17	India	55.7
2	Mexico	73.9	18	South Africa	55.6
3	Singapore	70.7	19	Netherlands	55.0
4	Canada	70.2	20	Luxembourg	52.3
5	Indonesia	67.4	21	Russia	51.3
6	Britain	65.8	22	Chinese Mainland	51.2
7	Switzerland	64.8	23	Austria	49.2
8	Australia	63.3	24	Portugal	44.8
9	The United Arab Emirates	63.1	25	Ireland	44.1
10	Saudi Arabia	60.5	26	Turkey	42.2
11	Korea	60.4	27	Brazil	39.0
12	Hong Kong, China	58.3	28	Japan	36.6
13	Finland	56.7	29	Spain	34.7
14	Germany	56.5	30	Argentina	32.1
15	Belgium	56.3	31	Greece	13.3
16	France	55.7	32	Italy	12.8

1.4.1 Bank Z-score

Table 28   Ranking of Tertiary Indicator for the Competitiveness of Financial Industry: Bank Z-score

Ranking	Economy	Bank Z-score	Ranking	Economy	Bank Z-score
1	Luxembourg	100.0	17	Australia	51.6
2	USA	99.3	18	Brazil	50.8
3	The United Arab Emirates	88.5	19	Portugal	47.2
4	Germany	88.0	20	Canada	47.1
5	Austria	87.1	21	Finland	46.3
6	France	85.1	22	Switzerland	42.0
7	Chinese Mainland	76.4	23	Italy	40.2
8	Singapore	74.0	24	Netherlands	36.2
9	Saudi Arabia	68.8	25	Korea	35.1
10	Mexico	67.3	26	Britain	33.2
11	Belgium	63.5	27	Ireland	32.2
12	Spain	60.4	28	Greece	27.6
13	South Africa	55.6	29	Turkey	27.2
14	Japan	54.3	30	Russia	23.2
15	Hong Kong, China	53.3	31	Argentina	21.7
16	India	53.2	32	Indonesia	20.8

1.4.2 Ratio of bank non-performing loan

Table 29   Ranking of Tertiary Indicator for the Competitiveness of Financial Industry: Ratio of Bank Non-Performing Loan

Ranking	Economy	Rating	Ranking	Economy	Rating
1	Canada	97.0	17	Indonesia	83.0
2	Finland	95.9	18	Turkey	81.0
3	Hong Kong, China	95.5	19	South Africa	80.9
4	Switzerland	94.8	20	Belgium	80.5

Ranking	Economy	Rating	Ranking	Economy	Rating
5	Luxembourg	94.7	21	France	79.5
6	Australia	94.1	22	Brazil	76.1
7	Britain	93.7	23	Germany	70.7
8	USA	92.5	24	Spain	70.3
9	Japan	92.1	25	The United Arab Emirates	57.1
10	Singapore	90.7	26	India	33.5
11	Saudi Arabia	89.2	27	Russia	33.3
12	Chinese Mainland	88.4	28	Ireland	23.6
13	Argentina	87.8	29	Portugal	21.1
14	Mexico	86.1	30	Italy	0.0
15	Netherlands	84.6	30	Korea	0.0
16	Austria	84.2	30	Greece	0.0

1.4.3 Ratio of bank capital to total assets

Table 30   Ranking of Tertiary Indicator for the Competitiveness of Financial Industry: Ratio of Bank Capital to Total Assets

Ranking	Economy	Rating	Ranking	Economy	Rating
1	Saudi Arabia	100.0	17	Chinese Mainland	31.0
1	Indonesia	100.0	18	Spain	26.2
3	Ireland	93.5	19	Korea	25.6
4	Greece	70.0	20	Belgium	25.5
5	USA	66.5	21	Austria	25.4
6	Argentina	65.7	22	India	23.9
7	Turkey	57.2	23	Britain	20.3
8	Russia	55.1	24	Australia	18.8
9	Mexico	54.0	25	Switzerland	17.4
10	Brazil	50.5	26	France	15.9
11	Hong Kong, China	48.3	27	Germany	13.3

Continued

Ranking	Economy	Rating	Ranking	Economy	Rating
12	Singapore	41.8	28	Netherlands	10.8
13	The United Arab Emirates	39.9	29	Finland	6.3
14	Portugal	34.2	30	Italy	4.9
15	Luxembourg	33.5	31	Japan	4.1
16	South Africa	32.0	32	Canada	2.2

1.4.4 Ratio of bank regulatory capital to risk weighted assets

Table 31 Ranking of Tertiary Indicator for the Competitiveness of Financial Industry: Ratio of Bank Regulatory Capital to Risk Weighted Assets

Ranking	Economy	Rating	Ranking	Economy	Rating
1	Ireland	100.0	17	Greece	46.8
1	Luxembourg	100.0	18	Turkey	45.7
3	Finland	87.2	19	Switzerland	45.2
4	Indonesia	86.7	20	Japan	44.4
5	Netherlands	80.2	21	South Africa	39.5
6	Britain	72.0	22	Argentina	37.2
7	Saudi Arabia	69.3	22	Mexico	37.2
8	Germany	62.5	24	Spain	37.0
9	Korea	61.1	25	Canada	32.1
10	Hong Kong, China	60.9	26	Australia	30.3
11	Belgium	59.8	27	USA	30.2
12	France	59.4	28	Italy	25.0
13	Austria	54.9	29	Chinese Mainland	20.8
14	Brazil	54.3	30	India	18.8
15	The United Arab Emirates	54.0	31	Portugal	16.8
16	Singapore	47.2	32	Russia	13.8

1.4.5 Ratio of current assets to deposits and short-term financing

Table 32 Ranking of Tertiary Indicator for the Competitiveness of Financial Industry: Ratio of Current Assets to Deposits and Short-Term Financing

Ranking	Economy	Rating	Ranking	Economy	Rating
1	Luxembourg	100.0	17	Ireland	33.5
2	Switzerland	94.1	18	Spain	28.4
3	Brazil	92.0	19	Belgium	28.1
4	France	90.0	20	Netherlands	25.3
5	Argentina	85.6	21	Turkey	23.8
6	Germany	75.6	22	Singapore	20.1
7	Britain	74.0	23	USA.	18.3
8	Mexico	51.2	24	South Africa	16.6
9	Canada	49.9	25	Australia	14.6
10	Finland	49.3	26	Portugal	11.4
11	Russia	43.5	26	Indonesia	11.4
12	Italy	42.9	28	Saudi Arabia	10.5
13	Japan	41.7	29	India	6.2
14	Austria	37.6	30	Chinese Mainland	5.1
15	Hong Kong, China	36.3	31	Korea	0.0
16	The United Arab Emirates	35.4	31	Greece	0.0

1.4.6 Ratio of the reserve for non-performing loan

Table 33 Ranking of Tertiary Indicators for The Competitiveness of Financial Industry: Ratio of the Reserve for Non-Performing Loan

Ranking	Economy	Rating	Ranking	Economy	Rating
1	Brazil	100.0	17	Netherlands	15.6
1	Mexico	100.0	17	Korea	15.6
1	Saudi Arabia	100.0	19	Greece	15.5
1	Chinese Mainland	100.0	20	India	11.9

Continued

Ranking	Economy	Rating	Ranking	Economy	Rating
5	Argentina	90.7	21	Japan	11.7
6	Turkey	41.1	21	Hong Kong, China	11.7
7	The United Arab Emirates	37.6	23	South Africa	11.6
8	Russia	34.4	24	Britain	11.4
9	Portugal	32.5	25	Belgium	10.6
10	Germany	29.3	26	Singapore	9.0
11	Spain	23.4	27	Luxembourg	5.8
12	USA.	21.7	28	Ireland	4.0
13	Austria	21.0	29	Switzerland	3.9
13	Indonesia	21.0	30	Canada	0.0
15	Italy	17.7	30	Finland	0.0
16	France	17.2	30	Australia	0.0

1.4.7 Bank robustness

Table 34 Ranking of Tertiary Indicator for the Competitiveness of Financial Industry: Bank Robustness

Ranking	Economy	Rating	Ranking	Economy	Rating
1	Finland	94.5	17	The United Arab Emirates	72.1
2	Canada	92.0	18	Belgium	71.3
3	Singapore	90.4	19	Germany	70.3
4	Australia	89.4	20	South Africa	69.3
5	Hong Kong, China	88.7	21	Indonesia	64.6
6	Luxembourg	87.9	22	Korea	64.1
7	Switzerland	86.0	23	Spain	61.9
8	USA	79.9	24	Argentina	61.0
9	Japan	79.7	25	India	60.5
10	Brazil	78.8	26	Turkey	60.3

Global Financial Competitiveness Report 2021

Continued

Ranking	Economy	Rating	Ranking	Economy	Rating
11	France	77.8	27	Chinese Mainland	58.1
12	Saudi Arabia	77.7	28	Ireland	49.7
13	Netherlands	76.5	29	Russia	45.1
14	Austria	75.9	30	Italy	44.9
15	Mexico	75.4	31	Portugal	38.7
16	Britain	75.1	32	Greece	26.1

1.4.8 Stock market volatility

Table 35 Ranking of Tertiary Indicator for the Competitiveness of Financial Industry: Stock Market Volatility

Ranking	Economy	Rating	Ranking	Economy	Rating
1	Canada	94.7	17	Hong Kong, China	60.2
2	USA.	93.2	18	Finland	59.2
3	Korea	92.0	19	Germany	54.5
4	Singapore	88.1	20	France	50.6
5	Australia	83.8	21	Chinese Mainland	48.1
6	India	81.6	22	Saudi Arabia	47.3
7	Mexico	80.4	23	Austria	43.3
8	Indonesia	79.4	24	Ireland	40.2
9	Britain	77.4	25	Turkey	36.3
10	Switzerland	74.9	26	Luxembourg	30.0
11	The United Arab Emirates	71.2	27	Japan	26.3
12	South Africa	67.5	28	Spain	25.5
13	Russia	67.2	29	Brazil	6.3
14	Belgium	64.2	30	Italy	0.6
15	Netherlands	63.0	31	Argentina	0.0
16	Portugal	60.7	31	Greece	0.0

Indicator 1.5: Availability of financial services

Table 36 shows the specific scores of the indicator for the availability of financial services in each economy. The larger the score, the stronger the ability of the financial system to gather financial resources and serve the real economy. Some studies have found that the improved availability of financial services can effectively reduce income inequality among countries. Concerning this indicator, Luxemburg ranked 1st, the United States 2nd, the UK 8th, and the Chinese Mainland 17th. In terms of sub-indicators, the number of commercial bank branches for every 100,000 adults in Chinese Mainland ranks 29th, and the ratio of stock market trading volume of the companies other than the top ten listed ranked 1st. The ratio of the value of the company outside the top ten listed companies to the total market value ranked 1st, and the number of listed companies per million people ranked 27th, SME financing ranked 18th and venture capital availability ranked 5th.

Table 36 Ranking of Secondary Indicator for the Competitiveness of Financial industry: availability of financial services

Ranking	Economy	Rating	Ranking	Economy	Rating
1	Luxembourg	74.3	17	Chinese Mainland	49.9
2	USA	72.4	18	Korea	48.8
3	Spain	65.8	19	Portugal	48.0
4	Japan	65.4	20	Indonesia	46.9
5	Switzerland	63.8	21	Italy	44.9
6	Hong Kong, China	63.3	22	The United Arab Emirates	40.0
7	Australia	62.5	23	Saudi Arabia	39.6
8	Britain	61.8	24	Turkey	39.4
9	Belgium	60.5	25	Austria	38.7
10	Canada	59.8	26	Russia	38.6
11	France	58.0	27	Mexico	36.7
12	Singapore	56.9	28	South Africa	35.8
13	Germany	53.8	29	Brazil	35.7
14	India	53.5	30	Ireland	33.6

Continued

Ranking	Economy	Rating	Ranking	Economy	Rating
15	Finland	53.1	31	Greece	28.9
16	Netherlands	51.2	32	Argentina	27.3

1.5.1 Number of commercial bank branches for every 100,000 adults

Table 37 Ranking of Tertiary Indicator for the Competitiveness of Financial Industry: Number of Commercial Bank Branches for Every 100,000 Adults

Ranking	Economy	Rating	Ranking	Economy	Rating
1	Luxembourg	100.0	17	Brazil	39.0
1	Spain	100.0	18	Turkey	34.8
3	Italy	89.3	19	Indonesia	33.7
4	Switzerland	81.5	20	Korea	30.9
5	Portugal	78.1	21	India	29.4
6	France	72.0	22	Mexico	28.3
7	Belgium	69.6	23	Argentina	27.1
8	Japan	68.1	24	Germany	25.8
9	USA	62.4	25	Austria	24.1
10	Australia	59.2	26	Netherlands	23.9
11	Russia	58.4	27	The United Arab Emirates	22.6
12	Britain	53.1	28	South Africa	20.9
13	Greece	45.7	29	Chinese Mainland	17.6
14	Hong Kong, China	42.1	30	Saudi Arabia	17.0
15	Canada	41.6	30	Singapore	17.0
16	Ireland	41.5	32	Finland	2.9

1.5.2 Ratio of stock market trading volume to total trading volume of the companies other than the top ten listed

Table 38 Ranking of Tertiary Indicator for the Competitiveness of Financial Industry: Ratio of Stock Market Trading Volume to Total Trading Volume Outside the Top Ten Listed Companies

Ranking	Economy	Rating	Ranking	Economy	Rating
1	France	100.0	17	Germany	70.5
1	Belgium	100.0	18	Turkey	68.0
1	Japan	100.0	19	Brazil	67.5
1	USA	100.0	20	Switzerland	67.3
1	Korea	100.0	21	Saudi Arabia	67.2
1	India	100.0	22	South Africa	62.3
1	Chinese Mainland	100.0	23	Spain	61.3
1	Finland	100.0	24	Argentina	57.1
9	Netherlands	99.7	25	Mexico	52.5
10	Canada	93.2	26	Russia	39.1
11	Luxembourg	91.9	27	Italy	36.9
12	Britain	91.4	27	Portugal	36.9
13	Hong Kong, China	86.3	27	Austria	36.9
14	Australia	82.5	30	Greece	21.4
15	Indonesia	73.8	31	The United Arab Emirates	7.7
16	Singapore	72.3	32	Ireland	5.8

1.5.3 Ratio of market value to total market value of companies other than the top ten listed companies

Table 39　Ranking of Tertiary Indicator for the Competitiveness of Financial Industry: Ratio of Market Value to Total Market Value of Companies Other than the Top Ten Listed Companies

Ranking	Economy	Rating	Ranking	Economy	Rating
1	Japan	100.0	17	Spain	72.7
1	Chinese Mainland	100.0	18	Indonesia	65.0
3	Netherlands	96.5	18	Mexico	65.0
4	USA	95.8	20	Singapore	64.2
5	India	95.0	21	Switzerland	63.4
6	France	89.4	22	South Africa	62.7
6	Belgium	89.4	23	Italy	56.3
6	Finland	89.4	23	Portugal	56.3
9	Canada	85.6	23	Austria	56.3
10	Korea	83.8	26	Brazil	53.8
11	Luxembourg	80.0	27	Saudi Arabia	50.9
11	Hong Kong, China	80.0	28	Greece	47.5
11	Britain	80.0	29	Russia	46.3
14	Australia	76.3	30	The United Arab Emirates	31.6
15	Turkey	74.8	31	Argentina	24.4
16	Germany	74.5	32	Ireland	11.3

1.5.4 Number of listed companies per million people

Table 40　Ranking of Tertiary Indicator for the Competitiveness of Financial Industry: Number of Listed Companies per Million People

Ranking	Economy	Rating	Ranking	Economy	Rating
1	Canada	100.0	17	Ireland	10.7
1	Hong Kong, China	100.0	18	Austria	9.5

Continued

Ranking	Economy	Rating	Ranking	Economy	Rating
1	Australia	100.0	19	France	8.7
1	Singapore	100.0	20	Netherlands	7.4
5	Spain	83.4	21	Saudi Arabia	7.1
6	Britain	62.1	22	Germany	6.8
7	Luxembourg	58.7	23	South Africa	6.4
8	Korea	51.3	24	Turkey	5.8
9	Japan	35.5	25	India	5.2
10	Switzerland	33.7	25	Portugal	5.2
11	Finland	30.0	27	Chinese Mainland	3.1
12	Greece	22.8	28	Argentina	2.7
13	The United Arab Emirates	16.7	28	Indonesia	2.7
13	USA	16.7	30	Brazil	2.0
15	Italy	14.0	30	Russia	2.0
16	Belgium	12.7	32	Mexico	1.4

1.5.5 SME Financing

Table 41   Ranking of Tertiary Indicators for the Competitiveness of Financial Industry: SME Financing

Ranking	Economy	Rating	Ranking	Economy	Rating
1	USA	79.7	17	Austria	57.9
2	Germany	71.9	18	Chinese Mainland	57.2
3	Finland	71.7	19	Saudi Arabia	53.3
4	Singapore	70.5	20	Korea	49.7
5	Hong Kong, China	66.8	21	Spain	49.3
6	Switzerland	66.3	22	France	48.7
7	Luxembourg	65.4	23	South Africa	45.6
8	Japan	63.4	24	Portugal	45.5
9	India	62.5	25	Ireland	44.8

		Continued			
Ranking	Economy	Rating	Ranking	Economy	Rating
10	Australia	61.9	26	Turkey	44.5
11	The United Arab Emirates	61.7	27	Mexico	43.2
12	Netherlands	61.6	28	Russia	39.0
13	Canada	59.7	29	Brazil	38.4
14	Britain	59.5	30	Italy	33.6
14	Indonesia	59.5	31	Argentina	30.1
16	Belgium	58.4	32	Greece	22.7

1.5.6 Availability of venture capital

Table 42　Ranking of Tertiary Indicator for the Competitiveness of Financial Industry: Availability of Venture Capital

Ranking	Economy	Rating	Ranking	Economy	Rating
1	USA	76.7	17	France	45.1
2	Germany	66.8	18	Canada	44.8
3	Finland	64.6	19	Australia	42.5
4	Singapore	61.3	20	Spain	41.6
5	The United Arab Emirates	57.0	21	Austria	38.7
5	Chinese Mainland	57.0	21	Ireland	38.7
7	Britain	56.8	23	Korea	36.0
8	Hong Kong, China	55.7	24	Mexico	35.9
9	India	55.3	25	Portugal	35.5
10	Luxembourg	54.9	26	South Africa	33.0
11	Switzerland	52.4	27	Turkey	28.7
12	Japan	51.5	28	Russia	27.9
13	Netherlands	51.4	29	Brazil	24.3
14	Indonesia	47.0	30	Argentina	24.1
15	Belgium	46.8	31	Italy	21.0
16	Saudi Arabia	46.3	32	Greece	16.8

Indicator 1.6: Status of the international financial center

Table 43 shows the specific scores of the indicator for the status of the international financial center of each economy. This indicator measures the comprehensive competitiveness of the international financial center. The larger the value, the richer the global financial resources. In terms of this indicator, the United States ranked 1st, represented by New York with an original score of 770 points, the United Kingdom ranked 2nd represented by London with an original score of 766 points, Chinese Mainland ranked 3rd represented by Shanghai with an original score of 748 points, and Japan ranked 4th represented by Tokyo with an original score of 747 points, with a difference of only 1 point to that of China. The financial centers of the other 17 economies are not listed in the top 30%, so they are all scored 0.

Table 43 Ranking of Secondary Indicator for the Competitiveness of Financial Industry: Status of the International Financial Center

Ranking	Economy	Rating	Ranking	Economy	Rating
1	USA	100.0	17	Belgium	89.1
2	Britain	99.5	18	Argentina	0.0
3	Chinese Mainland	97.1	18	Austria	0.0
4	Japan	97.0	18	Brazil	0.0
5	Hong Kong, China	96.5	18	Finland	0.0
6	Singapore	96.4	18	Greece	0.0
7	Switzerland	94.0	18	Indonesia	0.0
8	Luxembourg	93.4	18	India	0.0
9	Germany	92.9	18	Ireland	0.0
10	The United Arab Emirates	92.7	18	Italy	0.0
11	France	92.6	18	Mexico	0.0
12	Netherlands	91.0	18	Portugal	0.0
13	Canada	90.6	18	Russia	0.0
14	Korea	90.3	18	Saudi Arabia	0.0
15	Australia	90.0	18	Turkey	0.0
16	Spain	89.9	18	South Africa	0.0

ii Sub-indicators for the competitiveness of currency

Indicator 2.1: Store of value

Table 44 reflects the role of the currency of each nation as store of value internationally, with the United States and the Eurozone in the 1st echelon, far ahead of other countries. The US Dollar ranked 1st under both tertiary indicators of the "proportion of foreign exchange reserve currencies" and "SDR weights", so it scored 100 under the secondary indicator of "store of value". The Euro ranked 2nd under both tertiary indicators, and hence under "store of value", with a score of 55.05. The 2nd echelon is made up of Japan, Chinese Mainland and the United Kingdom. Japan and Chinese Mainland rank 3rd and 4th with close scores, and Britain is slightly behind them with a narrow gap. The 3rd echelon is composed of Canada, Australia and Switzerland. The currencies of these three countries also play the role of international reserve currency to a certain extent, but with low proportions. Furthermore, the currencies of these three countries are not included in the SDR basket, so the total scores for them are relatively low. The currencies of other countries, not identified in the IMF COFER database and not belonging to SDR currencies, get scores of zero for this indicator.

Table 44 Ranking of Secondary Indicator for the Competitiveness of Currency: Store of Value

Ranking	Economy	Rating	Ranking	Economy	Rating
1	USA	100	9	Russia	0
2	Eurozone	55.1	9	Korea	0
3	Japan	15.1	9	Mexico	0
4	Chinese Mainland	15.0	9	South Africa	0
5	Britain	13.7	9	Saudi Arabia	0
6	Canada	1.8	9	Turkey	0
7	Australia	1.6	9	Singapore	0
8	Switzerland	0.2	9	India	0
9	Argentina	0	9	Indonesia	0

Continued

Ranking	Economy	Rating	Ranking	Economy	Rating
9	The United Arab Emirates	0	9	Hong Kong, China	0
9	Brazil	0			

2.1.1 Proportion of foreign exchange reserve currencies

Table 45 shows that the US Dollar is still the main currency in international reserves. In the fourth quarter of 2020, the US Dollar accounted for 59.02% as foreign exchange reserves, far exceeding the currencies of other countries, so it got full marks. The Euro, accounting for 21.24% as foreign exchange reserves with a score of 36.0, ranked 2nd. The Yen and Pound also have their places as foreign exchange reserves, with scores of 10.2 and 8.0 respectively. RMB, accounting for 2.25% with a score of 3.8, ranked 5th, ahead of the Canadian dollar and Australian dollar.

Table 45 Ranking of Tertiary Indicator for the Competitiveness of Currency: Proportion of Foreign Exchange Reserve Currencies (2020 Q4)

Ranking	Economy	Rating	Ranking	Economy	Rating
1	USA	100.0	9	Russia	0.0
2	Eurozone	36.0	9	Korea	0.0
3	Japan	10.2	9	Mexico	0.0
4	Britain	8.0	9	South Africa	0.0
5	Chinese Mainland	3.8	9	Saudi Arabia	0.0
6	Canada	3.5	9	Turkey	0.0
7	Australia	3.1	9	Singapore	0.0
8	Switzerland	0.3	9	India	0.0
9	Argentina	0.0	9	Indonesia	0.0
9	The United Arab Emirates	0.0	9	Hong Kong, China	0.0
9	Brazil	0.0			

2.1.2 Currency weights in the SDR basket

Table 46 shows the IMF's latest adjustment to the weights of SDR basket currencies, with the ranking of the five basket currencies as US Dollar at the top, followed by Euro, RMB, Japanese Yen and Pound. According to the weights of these five currencies in the basket, the US Dollar and the Euro occupy the lion's share, accounting for more than 40% and 30% respectively, with scores of 100 and 74.1. RMB entered the basket for the first time, accounting for 10.92% with a score of 26.2, higher than Yen and Pound.

Table 46 Ranking of Tertiary Indicator for the Competitiveness of Currency: Currency Weights in the SDR Basket (Oct, 2016)

Ranking	Economy	Rating	Ranking	Economy	Rating
1	USA	100.0	6	South Africa	0.0
2	Eurozone	74.1	6	India	0.0
3	Chinese Mainland	26.2	6	Mexico	0.0
4	Japan	20.0	6	Russia	0.0
5	Britain	19.4	6	Turkey	0.0
6	Australia	0.0	6	Brazil	0.0
6	Canada	0.0	6	Indonesia	0.0
6	Switzerland	0.0	6	Saudi Arabia	0.0
6	Hong Kong, China	0.0	6	The United Arab Emirates	0.0
6	Singapore	0.0	6	Argentina	0.0
6	Korea	0.0			

Indicator 2.2: Medium of Exchange

It can be seen from Table 47 that the currencies of various countries are used asmedium for international exchanges. The United States got a score totaled 100 as the medium of exchange for its ranking 1st under the two tertiary indicators of the "proportion of cross-border payment currencies" and "proportion of currencies of foreign exchange market turnover". The Eurozone ranked 2nd under both tertiary indicators with a score of 65.7 as medium of exchange. Britain and Japan ranked 3rd and 4th respectively, more than 50 points behind the Eurozone, but still significantly higher than those of the other countries. Chinese Mainland and Hong Kong, China, ranked 7th and 8th, behind those of Australia and Canada, but higher than those of

Switzerland and Singapore, manifesting the potential of RMB and Hong Kong Dollar as the medium for exchange.

Table 47   Ranking of Secondary Indicator for the Competitiveness of Currency: Medium of Exchange

Ranking	Economy	Rating	Ranking	Economy	Rating
1	USA	100	12	Korea	1.15
2	Eurozone	65.7	13	South Africa	1.05
3	Britain	15.65	14	Russia	1
4	Japan	14.15	14	Turkey	1
5	Australia	5.7	16	India	0.95
6	Canada	5.15	17	Brazil	0.65
7	Chinese Mainland	4.9	18	Indonesia	0.25
8	Hong Kong, China	3.85	19	The United Arab Emirates	0.1
9	Switzerland	3.8	19	Saudi Arabia	0.1
10	Singapore	2.25	21	Argentina	0
11	Mexico	1.3			

2.2.1 Proportion of cross-border payment currencies

Table 48 shows the ranking of the currencies of various countries in cross-border payments. The US Dollar and Euro are still far ahead of currencies of the other countries. In December 2020, the proportion of USD and Euro in cross-border payments was 40.83% and 38.69% at the scores of 100 and 94.8 respectively, ranking the top two. Pound and Japanese Yen ranked 3rd and 4th, accounting for 6.85% and 3.78% at scores of 16.8 and 9.3 respectively. Chinese Mainland ranked 5th with its RMB accounting for 1.98% of cross-border payments at a score of 4.9, ahead of the Canadian Dollar and Australian Dollar.

Table 48   Ranking of Tertiary Indicator for the Competitiveness of Currency: Proportion of Cross-Border Payment Currencies (Dec, 2020)

Ranking	Economy	Rating	Ranking	Economy	Rating
1	USA	100.0	12	Turkey	0.7
2	Eurozone	94.8	12	Mexico	0.7

				Continued	
Ranking	Economy	Rating	Ranking	Economy	Rating
3	Britain	16.8	12	Russia	0.7
4	Japan	9.3	15	India	0.0
5	Chinese Mainland	4.9	15	Korea	0.0
6	Canada	4.6	15	Brazil	0.0
7	Australia	3.7	15	Indonesia	0.0
7	Hong Kong, China	3.7	15	Saudi Arabia	0.0
9	Singapore	2.5	15	Argentina	0.0
10	Switzerland	1.9	15	The United Arab Emirates	0.0
11	South Africa	0.8			

2.2.2 Proportion of currencies of foreign exchange market turnover

As seen from Table 49, the US Dollar is the dominant currency in the foreign exchange markets, and there is still a large gap between the RMB and the currencies of other key countries. In the transactions in foreign exchange markets in 2019, US Dollar accounted for 47.17% of the total turnover denominated by the currencies of the sample countries/regions, ranking 1st. The Euro sees 30 percentage points lower than the US dollar, though ranking 2nd, at a score of only 36.6. Japanese Yen, Pound and other international currencies also occupy significant shares, While Chinese Mainland ranks only 8th behind Australia, Canada and Switzerland.

Table 49 Ranking of Tertiary Indicator for the Competitiveness of Currency: Proportion of Currencies of Foreign Exchange Market Turnover(2019)

Ranking	Economy	Rating	Ranking	Economy	Rating
1	USA	100.0	12	Mexico	1.9
2	Eurozone	36.6	12	India	1.9
3	Japan	19.0	14	Russia	1.3
4	Britain	14.5	14	South Africa	1.3
5	Australia	7.7	14	Turkey	1.3
6	Canada	5.7	14	Brazil	1.3
6	Switzerland	5.7	18	Indonesia	0.5

Continued

Ranking	Economy	Rating	Ranking	Economy	Rating
8	Chinese Mainland	4.9	19	The United Arab Emirates	0.2
9	Hong Kong, China	4.0	19	Saudi Arabia	0.2
10	Korea	2.3	21	Argentina	0.0
11	Singapore	2.0			

Indicator 2.3: Unit of account

Table 50 shows the position of currencies of sample countries as unit of account internationally. The United States and the Eurozone remain rank the top two, with scores of 100 and 62.8 respectively. This is because the United States ranks 1st under the four tertiary indicators of the "exchange rate anchor", "basket currencies", "proportion of currencies for the international banking liabilities" and "proportion of currencies for the international debt securities", while Euro ranks 3rd under the "basket currencies" and 2nd under the other three tertiary indicators. Britain and Chinese Mainland ranked 3rd and 4th respectively, with scores of 11.4 and 9.4, significantly higher than those of Australia, Japan and other countries, though far behind the U.S. and Eurozone.

Table 50 Ranking of Secondary Indicator for the Competitiveness of Currency: Unit of Account

Ranking	Economy	Rating	Ranking	Economy	Rating
1	USA	100	12	Hong Kong, China	0.6
2	Eurozone	62.8	13	Mexico	0.2
3	Britain	11.4	13	Korea	0.2
4	Chinese Mainland	9.4	13	Turkey	0.2
5	Australia	3.2	16	Brazil	0.1
6	Japan	2.5	16	Russia	0.1
7	South Africa	2.1	16	Indonesia	0.1
8	India	1.5	19	The United Arab Emirates	0.0

					Continued
Ranking	Economy	Rating	Ranking	Economy	Rating
9	Switzerland	1.2	19	Saudi Arabia	0.0
10	Singapore	0.9	19	Argentina	0.0
11	Canada	0.8			

2.3.1 Exchange rate anchor

Table 51 shows the ranking of currencies of various countries/regions as currency anchors according to the de facto classification of exchange rate arrangements identified by the IMF. The US Dollar and the Euro bear the main currency anchor functions internationally. Among all the countries/regions surveyed by the IMF, 38 countries/regions anchored US Dollar, 25 anchored Euro, 3 anchored Australian Dollar, 1 anchored Singapore Dollar, 3 anchored South African Rand, 2 anchored Indian rupees, and 1 tracking Euro and US Dollar basket. According to the number of currency anchoring countries, the US Dollar scored 100 and the Euro scored 66.2, far ahead of the currencies of other countries/regions.

Table 51 Ranking of Tertiary Indicator for the Competitiveness of Currency: Exchange Rate Anchor (2019)

Ranking	Economy	Rating	Ranking	Economy	Rating
1	USA	100.0	7	Hong Kong, China	0.0
2	Eurozone	66.2	7	Korea	0.0
3	Australia	7.8	7	Mexico	0.0
3	South Africa	7.8	7	Russia	0.0
5	India	5.2	7	Turkey	0.0
6	Singapore	2.6	7	Brazil	0.0
7	Chinese Mainland	0.0	7	Indonesia	0.0
7	Japan	0.0	7	Saudi Arabia	0.0
7	Britain	0.0	7	The United Arab Emirates	0.0
7	Canada	0.0	7	Argentina	0.0
7	Switzerland	0.0			

2.3.2 Basket currencies

Table 52 shows the calculated scores of various currencies as basket currencies. The US Dollar gets full marks as the most important currency anchor, RMB scored 32.4 points and ranked 2nd, exceeding Euro with a score of 29.4, and British Pound ranked 4th at a score of 17.0. Although the Japanese Yen is included in the basket currencies, the overall score of its currency anchor effect is 0, while currencies of other countries are not included in the calculation.

Table 52 Ranking of Tertiary Indicator for the Competitiveness of Currency: Basket Currencies (Oct, 2016)

Ranking	Economy	Rating	Ranking	Economy	Rating
1	USA	100.0	5	South Africa	0.0
2	Chinese Mainland	32.4	5	India	0.0
3	Eurozone	29.4	5	Mexico	0.0
4	Britain	17.0	5	Russia	0.0
5	Japan	0.0	5	Turkey	0.0
5	Australia	0.0	5	Brazil	0.0
5	Canada	0.0	5	Indonesia	0.0
5	Switzerland	0.0	5	Saudi Arabia	0.0
5	Hong Kong, China	0.0	5	The United Arab Emirates	0.0
5	Singapore	0.0	5	Argentina	0.0
5	Korea	0.0			

2.3.3 Proportion of currencies for international banking liabilities

Table 53 shows the proportion of currencies of various countries as currencies for international banking liabilities. The US Dollar and Euro stayed far ahead of the currencies of the other countries. By the fourth quarter of 2020, the international banking liabilities denominated in US Dollar had reached $14.9 trillion, accounting for 49.65%, with the highest score. The international banking liabilities denominated in Euro totaled $9.94 trillion, accounting for 33.12% at a score of 66.7. The share of RMB denominated international banking liabilities was estimated to be 2.11% with a score of 4.3, ranking 5th after the Pound and Japanese Yen.

Table 53 Ranking of Tertiary Indicator for the Competitiveness of Currency:
Proportion of Currencies for International Banking Liabilities (2020 Q4)

Ranking	Economy	Rating	Ranking	Economy	Rating
1	USA	100.0	12	Mexico	0.6
2	Eurozone	66.7	12	India	0.6
3	Britain	10.9	14	Russia	0.4
4	Japan	6.3	14	South Africa	0.4
5	Chinese Mainland	4.3	14	Turkey	0.4
6	Switzerland	3.1	14	Brazil	0.4
7	Australia	2.5	18	Indonesia	0.2
8	Canada	1.9	19	The United Arab Emirates	0.1
9	Hong Kong, China	1.3	19	Saudi Arabia	0.1
10	Korea	0.7	21	Argentina	0.0
10	Singapore	0.7			

2.3.4 Proportion of currencies for international debt securities

As seen from Table 54, the US Dollar and Euro are also the dominant currencies of international debt securities. By the fourth quarter of 2020, the US Dollar denominated international debt securities was $12.18 trillion, accounting for 45.8%, with full marks; the Euro denominated international debt securities was $10.82 trillion, accounting for 40.7%, with a score of 88.9; Sterling also gained a significant share, about 8.02%, with a score of 17.5. The proportion of RMB denominated international debt securities is still low, only 0.42%, with a score of 0.9, ranking 9th.

Table 54 Ranking of Tertiary Indicator for the Competitiveness of Currency:
the Proportion of Currencies for International Debt Securities (2020 Q4)

Ranking	Economy	Rating	Ranking	Economy	Rating
1	USA	100.0	12	Turkey	0.2
2	Eurozone	88.9	13	Russia	0.1
3	Britain	17.5	13	India	0.1
4	Japan	3.7	13	Brazil	0.1
5	Australia	2.3	13	Indonesia	0.1

					Continued
Ranking	Economy	Rating	Ranking	Economy	Rating
6	Switzerland	1.7	17	Saudi Arabia	0.0
7	Canada	1.1	17	The United Arab Emirates	0.0
8	Hong Kong, China	1.0	17	Korea	0.0
9	Chinese Mainland	0.9	17	Argentina	0.0
10	Singapore	0.3	17	South Africa	0.0
10	Mexico	0.3			

iii Sub-indicators for the competitiveness of financial infrastructure

Indicator 3.1: Hardware of the financial infrastructure

Table 58 shows the ranking of the hardware of the financial infrastructure of different countries. In terms of the hardware of the financial infrastructure, the UK ranked 1st in the world with its score significantly higher than that of Mainland China who stood at the 2nd position, indicating that the UK, as the world's oldest financial center, was second to none concerning the number of its payment and settlement services system and terminal, the number of financial institutions that use SWIFT services, and the scale of business in selected clearing centers during the year. In 2018, the scale of the British cashless payment was 42.8 times that of GDP, and the scale of cashless payment in Chinese Mainland was 41.2 times that of GDP. In comparison, the scale of cashless payment in France, Germany and the United States is 11.5, 16.6 and 4.7 times of their GDP respectively. Therefore, Chinese Mainland has obvious advantages in terms of the amount of hardware and the scale of the business realized upon the financial infrastructure and is not inferior to other developed countries in Europe and America other than Britain.

Table 58 Ranking of Secondary Indicator of the Competitiveness of Financial Infrastructure: Hardware of the Financial Infrastructure

Ranking	Economy	Rating	Ranking	Economy	Rating
1	Britain	62.0	15	Portugal	19.9
2	Chinese Mainland	34.6	15	Greece	19.9
3	Hong Kong, China	33.3	15	Luxembourg	19.9
4	USA	32.5	15	Austria	19.9
5	Belgium	31.4	21	Japan	19.3
6	Switzerland	28.7	22	Canada	17.8
7	Korea	26.7	23	Spain	15.9
8	Germany	24.9	24	Russia	15.4
9	Singapore	24.1	25	Turkey	10.8
10	Netherlands	24.0	26	Saudi Arabia	10.5
11	France	23.5	27	Mexico	7.2
12	Australia	22.1	28	South Africa	6.6
13	Italy	21.3	29	Argentina	5.3
14	Brazil	20.2	30	India	2.1
15	Ireland	19.9	31	Indonesia	1.0
15	Finland	19.9	32	The United Arab Emirates	0.2

3.1.1 Number of institutions for payment services (per million residents)

Table 59 Ranking of Tertiary Indicator for the Hardware of Financial Infrastructure: Number of Institutions for Payment Services

Ranking	Economy	Rating	Ranking	Economy	Rating
1	Korea	100.0	17	India	1.1
2	Switzerland	41.8	18	Turkey	1.0
3	Singapore	39.4	19	Saudi Arabia	0.4
4	Hong Kong, China	34.1	20	South Africa	0.1
5	Russia	29.6	21	Indonesia	0.0

Continued

Ranking	Economy	Rating	Ranking	Economy	Rating
6	Germany	27.2	N/A	Britain	N/A
7	Canada	23.4	N/A	The United Arab Emirates	N/A
8	Belgium	12.5	N/A	USA	N/A
9	Italy	11.9	N/A	Australia	N/A
10	France	10.5	N/A	Ireland	N/A
11	Spain	7.2	N/A	Austria	N/A
12	Netherlands	7.0	N/A	Finland	N/A
13	Brazil	6.9	N/A	Portugal	N/A
14	China	4.2	N/A	Japan	N/A
15	Mexico	2.5	N/A	Greece	N/A
16	Argentina	2.0	N/A	Luxembourg	N/A

Note: the number is the standardized value of institutions providing payment services, with the original data from BIS. Many values are missing in terms of the hardware of the financial infrastructure. If a single indicator in a country or region is missing, the average weight of the values for the remaining indicator will be taken for the ranking. If all indicators in the country or region are missing, the average weight will be taken for ranking after supplementing them according to the average value of each indicator. The reason why this method, instead of the missing value processing method of similar indicators related to the competitiveness of the financial industry is taken mainly due to the large differences between countries of various indicators. If the average value of the front and rear ranking is taken after ranking based on an indicator (such as financial infrastructure software), it is possible to significantly overestimate/underestimate the value of the indicators to be filled. In comparison, it is smoother to take the overall average value. The same method will be applied for the below.

3.1.2 Proportion of cashless payment in GDP (%)

Table 60　Ranking of Tertiary Indicator for the Hardware of Financial Infrastructure: Proportion of Cashless Payment in GDP

Ranking	Economy	Rating	Ranking	Economy	Rating
1	Britain	100.0	17	Canada	3.7
2	Chinese Mainland	96.1	18	Singapore	1.5
3	Netherlands	56.9	19	Argentina	0.6
4	Saudi Arabia	37.3	20	Indonesia	0.2
5	Germany	35.9	21	India	0.0
6	Belgium	34.1	N/A	Hong Kong, China	N/A
7	Korea	29.2	N/A	The United Arab Emirates	N/A
8	Mexico	28.7	N/A	Ireland	N/A
9	France	23.6	N/A	Austria	N/A
10	Spain	17.5	N/A	Turkey	N/A
11	Brazil	14.7	N/A	Switzerland	N/A
12	Russia	14.1	N/A	Finland	N/A
13	South Africa	11.1	N/A	Portugal	N/A
13	Australia	11.1	N/A	Japan	N/A
15	Italy	7.6	N/A	Greece	N/A
16	USA	6.7	N/A	Luxembourg	N/A

3.1.3 Number of terminals (per resident)

Table 61　Ranking of Tertiary Indicator for the Hardware of Financial Infrastructure: Number of Terminals

Ranking	Economy	Rating	Ranking	Economy	Rating
1	Italy	100.0	17	Saudi Arabia	18.0
2	Singapore	92.0	18	South Africa	10.0
3	Britain	78.0	18	Mexico	10.0
3	Brazil	78.0	20	Indonesia	2.0

Continued

Ranking	Economy	Rating	Ranking	Economy	Rating
5	Switzerland	76.0	21	India	0.0
6	Australia	74.0	N/A	Hong Kong, China	N/A
6	Canada	74.0	N/A	The United Arab Emirates	N/A
8	Spain	66.0	N/A	Korea	N/A
9	Turkey	54.0	N/A	USA	N/A
9	Netherlands	54.0	N/A	Ireland	N/A
11	France	52.0	N/A	Austria	N/A
12	Chinese Mainland	44.0	N/A	Finland	N/A
13	Belgium	34.0	N/A	Portugal	N/A
14	Russia	32.0	N/A	Japan	N/A
15	Argentina	30.0	N/A	Greece	N/A
16	Germany	24.0	N/A	Luxembourg	N/A

3.1.4 Proportion of payment transactions processed by the selected payment system in GDP (%)

Table 62　Ranking of Tertiary Indicator for the Hardware of Financial Infrastructure: the Proportion of Payment Transactions Processed by the Selected Payment System in GDP

Ranking	Economy	Rating	Ranking	Economy	Rating
1	Hong Kong, China	100.0	17	Saudi Arabia	6.0
2	Japan	36.6	18	Russia	5.6
3	Netherlands	34.2	19	Spain	5.4
4	Germany	26.1	20	Mexico	3.7
5	Korea	25.3	21	Argentina	3.5
6	Brazil	23.7	22	Italy	3.4
7	USA	23.4	23	India	2.7
8	Switzerland	23.0	24	Indonesia	2.5
9	Chinese Mainland	22.7	25	Belgium	0.0

Ranking	Economy	Rating	Ranking	Economy	Rating
					Continued
10	Singapore	20.7	N/A	Ireland	N/A
11	Britain	17.0	N/A	Austria	N/A
12	France	15.3	N/A	Finland	N/A
13	South Africa	10.7	N/A	Portugal	N/A
14	Australia	10.6	N/A	Japan	N/A
15	Canada	9.4	N/A	Greece	N/A
16	Turkey	8.5	N/A	Luxembourg	N/A

3.1.5 Number of domestic institutions using SWIFT

Table 63　Ranking of Tertiary Indicators for the Hardware of Financial Infrastructure: Number of Domestic Institutions Using SWIFT

Ranking	Economy	Rating	Ranking	Economy	Rating
1	USA	100.0	17	India	5.9
2	Britain	65.2	18	Canada	5.7
3	France	45.7	19	Korea	5.1
4	Germany	43.5	20	Brazil	4.6
5	Chinese Mainland	40.2	21	Indonesia	2.3
6	Switzerland	27.0	22	Saudi Arabia	1.2
7	Russia	25.0	23	Turkey	0.8
8	Japan	19.3	24	Mexico	0.3
9	Hong Kong, China	18.7	25	Argentina	0.0
10	Italy	16.5	N/A	The United Arab Emirates	N/A
11	Singapore	14.6	N/A	Ireland	N/A
12	Spain	12.7	N/A	Austria	N/A
13	Netherlands	10.9	N/A	Finland	N/A
14	Belgium	7.9	N/A	Portugal	N/A
15	Australia	7.4	N/A	Greece	N/A
16	South Africa	6.6	N/A	Luxembourg	N/A

3.1.6 Proportion of clearing amount of selected central counterparties and clearing houses in GDP (%)

Table 64   Ranking of Tertiary Indicator for the Hardware of Financial
Infrastructure: the Proportion of Clearing Amount of Selected Central
Counterparties and Clearing Houses in GDP

Ranking	Economy	Rating	Ranking	Economy	Rating
1	Britain	100.0	16	Spain	0.4
2	USA	30.4	18	Singapore	0.1
3	Japan	17.4	18	Korea	0.1
4	Germany	15.9	20	Mexico	0.0
5	France	13.5	20	Indonesia	0.0
6	Hong Kong, China	11.8	N/A	The United Arab Emirates	N/A
7	Australia	7.6	N/A	Ireland	N/A
8	Italy	5.4	N/A	Belgium	N/A
9	Brazil	4.5	N/A	Chinese Mainland	N/A
10	Netherlands	4.3	N/A	Austria	N/A
11	India	4.0	N/A	Saudi Arabia	N/A
12	Switzerland	3.5	N/A	South Africa	N/A
13	Canada	1.8	N/A	Finland	N/A
14	Russia	1.2	N/A	Portugal	N/A
15	Turkey	0.5	N/A	Greece	N/A
16	Argentina	0.4	N/A	Luxembourg	N/A

3.1.7 Proportion of orders delivered by selected central securities depository institutions in GDP (%)

Table 65   Ranking of Tertiary Indicators for the Hardware of Financial
Infrastructure: the Proportion of Orders Delivered by Selected Central
Securities Depository Institutions in GDP

Ranking	Economy	Rating	Ranking	Economy	Rating
1	Belgium	100.0	16	Chinese Mainland	0.6
2	Britain	12.0	16	Netherlands	0.6

Continued

Ranking	Economy	Rating	Ranking	Economy	Rating
3	Brazil	9.4	19	Russia	0.4
4	Canada	6.4	19	Singapore	0.4
5	Mexico	5.3	21	Korea	0.3
6	Italy	4.6	21	Turkey	0.3
7	Japan	4.0	23	Indonesia	0.1
8	France	3.9	24	Saudi Arabia	0.0
9	Spain	2.2	N/A	The United Arab Emirates	N/A
10	Hong Kong, China	1.8	N/A	Australia	N/A
10	USA	1.8	N/A	Ireland	N/A
12	Germany	1.7	N/A	Austria	N/A
13	India	1.1	N/A	Finland	N/A
14	Switzerland	0.9	N/A	Portugal	N/A
15	South Africa	0.8	N/A	Greece	N/A
16	Argentina	0.6	N/A	Luxembourg	N/A

Indicator 3.2: Software of the financial infrastructure

Table 66 shows the ranking of the software of the financial infrastructure in various countries. In terms of the software of the financial infrastructure, Singapore ranked 1st. According to the sub-indicators of the business environment released by the World Bank, Singapore ranked 1st in the world in terms of the indicators for investor protection and contract enforcement, in addition to the highest score for the application of IFRS, indicating that the sound financial laws and regulations system in Singapore has laid the foundation for its superior software of the financial infrastructure. Singapore is followed by Hong Kong, China and Britain, both of which use the maritime law system. Comparatively, Chinese Mainland lagged concerning the indicators for the software of the financial infrastructure, ranking 23rd with a score of 52.3, 41.5 points lower than that of Singapore that ranked 1st, and lower than most North American and Western European countries as well, a piece of evidence that there is great potential for Chinese Mainland to improve its software of the financial infrastructure. Due to many variables in the business environment among recent years, the United States ranked 12th when it comes to the indicator for investor protection. At the same time, due to the low application of International Financial Reporting Standards, IFRS, the overall financial infrastructure software ranked 12th, out of the top 10. However, in terms of the indicator for credit access, the United States comes the 1st, clearly showcasing that the overall corporate financing environment in the United States is relatively favorable.

Table 66 Ranking of Secondary Indicator for the Competitiveness of Financial Infrastructure: Software of the Financial Infrastructure

Ranking	Economy	Rating	Ranking	Economy	Rating
1	Singapore	93.8	17	Germany	61.2
2	Hong Kong, China	83.5	18	France	58.8
3	Britain	83.2	19	Belgium	58.1
4	The United Arab Emirates	83.1	20	Brazil	57.5
5	Korea	73.7	21	Argentina	53.7
6	Australia	73.2	22	Finland	53.6
7	Ireland	72.7	23	Chinese Mainland	52.3
8	Canada	71.3	24	Portugal	49.8
9	Turkey	70.9	25	Switzerland	49.7
10	Saudi Arabia	69.6	26	Japan	48.6
11	South Africa	69.0	27	Italy	44.0
12	USA	66.9	28	Greece	43.9
13	Russia	66.0	29	Netherlands	42.4
14	Mexico	63.3	30	India	41.1
15	Spain	63.2	31	Luxembourg	38.0
16	Austria	62.9	32	Indonesia	35.6

Global Financial Competitiveness Report 2021 215

3.2.1 Access to credit

Table 67   Ranking of Tertiary Indicator for the Competitiveness of the Software of Financial Infrastructure: Access to Credit

Ranking	Economy	Rating	Ranking	Economy	Rating
1	USA	100.0	15	Switzerland	62.5
1	Australia	100.0	18	Chinese Mainland	56.3
3	Mexico	93.8	18	Finland	56.3
4	Canada	87.5	18	Saudi Arabia	56.3
5	India	81.3	18	South Africa	56.3
5	Russia	81.3	18	Spain	56.3
7	Hong Kong, China	75.0	24	Austria	50.0
7	Singapore	75.0	24	Japan	50.0
7	Turkey	75.0	26	Argentina	43.8
7	Britain	75.0	26	Brazil	43.8
11	Germany	68.8	26	France	43.8
11	Indonesia	68.8	29	Greece	37.5
11	Ireland	68.8	29	Italy	37.5
11	The United Arab Emirates	68.8	29	Netherlands	37.5
15	Belgium	62.5	29	Portugal	37.5
15	Korea	62.5	32	Luxembourg	0.0

Note: The data are standardized with the original from the sub-indicators of the World Bank's Business Environment Indicator. The same below.

3.2.2 Investor protection

Table 68   Ranking of Tertiary Indicator for the Competitiveness of the Software of Financial Infrastructure: Investor Protection

Ranking	Economy	Rating	Ranking	Economy	Rating
1	Singapore	100.0	15	Indonesia	55.6
1	Saudi Arabia	100.0	18	Belgium	50.0

Continued

Ranking	Economy	Rating	Ranking	Economy	Rating
3	Canada	94.4	18	France	50.0
3	Hong Kong, China	94.4	20	Italy	44.4
3	Britain	94.4	21	Australia	38.9
6	India	83.3	21	Japan	38.9
6	Ireland	83.3	23	Argentina	33.3
6	South Africa	83.3	23	Brazil	33.3
6	The United Arab Emirates	83.3	23	Finland	33.3
10	Turkey	72.2	23	Germany	33.3
11	Korea	66.7	23	Mexico	33.3
12	Chinese Mainland	61.1	23	Portugal	33.3
12	Spain	61.1	29	Russia	27.8
14	USA	60.0	30	Netherlands	22.2
15	Austria	55.6	31	Luxembourg	11.1
15	Greece	55.6	32	Switzerland	0.0

3.2.3 Contract enforcement

Table 69 Ranking of Tertiary Indicator for the Competitiveness of the Software of Financial Infrastructure: Contract Enforcement

Ranking	Economy	Rating	Ranking	Economy	Rating
1	Singapore	100.0	17	Mexico	59.6
2	Korea	99.1	18	Finland	58.2
3	Chinese Mainland	91.7	19	Japan	55.7
4	Australia	87.3	19	Saudi Arabia	55.7
5	The United Arab Emirates	80.1	21	Belgium	53.3
6	Austria	79.2	22	Brazil	52.9
7	Germany	76.0	22	Switzerland	52.9
8	France	74.6	24	Netherlands	43.2

					Continued
Ranking	Economy	Rating	Ranking	Economy	Rating
9	USA	74.4	25	Ireland	38.6
10	Luxembourg	74.1	26	Argentina	37.6
11	Russia	71.6	27	Canada	36.7
12	Turkey	69.7	28	South Africa	36.3
13	Spain	68.6	29	Italy	27.5
14	Hong Kong, China	64.4	30	Indonesia	18.2
15	Britain	63.5	31	Greece	15.9
16	Portugal	61.7	32	India	0.0

3.2.4 Application of IFRS

Table 70　Ranking of Tertiary Indicator for the Competitiveness of the Software of Financial Infrastructure: Application of IFRS

Ranking	Economy	Rating	Ranking	Economy	Rating
1	Britain	100.0	11	Germany	66.7
1	Hong Kong, China	100.0	11	Greece	66.7
1	Singapore	100.0	11	Italy	66.7
1	Ireland	100.0	11	Korea	66.7
1	Brazil	100.0	11	Luxembourg	66.7
1	South Africa	100.0	11	Mexico	66.7
1	The United Arab Emirates	100.0	11	Netherlands	66.7
1	Argentina	100.0	11	Portugal	66.7
9	Russia	83.3	11	Saudi Arabia	66.7
9	Switzerland	83.3	11	Spain	66.7
11	Australia	66.7	11	Turkey	66.7
11	Austria	66.7	28	Japan	50.0
11	Belgium	66.7	29	USA	33.3
11	Canada	66.7	30	Chinese Mainland	0.0
11	Finland	66.7	30	India	0.0
11	France	66.7	30	Indonesia	0.0

iv Sub-indicators for the competitiveness of financial technology

Indicator 4.1: Computing power

The indicator for computing power measures the computing power of the financial technology in various countries and shows the strength of their technical foundation. The table below reflects the ranking of the 32 countries in terms of computing power. The US ranks 1st in the world, followed by Chinese Mainland and Japan at the 2nd and the 3rd position, with the 4th to 10th going to Germany, Britain, Netherlands, France, Ireland, Canada and Italy. Among the 32 samples, the score for the United States, who ranked 1st, was set as 100 points, and the top ten countries were all found above the pass line by 60 points, with Chinese Mainland's computing power (84.2 points) being second only to that of the United States. The United States has been leading the world for a long time upon its scientific and technological strength, while China, as a developing country, has been catching up at a considerable speed in basic science and technology. Compared with the United States, China has a small gap in computing power (see table 72), while there is still a noticeable gap in computing efficiency, and especially in application and infrastructure support (see table 73, table 74 and table 75), which calls for further improvement.

Table 71 Ranking of Secondary Indicator for the Competitiveness of Financial Technology: Computing Power

Ranking	Economy	Rating	Ranking	Economy	Rating
1	USA	100.0	17	The United Arab Emirates	42.2
2	Chinese Mainland	84.2	17	South Africa	42.2
3	Japan	73.1	19	Finland	41.9
4	Germany	70.4	20	Brazil	41.4
5	Britain	65.3	21	Russia	39.1
6	Netherlands	65.1	22	Austria	34.2
7	France	64.9	23	Hong Kong, China	31.2

					Continued
Ranking	Economy	Rating	Ranking	Economy	Rating
8	Ireland	62.9	24	Spain	29.2
9	Canada	61.6	25	Luxembourg	24.1
10	Italy	60.2	26	Indonesia	18.1
11	Saudi Arabia	58.9	27	Argentina	15.1
12	Australia	57.5	28	Portugal	12.1
13	Singapore	43.6	29	Greece	9.1
14	Switzerland	43.3	30	Belgium	6.0
15	Korea	42.9	31	Turkey	3.0
16	India	42.6	32	Mexico	0.0

4.1.1 Computing power

Table 72　Ranking of Tertiary Indicator for the Competitiveness of Financial Technology: Computing Power

Ranking	Economy	Rating	Ranking	Economy	Rating
1	USA	100.0	17	India	44.2
2	Chinese Mainland	91.9	18	The United Arab Emirates	43.4
3	Japan	63.5	19	Finland	42.7
3	Germany	63.5	20	South Africa	41.9
5	Britain	58.1	21	Russia	40.5
6	Netherlands	57.4	22	Austria	37.2
7	France	56.8	23	Hong Kong, China	33.8
8	Ireland	56.0	24	Spain	32.1
9	Canada	55.1	25	Luxembourg	27.0
10	Italy	54.3	26	Indonesia	20.3
11	Saudi Arabia	53.5	27	Argentina	16.9
12	Australia	52.7	28	Portugal	13.5
13	Brazil	47.3	29	Greece	10.1
14	Singapore	46.5	30	Belgium	6.8

					Continued
Ranking	Economy	Rating	Ranking	Economy	Rating
15	Switzerland	45.7	31	Turkey	3.4
16	Korea	45.0	32	Mexico	0.0

4.1.2 Computing efficiency

Table 73　Ranking of Tertiary Indicator for the Competitiveness of Financial Technology: Computing Efficiency

Ranking	Economy	Rating	Ranking	Economy	Rating
1	USA	100.0	17	Korea	61.0
2	Japan	84.1	18	India	60.8
3	Germany	82.5	19	Finland	60.5
4	Chinese Mainland	81.0	20	The United Arab Emirates	60.3
5	Britain	77.8	21	South Africa	55.6
6	Netherlands	77.0	22	Austria	51.1
7	France	76.2	23	Hong Kong, China	46.4
8	Ireland	74.9	24	Spain	44.1
9	Canada	73.7	25	Luxembourg	37.2
10	Italy	72.4	26	Indonesia	27.9
11	Saudi Arabia	71.1	27	Argentina	23.2
12	Australia	69.8	28	Portugal	18.6
13	Russia	61.9	29	Greece	13.9
14	Brazil	61.7	30	Belgium	9.3
15	Singapore	61.4	31	Turkey	4.6
16	Switzerland	61.2	32	Mexico	0.0

4.1.3 Application

Table 74   Ranking of Tertiary Indicator for the Competitiveness of Financial Technology: Application

Ranking	Economy	Rating	Ranking	Economy	Rating
1	USA	100.0	17	Korea	36.0
2	Japan	83.5	18	India	35.8
3	Chinese Mainland	82.3	19	Finland	35.6
4	Germany	78.5	20	South Africa	35.4
5	France	73.4	21	Russia	25.3
6	Netherlands	72.2	22	Austria	23.4
7	Britain	70.9	23	Hong Kong, China	21.4
8	Ireland	69.6	24	Spain	19.5
9	Canada	68.4	25	Luxembourg	15.6
10	Italy	67.1	26	Indonesia	11.7
11	Saudi Arabia	65.8	27	Argentina	9.7
12	Australia	64.6	28	Portugal	7.8
13	The United Arab Emirates	36.7	29	Greece	5.9
14	Brazil	36.5	30	Belgium	3.9
15	Singapore	36.3	31	Turkey	2.0
16	Switzerland	36.2	32	Mexico	0.0

4.1.4 Infrastructure support

Table 75   Ranking of Tertiary Indicator for the Competitiveness of Financial Technology: Infrastructure Support

Ranking	Economy	Rating	Ranking	Economy	Rating
1	USA	100.0	17	Korea	29.1
2	Chinese Mainland	81.8	18	India	29.0
3	Japan	61.0	19	Finland	28.8
4	Germany	57.1	20	Russia	28.6

					Continued
Ranking	Economy	Rating	Ranking	Economy	Rating
5	Britain	54.6	21	South Africa	27.3
6	Netherlands	53.9	22	Austria	25.2
7	France	53.3	23	Hong Kong, China	23.1
8	Ireland	51.2	24	Spain	21.0
9	Canada	49.1	25	Luxembourg	16.8
10	Italy	47.0	26	Indonesia	12.6
11	Saudi Arabia	44.9	27	Argentina	10.5
12	Australia	42.9	28	Portugal	8.4
13	The United Arab Emirates	29.9	29	Greece	6.3
14	Brazil	29.7	30	Belgium	4.2
15	Singapore	29.5	31	Turkey	2.1
16	Switzerland	29.3	32	Mexico	0.0

Indicator 4.2: User access

The indicator for the user access measures the popularity and user base of the financial technology in various countries, with the ratio of the number of people connected to the financial technology in various countries to all potential users in the financial technology industry to show the current user access of the financial technology industry in various countries. Table 76 reflects the ranking of 32 countries in terms of digital financial user access (the users access in the field of financial technology). Canada, Netherlands, Germany, Luxembourg and Finland topped the list jointly. Countries with high access include Belgium, Switzerland, Australia, Britain, Austria, Japan, Ireland, Korea and France.

The U.S. ranked 15th concerning user access, and Chinese Mainland ranked 26th. The United States saw the accumulated high popularity of credit card payment thanks to its very early development. Due to the habit of payment through credit cards, the United States experienced low access in digital financial access. As a developing country and large economy that has just completed the task of poverty alleviation, China is still facing the problem of unbalanced and insufficient development. As an emerging form and means of business, the popularity of financial technology needs to be improved, on the condition of the very competitive potential users.

Table 76　Ranking of Secondary Indicator for the Competitiveness of Financial Technology: User Access

Ranking	Economy	Rating	Ranking	Economy	Rating
1	Canada	100.0	16	Spain	88.4
1	Netherlands	100.0	16	Italy	88.4
1	Germany	100.0	19	Portugal	82.6
1	Luxembourg	100.0	20	Hong Kong, China	81.2
1	Finland	100.0	21	The United Arab Emirates	79.7
6	Belgium	98.6	22	Greece	65.2
7	Switzerland	97.1	23	Russia	60.9
7	Australia	97.1	24	Chinese Mainland	56.5
7	Britain	97.1	25	Turkey	50.7
7	Austria	97.1	26	Saudi Arabia	46.4
11	Japan	95.7	27	South Africa	44.9
12	Ireland	94.2	28	Brazil	42.0
13	Korea	91.3	29	Argentina	15.9
13	France	91.3	30	Indonesia	8.7
15	USA	89.9	31	Mexico	4.4
16	Singapore	88.4	32	India	0.0

Indicator 4.3: The potential of the industry

The indicator for the potential of the industry measures the future development of the financial technology industry in various countries upon the development of the terminal industry in the financial technology industry. The two key factors determining the development potential of an industry are the input of labor and capital. Based on this, this report selects the recruitment and reserve of AI talents in various countries (see table 78) to reflect the labor input in the financial technology industry, and uses the financial technology credit of various countries (see table 79) to illustrate the capital input in the financial technology industry.

Table 77 shows the ranking of 32 countries in terms of the development potential of the financial technology industry. The United States ranked 1st in the world, Hong Kong China, ranks 6th and Chinese Mainland 18th. The United States has always maintained a leading position in the world in terms of investment and financing efficiency of emerging industries and high-tech talent reserve, so there is a huge potential for the development of its financial technology industry, comparatively, China's reserve of high-tech professionals, especially high-tech engineers, is still insufficient. The industrial investment and financing efficiency of China's capital market also represents an ability that needs urgently to be improved for better financial services for the entities.

It should be noted that Italy showed its great strength of credit in the field of financial technology as a traditional financial power, with Florence of Italy as one of the earliest financial centers in Europe. It has been playing a leading role in trade and finance for a long time in history and its traditional advantages and historical heritage in the financial field still remain dynamic despite the impact of the European debt crisis, so facing the emerging industry of financial technology, Italy managed to seize this new industrial development opportunity at least concerning the credit. In addition, due to the great reserve of professionals in the high-end manufacturing industry, the indicator for AI recruitment is also relatively high for Italy according to the manner adopted for statistics. Therefore, the power of Italy in financial service and talent service in the financial technology industry cannot be underestimated although there is the possibility that the potential of the financial technology industry of Italy may be exaggerated due to the availability of data and the selection of indicators.

Table 77   Ranking of Secondary Indicator for the Competitiveness of Financial Technology: Potential of the Industry

Ranking	Economy	Rating	Ranking	Economy	Rating
1	USA	82.4	17	Switzerland	18.7
2	Italy	65.8	18	Argentina	16.1
3	The United Arab Emirates	48.5	18	Chinese Mainland	16.1
4	Singapore	41.1	20	Austria	15.6

Continued

Ranking	Economy	Rating	Ranking	Economy	Rating
5	Canada	39.7	21	South Africa	14.3
6	Hong Kong, China	37.5	22	Russia	13.5
7	India	36.6	23	Belgium	12.3
8	Germany	35.9	23	Turkey	12.3
9	Brazil	35.2	25	Luxembourg	11.8
10	Australia	32.1	26	Portugal	10.9
11	Britain	30.7	27	Mexico	10.8
12	Korea	29.3	28	Ireland	10.5
13	Netherlands	29.0	29	Spain	9.0
14	France	28.7	30	Greece	5.6
15	Japan	27.8	31	Indonesia	4.9
16	Finland	23.9	32	Saudi Arabia	2.2

4.3.1 Indicator for AI recruitment

Table 78   Ranking of Tertiary Indicator of the Competitiveness of Financial Technology: Indicator for AI Recruitment

Ranking	Economy	Rating	Ranking	Economy	Rating
1	Singapore	78.6	17	The United Arab Emirates	30.3
2	Canada	77.5	18	Chinese Mainland	29.4
3	Hong Kong, China	75.0	19	South Africa	28.0
4	Germany	67.2	20	Argentina	26.9
5	India	66.8	21	Turkey	24.4
6	Brazil	65.6	22	Belgium	23.6
7	USA	64.7	22	Luxembourg	23.6
8	Australia	62.2	24	Korea	23.4
9	Britain	60.6	25	Russia	22.3
10	France	50.6	26	Portugal	21.7
11	Finland	45.3	27	Mexico	21.4

					Continued
Ranking	Economy	Rating	Ranking	Economy	Rating
12	Japan	43.2	28	Ireland	20.0
13	Italy	40.8	29	Spain	17.6
14	Netherlands	32.7	30	Greece	11.1
15	Austria	31.2	31	Indonesia	7.3
16	Switzerland	30.4	32	Saudi Arabia	0.0

4.3.2 Credit of the financial technology

Table 79　Ranking of Tertiary Indicator for the Competitiveness of Financial Technology: Credit of the Financial Technology

Ranking	Economy	Rating	Ranking	Economy	Rating
1	USA	100.0	17	Indonesia	2.5
2	Italy	90.8	17	Finland	2.5
3	The United Arab Emirates	66.7	19	Australia	1.9
4	Korea	35.3	20	Canada	1.8
5	Netherlands	25.2	21	Belgium	1.1
6	Japan	12.4	22	Ireland	1.0
7	Switzerland	6.9	23	Britain	0.9
7	France	6.9	24	South Africa	0.5
9	India	6.5	25	Spain	0.3
10	Argentina	5.3	26	Mexico	0.2
11	Brazil	4.9	26	Turkey	0.2
12	Russia	4.7	28	Luxembourg	0.0
13	Germany	4.5	28	Portugal	0.0
14	Saudi Arabia	4.4	28	Hong Kong, China	0.0
15	Singapore	3.6	28	Austria	0.0
16	Chinese Mainland	2.7	28	Greece	0.0

v. Sub-indicators for the competitiveness in international financial governance

Table 80, Table 83 and Table 86 show the ranking in terms of the three secondary indicators for the competitiveness in international financial governance.

Indicator 5.1: Competitiveness of global financial organizations

Table 80   Ranking of Secondary Indicator for the Competitiveness in International Financial Governance: Competitiveness of Global Economic and Financial Organizations

Ranking	Economy	Rating	Ranking	Economy	Rating
1	USA	100.0	17	Austria	40.8
2	Japan	64.3	18	Ireland	39.9
3	Germany	56.6	19	Finland	39.8
4	Britain	52.8	20	Portugal	39.4
5	France	52.7	21	Greece	39.2
6	Italy	48.5	22	India	33.6
7	Canada	47.3	23	Russia	33.0
8	Spain	45.2	24	Saudi Arabia	32.1
9	Korea	44.6	25	Brazil	31.6
10	Mexico	44.3	26	Indonesia	27.9
11	Netherlands	43.9	27	Argentina	27.6
12	Australia	43.5	28	Singapore	26.6
13	Belgium	42.9	29	Luxembourg	13.6
14	Switzerland	42.8	30	South Africa	2.1
15	Chinese Mainland	42.2	31	The United Arab Emirates	1.1
16	Turkey	42.0	32	Hong Kong, China	0.0

As can be seen from Table 80, among the secondary indicators for the competitiveness of global economic and financial organizations, those of developed countries are more prominent. Among them, the United States ranked 1st with a full mark at 100, which shows the strong voice of the United States in global economic and financial organizations. Chinese Mainland and India, as representatives of developing countries, merely ranked 15th and 22nd in this regard. It is worth mentioning that Mexico ranked 10th with a score of 44.31, not only higher than Chinese Mainland, but higher than the traditional developed country Australia. Mexico ranked higher than Chinese Mainland because Chinese Mainland only has three seats in the four largest global economic and financial organizations. Mexico stayed ahead of Australia in that Mexico is stronger concerning its foreign trade and international reserves than those of Australia, although the two countries remain a Roland for an Oliver when it comes to the scale of GDP, and these three perspectives are the main basis for the allocation of shares by global financial organizations. Therefore, Mexico ranked slightly higher than Australia.

From the perspective of the competitiveness of global economic and financial organizations, international financial governance is yet to go from the hegemonic model to the real multilateral model, which is manifested in that global economic and financial organizations are still controlled by the developed countries, and there is still a large gap between the voice of emerging and developing countries in international financial affairs and their economic scale. This shows that significant progress has yet to be made in the series of reforms of the international financial governance system after the 2008 financial crisis and the emerging and developing countries saw the limited promotion of their voice in formal international economic and financial organizations.

5.1.1 Membership of global economic and financial organizations

Table 81　　Ranking of Tertiary Indicator for the Competitiveness in
International Financial Governance: Membership of Global Economic
and Financial Organizations

Ranking	Economy	Rating	Ranking	Economy	Rating
1	USA	100.0	17	Brazil	31.6
2	Japan	57.5	18	Switzerland	31.6
3	Germany	48.5	19	Belgium	31.3
4	Britain	43.6	20	Turkey	30.8
5	France	43.3	21	Austria	29.1
6	Chinese Mainland	42.1	22	Ireland	28.1

Continued

Ranking	Economy	Rating	Ranking	Economy	Rating
7	Italy	38.4	23	Finland	28.0
8	Canada	36.9	24	Indonesia	27.9
9	Spain	34.5	25	Argentina	27.6
10	Korea	34.1	26	Portugal	27.5
11	India	33.6	27	Greece	27.3
12	Mexico	33.4	28	Singapore	26.6
13	Russia	32.9	29	South Africa	2.0
14	Australia	32.9	30	Luxembourg	1.5
15	Netherlands	32.1	31	The United Arab Emirates	1.1
16	Saudi Arabia	32.0	32	Hong Kong, China	0.0

5.1.2 Voting weight in global economic and financial organizations

Table 82   Ranking of Tertiary Indicator for the Competitiveness in International Financial Governance: Voting Weight in Global Economic and Financial Organizations

Ranking	Economy	Rating	Ranking	Economy	Rating
1	USA	100.0	17	Ireland	51.6
2	Japan	71.1	18	Finland	51.5
3	Germany	64.8	19	Portugal	51.2
4	France	62.1	20	Greece	51.1
5	Britain	62.1	21	Chinese Mainland	42.2
6	Italy	58.6	22	India	33.6
7	Canada	57.7	23	Russia	33.0
8	Spain	55.9	24	Saudi Arabia	32.1
9	Netherlands	55.8	25	Brazil	31.7
10	Mexico	55.2	26	Indonesia	27.9
11	Korea	55.1	27	Argentina	27.7
12	Belgium	54.4	28	Singapore	26.7
13	Australia	54.2	29	Luxembourg	25.7
14	Switzerland	53.9	30	South Africa	2.1

Continued

Ranking	Economy	Rating	Ranking	Economy	Rating
15	Turkey	53.2	31	The United Arab Emirates	1.2
16	Austria	52.4	32	Hong Kong, China	0.0

Taking the IMF as an example, this paper analyzes the reasons why the reform of formal international organizations turned out difficult. The IMF adopts a weighted voting system, that is, the voting right is consisted of basic voting rights and share voting right. Among them, the basic voting rights and are evenly distributed among the Member States upon the principle of equality of its sovereign nations. However, with the repeated capital increase of IMF and the continuous accession of new members, the basic voting rights are gradually diluted and give way to share-based voting rights. The fund share is determined according to multiple factors such as the gross national income, economic openness, economic volatility, international reserves of a country, which is basically linked to the economic strength of a country. With the development of financial globalization, developing countries are growing strongerinto big powers. The 2008 international financial crisis has significantly enhanced the economic strength of emerging markets and developing countries and made them the locomotive for the recovery of the world economy. However, their membership in the IMF has been greatly underestimated and seriously underrepresented. In October 2010, the membership share of the United States in the International Monetary Fund was 17.09%, with a voting weight of 16.74%; and the share of Japanese is 6.12%, with the voting weight of 6.01%, while the share of Chinese Mainland is only 3.72%, with the voting weight of 3.65%. After a long period of reforms, by the end of 2020, the share of the Chinese Mainland was increased to 6.41%, and the voting weight to 6.08%, but with the membership share of Japan increased slightly to 6.48%, and the voting weight to 6.12%. The voting weight of the United States decreased slightly to 16.51%, while the membership shares of it increased to 17.51%, which helped keep the absolute competitiveness of the United States under the "one vote veto" (that is, more than 85% of the voting power) system, in addition to the maintenance of the competitiveness of developed countries such as Japan.

Indicator 5.2: Competitiveness over the informal coordination platforms

As can be seen from Table 83, among the secondary indicator for the competitiveness of the informal coordination platforms, the strength of all countries is relatively average, with that of the major developed countries staying in the first echelon. Emerging developing countries are divided, with BRICS countries like Brazil and Russia taking the lead in becoming unequally competitive in the informal coordination platform with those developed countries, while Chinese Mainland and India, also as the BRICS members, staying in the second echelon, largely due to the reason that they are merely special participants but not permanent members of the Paris Club.

Table 83   Ranking of Secondary Indicator for the Competitiveness in International Financial Governance: the Competitiveness over Informal Coordination Platform

Ranking	Economy	Rating	Ranking	Economy	Rating
1	Australia	100.0	12	Netherlands	66.7
1	Brazil	100.0	12	Saudi Arabia	66.7
1	Canada	100.0	12	South Africa	66.7
1	France	100.0	12	Spain	66.7
1	Germany	100.0	12	Switzerland	66.7
1	Italy	100.0	12	Turkey	66.7
1	Japan	100.0	23	Austria	33.3
1	Korea	100.0	23	Belgium	33.3
1	Russia	100.0	23	Finland	33.3
1	Britain	100.0	23	Hong Kong, China	33.3
1	USA	100.0	23	Ireland	33.3
12	Argentina	66.7	23	Singapore	33.3
12	Chinese Mainland	66.7	29	Greece	0.0
12	India	66.7	30	Luxembourg	0.0
12	Indonesia	66.7	31	Portugal	0.0
12	Mexico	66.7	32	The United Arab Emirates	0.0

5.2.1 Membership of informal coordination platform

Table 84　Ranking of Tertiary Indicator for the Competitiveness in International Financial Governance: Membership of Informal Coordination Platform

Ranking	Economy	Rating	Ranking	Economy	Rating
1	Australia	100	17	India	66.7
2	Brazil	100	18	Mexico	66.7
3	Canada	100	19	Netherlands	66.7
4	Germany	100	20	Saudi Arabia	66.7
5	France	100	21	Turkey	66.7
6	Britain	100	22	South Africa	66.7
7	Italy	100	23	Austria	33.3
8	Japan	100	24	Belgium	33.3
9	Korea	100	25	Finland	33.3
10	Russia	100	26	Hong Kong, China	33.3
11	USA	100	27	Ireland	33.3
12	Argentina	66.7	28	Singapore	33.3
13	Switzerland	66.7	29	The United Arab Emirates	0.0
14	China	66.7	30	Greece	0.0
15	Spain	66.7	31	Luxembourg	0.0
16	Indonesia	66.7	32	Portugal	0.0

5.2.2 Voting weight over informal coordination platform

Table 85　Ranking of Tertiary Indicator for the Competitiveness in International Financial Governance: Voting Weightover Informal Coordination Platform

Ranking	Economy	Rating	Ranking	Economy	Rating
1	Australia	100	12	India	66.7
1	Brazil	100	12	Mexico	66.7
1	Canada	100	12	Netherlands	66.7

Continued

Ranking	Economy	Rating	Ranking	Economy	Rating
1	Germany	100	12	Saudi Arabia	66.7
1	France	100	12	Turkey	66.7
1	Britain	100	12	South Africa	66.7
1	Italy	100	23	Austria	33.3
1	Japan	100	23	Belgium	33.3
1	Korea	100	23	Finland	33.3
1	Russia	100	23	Hong Kong, China	33.3
1	USA	100	23	Ireland	33.3
12	Argentina	66.7	23	Singapore	33.3
12	Switzerland	66.7	29	The United Arab Emirates	0.0
12	Chinese Mainland	66.7	29	Greece	0.0
12	Spain	66.7	29	Luxembourg	0.0
12	Indonesia	66.7	29	Portugal	0.0

Generally, compared with the competitiveness of global financial organizations, the competitiveness of informal coordination platforms is less affected by power hegemony, which reflects the flexibility of diversified governance and informal mechanisms to a certain extent. Take G20 as an example, compared to formal international organizations, informal international organizations can quickly improve the competitiveness of emerging developing countries in international financial governance. Generally, countries often adopt informal mechanisms when the international environment changes rapidly with vast uncertainties, because this makes it easy for the countries to modify or even withdraw from the reached international agreements and maintain the flexibility of the mechanism[①]. After the financial crisis in 2008, the informal flexible mechanism of G20 helps to enhance the voice of emerging developing countries to a certain extent, and also provides a time window for the formation of follow-up formal mechanisms. It can be safe to say that the G20 offers the only economic platform of global

---

① Charles Lipson, "Why are Some International Agreements Informal?", *International Organization*, Vol. 45, No. 4, 1991, pp. 495–512.

co-governance taking into account the effectiveness of deliberations and the common interests of the North and the South after the financial crisis, as well as the only highest coordination mechanism for equal dialogue between leaders of developed and developing countries. It represents the attempt of a shift from the hegemonic model to the multilateral model in the system of international financial governance and provides a platform and channel for the presence of emerging developing countries in international financial governance with enhanced voices. Since 2013, Chinese Mainland, with a greater voice, has been increasingly influential in the global economy and international financial governance, when more issues concerning inclusiveness and sustainable development gradually became the topic and field of cooperation in G20. G20 has expanded the participation rights of emerging countries, yet its efficiency in international economic coordination and decision-making still remained frequently questioned by the international community. Besides the repetition, again and another time, of the principled consensus reached by countries during the crisis and demonstration of the determination of Member States to promote global economic recovery, there have been few breakthroughs in actions. On the one hand, the G20 is a consultative platform but not an implementation platform for global economic and financial governance, with neither a permanent secretariat nor an entity for the governance over implementation or supervision. It was established on legal documents, and the subsequent international agreements would not be legally binding, with the communiqués, declarations and action plans adopted only playing guiding roles with no international legal obligations to its Member States[1]. On the other hand, the G20 is still operating under the leadership of developed countries, with developing countries still in a secondary position. The United States and European countries try to maintain or even expand their leadership in global economic and financial governance, and turn negative towards the transformation of G20, and even tougher when coordinating with emerging countries. Furthermore, emerging developing countries, not united closely, are still to meet major obstacles in effectively enhancing their voice in the international financial governance system in the future.

At the same time, as an informal mechanism, to maintain frank, open and effective informal exchanges between leaders, the number of members participating in the meeting must be limited, that is, the principle of "selective" membership must be adopted to maintain the characteristics of the

---

[1] Liu Hongsong, "The Expansion of G20 Issues and Its Impact on the Effectiveness of the Mechanism", *International Forum*, 2015, No. 3, p. 7.

"small group". This principle of "selective" membership will also bring serious legitimacy defects to it, especially paying too much attention to the standard of economic strength when selecting members, which will make the majority of developing countries, especially African countries, question the legitimacy and representativeness of the mechanism, and objectively make themselves fall into the dilemma of "effectiveness" (by cutting members) and "legitimacy" (by adding members).

Indicator 5.3 Competitiveness in regional multilateral financial organizations

Table 86   Ranking of Secondary Indicator for the Competitiveness in International Financial Governance: Competitiveness in Regional Multilateral Financial Organizations

Ranking	Economy	Rating	Ranking	Economy	Rating
1	Chinese Mainland	64.2	17	Brazil	36.0
2	Germany	62.4	18	Switzerland	32.5
3	France	55.9	19	Russia	27.5
4	USA	55.3	20	South Africa	25.4
5	Italy	54.0	21	Luxembourg	22.3
6	Japan	53.3	22	Argentina	22.3
7	Spain	44.6	23	Mexico	21.5
8	Netherlands	41.8	24	Ireland	15.7
9	Belgium	40.5	25	Australia	15.1
10	Britain	39.6	26	Turkey	9.7
11	Canada	39.5	27	Saudi Arabia	8.6
12	Austria	39.5	28	Greece	7.6
13	India	38.8	29	Indonesia	6.8
14	Finland	38.2	30	Hong Kong, China	1.1
15	Portugal	37.1	31	Singapore	0.6
16	Korea	36.2	32	The United Arab Emirates	0.6

As can be seen from Table 86, among the secondary indicators for the competitiveness in regional multilateral financial organizations, the ranking of developing countries has increased significantly. In terms of the competitiveness in regional multilateral financial organizations, Chinese Mainland scored 64.2 in the 1st place, slightly higher than Germany that ranked 2nd, and the United States, which has an absolute voice in the global economic and financial organizations, ranking only 4th with a score of 55.3. Brazil and India, also as emerging developing countries, jumped from 22nd and 25th to 17th and 13th respectively when related to the competitiveness in global economic and financial organizations.

5.3.1 Membership of regional multilateral financial organizations

Table 87　　Ranking of Tertiary Indicator for the Competitiveness in International Financial Governance: Membership of Regional Multilateral Financial Organizations

Ranking	Economy	Rating	Ranking	Economy	Rating
1	Chinese Mainland	63.2	17	Finland	31.9
2	Germany	61.1	18	Portugal	30.2
3	France	58.8	19	Argentina	28.6
4	Italy	57.9	20	South Africa	28.6
5	USA	57.1	21	Russia	23.1
6	Japan	55.0	22	Saudi Arabia	15.5
7	Britain	44.1	23	Ireland	15.1
8	Spain	43.2	24	Luxembourg	15.0
9	Brazil	42.9	25	Mexico	14.5
10	Canada	38.7	26	Australia	8.5
11	India	38.4	27	Indonesia	6.6
12	Netherlands	37.5	28	Turkey	3.2
13	Korea	36.4	29	Greece	0.9
14	Belgium	36.2	30	Hong Kong, China	0.9
15	Austria	34.3	31	The United Arab Emirates	0.6
16	Switzerland	32.7	32	Singapore	0.4

5.3.2 Voting weight in regional multilateral financial organizations

Table 88　Ranking of Tertiary Indicator for the Competitiveness in International Financial Governance: Voting Weight in Regional Multilateral Financial Organizations

Ranking	Economy	Rating	Ranking	Economy	Rating
1	Chinese Mainland	65.2	17	Switzerland	32.2
2	Germany	63.6	18	Russia	31.8
3	USA	53.4	19	Luxembourg	29.7
4	France	53.0	20	Brazil	29.2
5	Japan	51.6	21	Mexico	28.6
6	Italy	50.0	22	South Africa	22.3
7	Spain	46.1	23	Australia	21.7
8	Netherlands	46.1	24	Ireland	16.3
9	Belgium	44.7	25	Turkey	16.3
10	Austria	44.6	26	Argentina	15.9
11	Finland	44.5	27	Greece	14.4
12	Portugal	44.0	28	Indonesia	6.9
13	Canada	40.2	29	Saudi Arabia	1.6
14	India	39.1	30	Hong Kong, China	1.3
15	Korea	36.1	31	Singapore	0.9
16	Britain	35.1	32	The United Arab Emirates	0.7

When it is difficult to promote or make substantive progress in financial governance at the global level, regional financial governance absorbed every one's attention. Successful financial governance at the regional level will greatly promote financial governance at the global level. It can be reasonable to say that regional financial cooperation serves also as an important step or a circuitous path in thereform of international financial governance. From this perspective, Chinese Mainland has already assumed the responsibility of matching itself with regional multilateral governance and has also won equal voice as those for the major developed countries in regional multilateral cooperation. In the future, how to promote international financial governance through regional multilateral financial cooperation lays the key to enhancing its competitiveness in international financial governance through its involvement in it.

参考文献

焦瑾璞:《中国金融基础设施功能与建设研究》,社会科学文献出版社 2019 年版。

刘轶:《国际金融中心衡量指标体系的构建及实证分析》,《经济研究导刊》2010 年第 26 期。

倪鹏飞:《构建国际金融中心:全球眼光、国际标准与世界经验》,《开放导报》2004 年第 2 期。

倪鹏飞:《中国国家竞争力报告 No.2》,广东经济出版社 2016 年版。

上海发展研究基金会全球金融治理课题组:《全球金融治理:挑战,目标和改革——关于 2016 年 G20 峰会议题的研究报告》,《国际经济评论》2016 年第 3 期。

吴念鲁、郧会梅:《对我国金融稳定性的再认识》,《金融研究》2005 年第 2 期。

熊北辰:《国际金融组织在全球金融治理中的作用》,《学习时报》2021 年第 1 期。

徐奇渊、杨盼盼:《东亚货币转向钉住新的货币篮子?》,《金融研究》2016 年第 3 期。

詹继生:《金融竞争力研究》,江西人民出版社 2007 年版。

张礼卿:《全球金融治理面临的八个问题》,《中国外汇》2021 年第 4 期。

Allen F., Gale D., "Financial Contagion", *Journal of Political Economy*, 2000, 108(1).

Beck T., Demirgüç-Kunt A., Honohan P., "Access to Financial Services: Measurement, Impact, and Policies", *The World Bank Research Observer*, 2009, 24(1).

Beck T., Levine R., Loayza N., "Inance and the Sources of Growth", *Journal of Financial Economics*, 2000, 58(1-2).

Beck, T., Demirgüç-Kunt, A., & Levine, R., *A New Database on Financial Development and Structure*, The World Bank, 1999.

Bradlow D., *Materials for a 4-Part On-Line Course on Global Financial Governance Offered by United Nations Institute on Training and Research (UNITAR)*, UNITAR, On-Line Training Courses in Public Finance and Trade, 2009.

Diamond D. W., "Financial Intermediation and Delegated Monitoring", *The Review of Economic Studies*, 1984, 51(3).

Fankel, Jeffrey A., Shangjin Wei, 1994, "Yen Bloc or Dollar Bloc? Exchange Rate Policies of the East Asian Economies", *Macroeconomic Linkage: Savings, Exchange Rates, and Capital Flows*, NBER-EASE 3.

IMD, *IMD World Competitiveness Yearbook*, IMD World Competitiveness Center, 2019.

IMF, *Financial Soundness Indicators Compilation Guide*, International Monetary Fund, 2006.

IMF, *Review of the Method of Valuation of the SDR*, IMF Policy Paper, 2015.

IMF, *Annual Report on Exchange Arrangements and Exchange Restrictions*, International Monetary Fund, 2019.

Levine R., Loayza N., Beck T., "Financial Intermediation and Growth: Causality and Causes", *Journal of Monetary Economics*, 2000, 46(1).

Levine R., Zervos S., "Stock Markets, Banks, and Economic Growth", *American economic review*, 1998.

Levine R., "Finance and Growth: Theory and Evidence", *Handbook of Economic Growth*, 2005, 1.

Merton R. C., "A Functional Perspective of Financial Intermediation", *Financial Management*, 1995.

Mookerjee R., Kalipioni P., "Availability of Financial Services and Income Inequality: The Evidence from Many Countries", *Emerging Markets Review*, 2010, 11(4).

Peter B. Kenen, *The Role of the Dollar as an International Currency*, Group of Thirty, New York, 1983.

Rajan R. G., Zingales L., "Which capitalism? Lessons form the east Asian crisis", *Journal of Applied Corporate Finance*, 1998, 11(3).

Rosenau J. N., "Governance in the Twenty-first Century", *Palgrave Advances in Global Governance*, 2009.

Solovjova I., Rupeika-Apoga R., Romanova I., *Competitiveness Enhancement of International Financial Centres*, 2018.

WEF, *The Global Competitiveness Report*, World Economic Forum, 2019.